The

Human
Antenna

Dr. Robin Kelly
www.HumanAntenna.com

Energy Psychology Press
Santa Rosa, CA 95439
www.EnergyPsychologyPress.com

Library of Congress Cataloging-in-Publication Data

Kelly, Robin, 1951—
    The Human Antenna: reading the language of the universe in the songs of our cells /
Robin Kelly. — 2nd ed.
        p. cm.
Rev. ed. of: The human aerial / Robin Kelly, 2006.
Includes bibliographical references and index.
ISBN-13: 978-1-60415-014-8
1. Holistic medicine. 2. Mind and body. 3. Healing. I. Kelly, Robin, 1951—Human aerial.
II. Title.
[DNLM: 1. Holistic Health. 2. Mental Healing. 3. Mind-Body Relations (Metaphysics)
W 61 K29h 2007]

R733.K45 2007
610—dc22

2007037170

© 2008, 2009 Robin Kelly

Typeset in Kozuka Mincho & Lucida Console by Adrian Wright
Printed in USA by Bang Printing
Second Edition

10 9 8 7 6 5 4 3 2 1

For Trish

For updates and more information about this book, visit:
www.HumanAntenna.com

For more information about the author, visit:

www.RobinKelly.co.nz

About the Author

Robin Kelly runs a medical practice in which he integrates Western, Eastern and modern mindbody concepts of health. He qualified as a doctor in London, moving to Auckland, New Zealand in the late 1970s.

Soon after starting in general practice, he started to practise and study acupuncture. Impressed by the safety and effectiveness of this ancient Chinese healing art, he studied its roots in traditional Chinese medicine. He became president of the New Zealand Medical Acupuncture Society, and by the early 90s had established a full time practice in Medical Acupuncture on Auckland's North Shore.

Since this time, Robin's practice has broadened to focus on the concept of deep healing, and the drawing up of individualized healing plans. He runs MindBody Healing workshops in New Zealand and overseas for the sufferers of chronic illness, health professionals, and the general public.

The Human Antenna is Robin's second book, and explores his interest in the science of consciousness, and the role intuition plays in our lives. He draws from his everyday experiences, explaining these exciting but sometimes bewildering concepts in a simple and entertaining way.

Robin is also a passionate musician and singer-songwriter, currently recording his fourth CD. His previous albums *Black Ice (1998), Silk and Knives (2002),* and *Shimmer* (2006) have been featured on local and national radio stations, and he has performed live on national television.

He has recently written a stage musical, *Chakramor,* a celebration of the growth of human consciousness.

Robin works from home with his wife, Trish, a registered nurse and midwife. They have three children, a lively Cavoodle puppy, and two beautiful but emotionally distant cats.

When not working, he can be found pottering around either his garden or the golf course.

His overriding ambition is to be the last person on earth to own a mobile phone.

Contents

Acknowledgments

I am indebted to those special people who have gifted me the space from which this book has emerged.

In particular, to my eldest daughter Sophie, who graciously allowed me to convert her orange bedroom into my writing retreat.

And to Gabrielle Graham, who together with the staff of the Student Health and Counseling Center at Albany's Massey University, unselfishly allowed me to cut back on my duties for several months to write my book.

Throughout the book, I mention many friends and colleagues who have guided me in my life and work. It is heartening to experience at first hand the support now in place for all doctors who are compelled to extend the boundaries of healthcare, and to embrace new paradigms of healing. I owe special thanks to Miriam and Gerald Gibb, and Julie and Tim Ewer, who continue to inspire me with their wisdom and cheerful encouragement.

I am also grateful to Dawson Church, Courtney Arnold, Deburah Tribbey and Jeff Anderson – all at Energy Psychology Press. I am fortunate indeed to have found you all. Special thanks also to artist Karla Vink who has converted my rough sketches into such clear and satisfying images, to cover designer Victoria Valentine for her stunning work, and to Karin Kinsey for the changes made to this edition.

I am also grateful for the unending patience and literary skills of my editors, Graeme Beals and Paula Reid, who have helped make writing *The Human Antenna* such a happy and fulfilling experience.

Robin Kelly
Auckland 2009

Introduction –
The Journey Begins

This book is an accurate, truthful account of my personal experiences. It is not a textbook in the traditional sense, as textbooks reveal little of the writer. Rather they separate the writer from the text, the subject from the object. I am unable to make these distinctions; my life and my health, and the lives and health of my family and of those seeking my help over the years are so delicately entwined that their separation would undoubtedly represent a departure from this truth.

Similarly any knowledge I have gleaned from any sources, be they academic lectures, learned journals, all manner of books or Internet sites, reflects the warm generosity of others who have shared their wisdom unselfishly with the world. My intent is to fully acknowledge all these wise researchers, but also to avoid weighty and distracting lists of references. I have strived to achieve a happy balance here, erring on the side of simplicity. Much of my working life has involved translating the hard-earned knowledge of others into a language I can personally understand. There is a good chance that by passing on my personal interpretations of this universal wisdom I can be a help to others.

I am also grateful for those who have given me permission to use their own powerful healing stories in this book. Hopefully I have retained their essence as, for confidentiality reasons, I have used alternative names, nationalities and locations. I am grateful for the confidence these generous people have shown in me; they come from all walks of life and this book would not be possible without them. Every day I hear stories that are extraordinary; experiences I would have regarded years ago as supernatural, appear now as perfectly natural.

The short biography that opens this book highlights certain events in my personal and early practising life that eased open the door to this place of wonder; episodes that gave me the confidence to pursue topics in an intimate setting that may have been viewed by some as being taboo. I have taken care in my work to remain an integral member of the medical profession. I perceive my role to be more helpful if I maintain clinical competence within the framework of 'orthodox' medicine. This somehow has helped reassure those who have felt destabilized by their experiences – 'Please tell me; I'm not mad, am I doctor?'

I can empathize with them as I too have asked myself such questions, and at times felt the judgment of a conservative profession.

In retrospect, the experiences that have proved formative and the most pivotal have not been the dramatic 'road to Damascus' peak experiences. Rather they have been everyday events, sequences and synchronicities. An epiphany occurs far more rarely – and then as a vivid confirmation of wisdom already held within. As we begin to experience the spiritual dimensions in everyday life, the ordinary becomes wonderful, the mundane miraculous. Further confirmation is no longer needed, as we are now tuned to perfection.

My personal experiences as recounted here are no more nor less valid than your own. Each of us has our unique, compelling story and I hope this book encourages you to examine your life's experiences and to draw your own conclusions. I am sure you will find your own special journey equally fascinating.

I am trained professionally in the material sciences. Becoming a doctor, and remaining one, has been both arduous and deeply satisfying. It has provided a perfect platform for all aspects of my life with its joyful exploration of what has been called non-material science. This new paradigm sees science and spirit merge, but in no way implies that our physical beings are any the less spiritual. In fact, our earth-bound, time-bound, physical presence appears all the more miraculous by our new awareness of the non-material world. It has often been said that our bodies are sacred temples.

I feel it is important for us to have an understanding of this new science. To me it is both fascinating and less complicated than the science governed by bewildering laws and formulae. This new science is, as the evolutionary biologist Rupert Sheldrake has termed, the *true science of life*. It lives more in the universal world of patterns and codes appealing as much to the artist in me as the scientist. It is a world I find fascinating and fun. It would be deeply satisfying to me if I were able, through this book, to infect you with a large dose of this joy.

My own life and the lives of my family members have been greatly enhanced by standard Western medical care. However, I have found the emphasis on the purely physical at the expense of the emotional and spiritual an unsatisfactory way to practise medicine. So rather than delivering in this foreword a bland disclaimer along the lines of, 'this book in no way is a substitute for orthodox medical care,' I would prefer to emphasise the remarkable health benefits of integrating the spiritual with the physical. It certainly appears to work for me.

So if my orthodox training has provided me with a solid platform, my ongoing life could be regarded as a mysterious train journey – in a train that at this very moment is pulling out of the station, bound for an undisclosed destination.

As I peer out of the carriage window, I see many who choose to stay behind on the platform. Some work diligently on the platform structure, keeping it sturdy and safe. Others help guide me and my fellow passengers onto the train, checking our tickets and ensuring we are not injured on the way. A number are passengers waiting for other trains, going to places they already know and love, naturally wary of heading out into the unknown. Maybe they too will make this journey at a time when they are ready.

There are even a few that never leave the safety of the platform – and question us skeptically about our intentions, warning us of our folly.

Every one of these folk in their own special way helps us on our journey – and by remaining behind they create comfort and space for us in our carriage. Together we wave to all our friends in the station – bidding them a fond farewell. I feel privileged we have chosen to travel together. As our journey proceeds, each of us will have the opportunity to recount just how and why we came to be here.

You have kindly allowed me to speak first.

1: An Awakening

It was 1985 and my two-and-a-half-year-old daughter was looking for something behind the television.

'Where did the Wombles get in to the TV, Daddy?'

It was very dark in the corner of our living room. I fetched a flashlight and together we looked in vain for a trap door at the back of the set.

'Oh dear,' I said, 'I can't see any door.' I pointed to two wires. 'Maybe the Wombles got in there, Sophie?'

'Silly Daddy – too squeezy for Wombles,' she said dismissively.

I admitted she had a good point. Floundering, I decided to perform a practical demonstration, yanking the antenna connection lead out of its socket at the back of the television.

This proved to be not such a good move.

In the ensuing commotion, I could just decipher 'Naughty naughty Daddy' amid the screams and the tears, as my daughter scampered off to be comforted by my wife. We agreed there could have been more gentle ways of teaching my daughter the intricate workings of one of the true marvels of the modern age.

My daughter's perception that TV characters lived inside the set was of course completely natural. A few years later my second daughter and my son embarked on precisely the same line of enquiry. Happily my approach had become refined through experience, and on these occasions there were no tears as a result.

My life as a family doctor had taken an unlikely turn in the early eighties. Up until then I had been trained to expect that our illnesses could be helped mainly by first looking inside our bodies, and then corrected by either adding a chemical or taking away a diseased part through surgery. By and large this model still remained strong within me – but I had fallen on a totally different approach, in many ways foreign to this mainstream teaching. The evening following the Wombles incident, I couldn't help but reflect on how my own world view had been challenged by observing the effects a few acupuncture needles had on a human body; a view that had been no less naïve than demonstrated by my two-year-old daughter's search for bizarre furry animals deep inside the body of our television.

It was then that an idea seeded in my mind; could these tiny metal needles be acting as conducting antennas, somehow transmitting information in and out of the body?

It was several years later that I began to realize that our very bodies, in a state of balance, could be antennas, receiving and transmitting information somehow, 'to and from' – but more accurately 'within' – a dimension beyond time and space.

Despite a mood of skepticism within my profession at this time, acupuncture had been shown by science to change the chemical make up of the body. Most notably the body's natural painkilling *endorphins* had been shown to increase after stimulating acupuncture needles electrically. This was certainly a help in convincing my colleagues that I had not completely 'lost it'.

But this did not satisfy my curiosity. I was keen to know why women told me that after an acupuncture treatment not only had their headache got better, but that they had no pain with their period for the first time ever; how they had the best night's sleep in ages and why the Chinese advised never to perform acupuncture on someone when there was thunder and lightning around.

Together with a few similarly intrigued doctors, I had begun to study Traditional Chinese Medicine to help answer some of these questions. As I poured through volume after volume of poorly translated texts, I was surprised to feel enlightened rather than overwhelmed. I was fascinated by the way emotional states were linked to organs and illnesses, and was even comfortable with the view that the body was primarily an energetic entity rather than a purely physical machine.

In fact, it all seemed strangely familiar to me.

I had a happy childhood – my father was a family doctor in a small suburb – Eastcote – on the outskirts of London. He worked from home. We had to keep quiet during evening surgery, as our dining room was right next to the consulting room.

Despite going to Epsom College – a public school with many doctors' sons, and with a focus on producing doctors – I felt no pressure to follow my father's profession. If anything, the long hours and modest pay would very likely have put me off if I hadn't had a strong vocational urge to practise medicine.

As a young doctor, I worked in hospitals in and around London, firstly in general surgery and medicine, and then in more senior positions with sick children and cancer patients. Trish and I married as soon as I had qualified, and after three years we decided to spend a year in Auckland, New Zealand, after reading an advertisement in the British Medical Journal for the post of a medical registrar in Paediatric Oncology – combining my two interests in children and cancer. Trish, a registered nurse and midwife, quickly found a fulfilling job on a surgical ward at a local private hospital. It turned out we loved New Zealand so much that the year's trip became two years and so on. After twenty-seven years here, we have no desire to leave Aotearoa – the Land of the Long White Cloud.

My decision to become a general practitioner after six years in hospital seemed natural for me. I knew that pursuing a specialist career would take me away from New Zealand to centers of world excellence, and after many years of sleepless nights and study, the promise of settling down in a beautiful part of the world was more attractive. I also had become aware that advancing up the specialist ladder also brought with it a focus on research, and a distancing from the intimate relationships family doctors could nurture with their patients.

In New Zealand, most family doctors had longer appointment times than those within the British National Health Service. My friends in England were immensely jealous of my quarter of an hour time slots

– three times longer than many of them were allowed. There were still many city doctors practising in the UK in those days without examination couches in their consulting rooms.

It is still a major concern to me that doctors try to solve complex problems in an impossibly short time. In 5–10 minutes, a doctor is severely limited in what she or he can achieve. It is one of the reasons there has been so much inappropriate over-prescribing in the past fifty years. If a doctor wants to delve beneath the surface, agitated patients pile up in the waiting room. This is the major cause of stress I have experienced when working in general practices. It's also one that I struggled to address while adapting my practice to cope with the search for the roots of illness that accompanied my immersion in Chinese medicine.

As the years have gone by, the time I have made available to spend with people has steadily increased. Unfortunately, this doesn't equate with a similar rise in income and at present, doctors pursuing holistic models of healing have had to make many sacrifices along the way. Luckily, my love for practising at home with my wife as nurse, thereby avoiding heavy financial overheads, has been the essential ingredient that has allowed me to continue to enjoy a taste of the sweet life.

It is often said that doctors get rich treating the top few millimeters of the body, and that their remuneration declines proportionally as they delve deeper and deeper within. It is perhaps understandable that so many are drawn to injecting surface skin wrinkles with Botulinum toxin, a product used in biological warfare.

I instantly took to my life in general practice in Takapuna, on Auckland's sunny North Shore. However, one aspect of general practice concerned me greatly – the quantity of drugs being swallowed every day by people who, to my observation, would be better off without them.

It was not that I was against drugs on principle. My six years in hospitals in England and New Zealand had confirmed how powerful, and life saving many drugs could be. Even in those earlier days, potent cancer drugs were resulting in cures for childhood cancers, and much of our focus in the acute children's wards had been on the diagnosis and treatment of potentially lethal diseases such as meningitis and tuberculosis that could be cured with antibiotics. My working life had involved many days and nights of inserting drips, prescribing strong drugs and assisting in major operations. But I harboured deep concerns.

On one occasion in London, a slim, middle-aged lady presented with a blockage in her intestines. She was in immense pain, and on palpating her abdomen I was concerned and puzzled to feel something I have never felt either before or since. Under her skin I could feel bizarre tight coils of tissue, as if somehow stuck together by thick glue that had set hard. I ordered an X-ray, but this proved just as puzzling. The whole bowel had the appearance of a cocoon – something none of the other doctors I showed it to had ever seen. The lady became more distressed and started to vomit – so the consultant surgeon decided there was no other option but to operate. Nowadays we would have the option of using a laparoscope, a flexible tube passed through a small incision through which we could view the area close up. But these were days before valuable inventions such as this and the sophisticated scanners of today.

In the operating theater, our initial fears were confirmed – the bowel was completely glued together in a cocoon with the connecting tissue known as the mesentery – normally a soft translucent skin housing blood vessels – transformed into something that resembled dried polyurethane paint. All this was stuck to the back wall of the abdomen, rendering it completely inoperable. All we could do was sew her up. Sadly the lady was to die soon afterwards.

On researching this tragic case, I discovered that similar cases were being recorded around the world. A linking factor had been that all had at one time been taking a new type of blood pressure medication known as *practolol*. This was the first of a new class of drugs known as the *beta-blockers*. Its link with this condition – known medically as *sclerosing peritonitis* – was subsequently confirmed, and it was immediately withdrawn. I would like to stress that no other *beta-blockers*, still in common usage, have been shown to produce this devastating side effect.

This experience, however, had a powerful effect on me. On starting in general practice five years later, I discovered many of the elderly and middle-aged male patients were on large doses of beta-blocking drugs. Although I didn't feel they were at risk of this terrible bowel condition, I was concerned how sluggish they all felt. Not only that, most were impotent.

My predecessor, like many doctors of the time would have done, had found their blood pressure readings to be raised, and informed them they should take these pills unerringly for the rest of their life. Not to do so, they had been told, would result in them running the real risk of dying suddenly of a stroke or heart attack. They would come religiously to the doctor every three months for a blood pressure check by the doctor, and to collect a prescription for a further batch of pills. For most of them their sex life was but a happy memory, but as one told me 'even my memory will fade if I'm six foot under'.

On close questioning, I discovered that many of these men, who incidentally contributed considerably to my weekly income, had been diagnosed some years before while going through what many would now call mid-life crises. These crises, whether financial or marital, had by and large resolved over the years, yet they continued to take the pills for fear of the dire consequences that would result from stopping.

Doctors too, practise within a state of fear; many a time have I answered the phone while on night call and given someone advice, only to toss and turn in bed, imagining all the worst case scenarios. Inevitably I would phone them back within a few minutes and head to their home with a jumper and baggy jeans over my pajamas.

So as well as our concern for patients' well-being and survival, as doctors we have always had our own insecurities to deal with. Major life-threatening practices could get us struck off, shamefully demoted, socially and financially ruined. Our families would suffer too. The fear is not solely within the patient; in my experience it is often greater in the doctor.

But I had discovered in acupuncture another healing tool. I had noticed that blood pressures frequently settled when the person relaxed in my rooms. Acupuncture seemed to enhance this effect, with people telling me of a newfound sense of calm during and after treatments. Many people I would normally have started on blood-pressure pills no longer needed them. So with caution, and some considerable trepidation, I approached several of my regular patients whose lives had settled, who had no history of heart disease but who remained on blood pressure medication, and I suggested we wean them off their pills over several weeks, checking their readings carefully along the way. Some, who had already had acupuncture, opted to have treatments during this time, but most just carried on their normal lives, hoping for an improvement in their energy and libido. Well over half ended up off their pills. Many are now into their eighties, and remain drug free.

Many middle-aged and older women in my practice were also overmedicated but this group proved to be more difficult to help. In the sixties and seventies they had been started on tranquillisers – in Mick Jagger's words, 'Mother's Little Helpers'. As the Rolling Stones song explained, these pills, 'helped them on their way, helped them through their busy day'. The benzodiazepines were heralded as safe, non-addictive alternatives to barbiturates. Valium was a chemically refined version of the herb *valerian* and generically the common drugs were known as diazepam (for day time relief of tension), and nitrazepam (for night sedation).

These drugs stayed in the body for a long time; the effects of nitrazepam lasted well into the next day, and so the dulling of mind and body became cumulative. Newer versions were introduced that worked more quickly, and were excreted from the body more quickly, and we were encouraged as doctors to change patients over to these. This still concerned me, however. Everything I was learning strongly supported that it was unhealthy to bottle up and block emotions. I would see people get better after they had talked about problems, and Chinese medicine equated physical illnesses with emotional blocks. It became obvious to me that the real issue was that of the unhealthy repression of feelings produced by these medications, and no amount of 'refining' these drugs addressed this cardinal issue. In common with all addictive substances including cigarettes and excessive alcohol, these drugs had the effect of driving feelings underground. Feelings would be further suppressed at night with more medication. We have since come to discover that the benzodiazepines are some of the most addictive drugs ever known. Drug withdrawal experts experience more difficulty in weaning people off these than either heroin or cocaine.

So even with acupuncture, I found this a near impossible task. In truth, many were locked into unhealthy marriages that had in some ways been propped up by these pills. There were real fears – some expressed, but more hidden – about what the effects would be of exposing years and years of repressed feelings.

In my practice today, I see many such casualties of these times. One lady who did wean herself off these drugs over three years in the eighties is left with chronic widespread pain. For fifteen years she had suffered an abusive relationship with her alcoholic husband, whom she had the courage to leave once she had finally stopped her medication.

Feelings, I was learning, were closely aligned to *being*. And many, myself included, had little time to simply be. We were human doings, not human beings, and the effects of busy-ness and time pressure are even more marked today.

Recently I saw a 22-year-old mother struggling to cope with finishing a university assignment, looking after her sick toddler while holding down a job at the supermarket to help pay for her student loan. She had developed a bad cough, and wanted antibiotics to 'knock it on the head'. Clearly, far more than this needed attending to.

In those early days of general practice, I felt a sense of isolation. I had to lengthen my appointment times, but still felt the pressure of consulting with 35 patients a day. The more patients a doctor saw a day, the more money he made. There were still many doctors in Auckland who were seeing over 80 patients each day, and I wondered what on earth was happening in these consultations. Even around me there were doctors who were disgruntled if they saw less than 40 patients a day.

My frustrations came to a head, at an evening clinical meeting with a group of local doctors, led by a local specialist. As an exercise, we were all given a case study describing a middle-aged man who presented with high blood pressure, insomnia, and anxiety symptoms. We were asked what our ideal management would be. Around this time, beta-blocking drugs were being prescribed to many business executive and community leaders to reduce the anxiety associated with public speaking. So to all but me at this meeting, the answer was obvious.

As the specialist explained, a beta-blocker would 'kill two birds with one stone'. My own suggestion that the course of action could be a lengthy chat with his doctor, followed by either acupuncture or his learning to meditate, was met with a stony silence.

Despite my concerns about pharmaceuticals, I was not about to turn my back on Western medicine. I freely admit enjoying the lavish meals at luxury hotels and golfing weekends generously provided in those years by the thriving drug companies. It was a lovely way to be educated. In 1988 I was selected by a well-known drug company to travel business class, all expenses paid to an international conference on blood pressure in Kyoto, Japan. This allowed me to visit the beautiful temples and Zen gardens, and gave me my first taste of Karaoke singing – a craze that was yet to reach the West.

After an initial embarrassing failure in a student bar in central Kyoto – where there was no video screen, and a choice of Japanese or poorly translated English lyrics held loosely in a frayed, beer-stained folder – I well and truly nailed Elvis Presley's *Heartbreak Hotel*. This rekindled my passion for singing and songwriting that has remained with me, even grown, to this day.

At the conference I attended as many lectures as I could. The Kyoto Conference Center was a huge, ugly, concrete building surrounded by magnificent gardens. A central lake was home to hundreds of gigantic, golden, coy carp. Many lectures were complex descriptions of animal experiments using a new class of blood pressure pills, the ACE inhibitors. There were also reports of controlled trials using these and other drugs. The auditorium was packed out for these sessions with doctors from all around the world. Their interest was intense and the general mood highly focused. As I looked around I felt I had definitely made the right decision in leaving the demands and exactitudes of specialist medicine to these highly intelligent (mainly) men.

My mind wandered. If one of those giant goldfish had been taken out of the lake outside, and placed on the seat beside me, I at least would have found a colleague who might understand.

I was waiting for an intriguing session at the end of the morning describing the effects of meditation on lowering blood pressure. I had started to do my own version of meditation, and to teach as simple a version as I could to patients who were keen to keep off medication. After two hours of rats' adrenal glands, I couldn't wait.

As the focus turned from rats to humans, however, the auditorium rapidly cleared. It reminded me of a crowd dispersing at the end of an All Black test in Eden Park, Auckland. There were a few solitary souls dotted around the vast theater. This time, women outnumbered men. The lecturer was an Indian trained physician who practised Yoga and meditation. As I listened to this learned man talk, I felt the relief and exhilaration my friend the fish would have felt if he were to be placed gently back into the water.

As I began to appreciate our interconnectivity with other humans, and nature (the Chinese would explain it as the macrocosm of the universe expressed in the microcosm of our bodies) I also began to see the possibilities of blending this into an altogether better style of medicine.

Five years later I was to leave the constraints of 'orthodox' general practice, to focus on a combination of Eastern and Western approaches to healing. I had two specialist friends contact me. Both were genuinely concerned. One said how sad it was that 'such a good doctor' was leaving medicine. The other, alluding to my acupuncture, wondered how I would cope 'leaving a profession for a trade'. But there were other seeds of awareness being planted early in my general practice career. Soon after I had started in Takapuna, Archie, a red faced Scottish man in his early sixties came to see me. The atmosphere in the consultation was decidedly frosty. Despite my never meeting him before, he seemed cross with me. He was there to pick up his heart pills and have a general check up.

'I can't help feeling you are annoyed with me, even though I can't remember seeing you before. Have I done anything wrong?' I asked nervously.

After a long pause during which he appeared to be eyeing me up and down, he replied, 'it's not you really . . . well not you personally. It's your lot . . . you doctors.'

He went on to recount that a year before, he had been admitted to hospital with chest pain and was kept in overnight. In the early hours, he had more severe pain and his heart stopped. The emergency team of doctors and nurses gave him CPR and restarted his heart with a defibrillator. He was literally brought back from the dead.

'Surely this is a reason to be thankful for the skill and dedication of the doctors and nurses,' I suggested.

He then began to describe his near-death experience; how he was floating above his hospital bed, completely pain free, and care free. There was the white light, and the loving welcome from his parents who had died thirty years before. As well as that, every detail of his life compressed into a moment's review that somehow managed to leave nothing out. It was a feeling of peace he had never experienced in life.

'And those buggers went and screwed it all up,' he said angrily. 'Before I knew it I was back in my body with this excruciating pain in my chest, and two cracked ribs to boot!'

His anger was turning to sadness; his red face softened, and tears formed in his eyes.

'I'm so sorry,' he said, touching my hand, 'but this has been bottling up inside me for months. I couldn't tell them in hospital, or Hettie my wife. I do love her but how could I explain how nice this feeling was, while at the same time I was leaving her behind.'

We agreed to mull all this over for a few days, and to meet up again a week later. For my part, I went to the library and found similar reports of near-death experiences. One even involved a mother of two young children who had been resuscitated after a serious car crash. She had felt the same blissful peace Archie had described, only to later be wracked by guilt that she had been so ready to abandon them.

These feelings had been later reconciled after a skilled counsellor had suggested she was not yet ready to 'move on' – that she truly had an important role here on earth. She ended up retaining some of the peace she had picked up in her near-death journey, with a comforting view that somehow death didn't represent the end of everything.

It was then that I started to question our engrained views on death. Although I was yet to embrace the view that consciousness survived death, none of these first-hand accounts mentioned the haunting presence of a sinister grim reaper. In fact many of the reports I was reading were positively upbeat, leaving the person with an enhanced view of life valuing every new day like never before.

I began to wonder whether our fear of dying was having a negative impact on how we were living. And how as a doctor I was practising medicine. After all, many treatments revolved around evidence that patients would live longer if they complied with them; that their death would be delayed. I wrestled with all the paradoxes this argument uncovered.

In many ways this book tracks my journey of discovery of this issue. I started to ask patients about their views of death, and found the vast majority relieved, and grateful to be asked. I found it easier to talk to patients than colleagues, and I wondered whether our conditioning as doctors was contributing to death's taboo status.

We had all spent our first two years of medical school studying and dissecting preserved dead bodies; in my own case I was barely 18 years old when first confronted by rows and rows of stiff grey cadavers lying on metal trolleys in the dissecting room. The overwhelming smell of formalin lingers to this day.

Over the years that followed, I began to seriously consider that our living bodies existed not simply as individual isolated structures, but as *human antennas* – the transmitters and receivers of subtle energy or consciousness; a timeless, interconnected consciousness that somehow comprised the very foundation of our universe.

One morning in 1979 I woke with a strange feeling. I felt truly awful; a heavy tiredness like nothing I had experienced before. Of course, there had been many times I had felt exhausted after a night on call, but an early night would then restore my energies. This was different.

It hung around for several days. I'd go to sleep with it, and wake up with it. Every muscle in my body seemed made of lead. It was as if a stiff wire coat hanger had somehow burrowed itself inside my shoulders with its hook skewering through the spinal cord of my neck up to the base of my skull.

I had no idea what the cause of this was. The night call-roster at Auckland Hospital was kinder than I had experienced in English hospitals, and we were really enjoying our new life in Auckland. At the same time I developed an intensely itchy rash on my arms and legs, thick red patches the size of small coins.

I showed it to a skin specialist friend who diagnosed discoid eczema, and prescribed a strong steroid cream and a soap substitute. I asked him about my awful feelings, but he looked blank.

I was wary about doing blood tests; a doctor I had known in a hospital in England had felt tired and sent a sample of his blood to the hospital laboratory under the name of an imaginary patient, Frank Smith. He signed the request form himself. Later that day the pathologist phoned to say that his patient, Mr. Smith, had a 'very nasty' advanced stage of leukaemia that was likely to prove fatal.

So, tentatively I asked a friend to check my blood pressure, look at the blood vessels at the back of my eyes and to give me a general physical check up. He found nothing unusual, and a full set of blood tests also proved to be completely normal. I had no idea someone could feel this bad and have normal tests.

These symptoms, with the accompanying extreme fatigue, were to last with me for the next twelve years. They were not there all the time; I would often go some weeks feeling completely well, only to relapse for no obvious reason. There seemed to be no pattern, although the symptoms were the most severe when I was in a state of jetlag visiting my family in England.

During my early years in general practice, I would frequently return home after a morning's consultation to crash exhausted on my bed, much to the concern of my wife Trish. It was even worse for her. Nothing she could do or say seemed to make a difference. I carried on working in this state, unable to notice any pattern to the symptoms. I changed my diet several times, gave up coffee and visited a whole range of therapists: orthodox doctors, naturopaths, osteopaths and massage therapists. I took pills, herbs, had acupuncture, gave myself acupuncture and tried to meditate. I had all my mercury fillings removed.

The closest I could get to a diagnosis was that I had a combination of chronic fatigue syndrome or *ME (myalgic encephalomyelitis),* and *fibromyalgia.* In those days, many in my own profession did not think that this was a real diagnosis, so very few people knew how I felt. Certainly it was several years before I told patients about my suffering, only to find that it was to prove the single most effective way to help them.

Even more confusingly, all these strange symptoms were occurring in me at a time when my own perceptions of the world were expanding. I was learning to think of energy in my work – of the Chinese concepts of *yin* and *yang* (balance in life) and the life force *qi*. People were coming to see me feeling awful, but with normal tests. I began to notice that I shared several traits with these people. By and large we seemed to be sensitive souls, as if we were thin-skinned, indiscriminately absorbing into our bodies all that surrounded us. Our bodies had become clogged, and all our energies were being used up trying to cope with this.

I began to reflect whether my empathy for patients was worsening the situation. Within a typical 15 minute consultation, I had to establish rapport, ask questions, examine and order tests and explain. In addition, I was often trying to apply a Chinese energetic diagnosis. The more interest I took, the more I would unravel. I wondered if I was also absorbing their pain, and whether some were draining me of my own life force.

Many people were coming to see me with problems Western medicine could not fix; that doctors couldn't understand. My head was literally spinning all day. I noticed my breathing was shallow in my chest, and this contributed to tension and pain in my neck and shoulders. I probably was not absorbing enough oxygen in my body, and this was making my tiredness worse.

The whole medical system seemed to exist in this state of constant rush and tension. How on earth could we begin to uncover the roots of ill health, if as doctors we were setting such a bad example ourselves?

It is only now that I have gained some true perspective on these times. As I learned to assert myself within my practising life, and to achieve more balance in my life, my symptoms have gradually subsided. In those early days, I had tried constructing an imaginary 'protective wall' around me, a rhinoceros hide to deflect noxious invading energies, but this never worked for me. In fact, this is the main reason we hyperventilate as we defiantly puff out our chests. We try to create a defensive plate of armour around our heart, only to end up breathing rapidly and shallowly.

The answers, I was gradually to find over the next twenty years. I have mentioned that those of us who are thin-skinned *human antennas* absorb a wide range of wavelengths and as a result our systems become overloaded. So we have to learn to say no politely and assertively. We have to learn to worry less, as our brains use up so much energy. And we need to build up our inner strength by using our special gift of being good absorbers. We must take in nature's goodies, and discard what we don't need. And we must learn to love and respect ourselves.

Early on, my symptoms were chaotic; devoid of meaning. But gradually, I was to learn that a 'knowing' about myself was being cemented deep within me, and a knowing about others who suffered chronic debilitating ill health. I learned to recognize that I could feel the pain of others (I was *clairsentient*) and how important it was to learn to let this pain go. I was also beginning to understand that the very thing that was at the root of my suffering – my open absorbent body – was also a subtle and powerful healing tool. It was my own version of intuition, allowing me to tune in to others and myself.

It has been said that on the uneven ground of human suffering, a seed is sown, takes root and begins to grow. I began to regard bodily symptoms as intuitive messages; messages to be listened to intently before any action was taken. But enlightening as all this was, I was also realizing how difficult it was to honor these insights within the constraints of a medical system built around quick consultations. It appeared I would have to make major changes to my working life if I was to feel fulfilled, and healed in a deep sense. I would have to leave the securities of recognized general practice for uncharted waters at a time when I had two young school-aged children.

My wife Trish was wonderful. In many ways she had to endure all my pain and suffering and her support at this time was unflinching. She supported any move that would help my health, even if that meant risking our security. She wanted to see me happy.

But my cautious, conservative, conditioned self needed some further persuading. After all, it was a rash fool that rushed in where a sensible angel feared to tread. I needed help with this decision.

In New Zealand in the late eighties, a large number of doctors had learned acupuncture. Many were using it effectively, but only a few were keen to explore the philosophies behind Chinese medicine. Most doctors found it confusing, fanciful and mystical. They found it difficult to come to terms with the traditional Chinese view, based on Taoist principles, that the body is primarily energy, and that our organs, for instance our heart, liver and kidney, could also be linked with our emotions. Also hard to accept was the idea that an imbalance in one organ could affect another in ways foreign to our Western understanding.

But a few of us were deeply intrigued. Some travelled to China; others read translated textbooks in great detail. There were also books that linked Eastern philosophy with modern physics, such as Fritjof Capra's *The Tao of Physics,* and Deepak Chopra's *Quantum Healing.* Both these books struck a deep chord in me. Most of us were unable to leave our practices for three months to travel to China. Instead, we joined forces, and invited world experts in acupuncture to give small workshops on deeper aspects of Chinese medicine.

In 1990, we invited Dr. Anita Cignolini from Milan. Anita was a world authority on Zang Fu, the Mind-Body-Spirit connections of our organ systems. Her workshop was very detailed but I remember being completely transfixed.

It was all so familiar to me; a total confirmation of much I had observed in my work. I had observed how lung diseases could reflect repressed grief, how heart diseases could have their roots in blocked love and acceptance of self, and how over-thinking and worry could damage our immune system.

I was also intrigued by the detailed descriptions of how weather could affect our health. Our bodies were affected by wind, cold and damp, sensitively responding to our environment in ways not explained by my medical training. Much of it repeated exactly my grandmother's wise words to me many years before.

It was apparent that this model of health acknowledged a direct connection between nature and our bodies. But not only could weather have an effect on our bodies; so too could the emotional 'field' of others. The positive and negative energy of other people could have a definite impact on our well-being. We were true transmitters and receivers of this energy – *human antennas.*

This book tells the story of my discoveries from this point. It explains the steps that I have taken, the signs I have followed, and the synchronicities I have acknowledged. Steps that have led me to a place of wonder; an appreciation that we are all unique, sacred beings reflecting the very consciousness of our universe. Moreover, it explains my continued quest of how best to translate this growing awareness, now shared by so many, into practical ways that facilitate a process of deep healing, so we can be totally fulfilled in this life.

I lay on my bed at the end of the final day of Anita's workshop, exhausted but happy. Trish came into the bedroom and started to massage me gently. Closing my eyes, I drifted in to a blissful state of deep relaxation, my body so light it seemed to float. Everywhere Trish touched sparked off showers of multi-colored light, somehow flowing from deep inside me to the outermost reaches of the universe. Then in an instant all my body's meridians lit up, all the connections inside and outside my body were displayed in perfect detail. I fell into a deep sleep.

Over breakfast the next day, I talked it over with Trish. We decided to sell my general practice, sell our home and to move to a central location, so we could set up a home-based practice combining the best of Western and Eastern medicine.

Three months later, we opened the door of our new home to our first patient.

2: Signs, Symbols and Science

Wonderful things can happen when we create space in our lives.

Extending my consultation times from 15 to 20 minutes may not sound dramatic, and for the way I practise now it is far too short, but for me in the early nineties this extra time was a godsend.

What was to gradually unfold was a revelation.

This chapter illustrates key personal experiences that have guided me towards a deeper understanding of a process that continues to gently envelope me. I have arranged them in a sequence that seems to make sense to people attending my workshops and talks. In reality these insights have been acquired in a rather random, haphazard way. My intent is to 'help the penny drop' for you in a simpler, more orderly way than it did for me.

My only request is that those of you whose hearts sink at the very mention of the word *science* stay with me a while, because I am not about to feed you a heavy main course of stodgy scientific laws followed by a dessert of endless unpalatable equations and formulae. Rather I am serving a sumptuous smorgasbord of symbols and space. This new science is rather fun. Doctors of medicine are not pure scientists. The drugs we prescribe have been developed by scientists, and have gone through a trial process where they have been shown to be statistically effective. At medical school we have studied the chemistry and the scientific workings (the physiology) of the body, but as if the body was an isolated structure somehow separated from the rest of the world. The art of medicine has been to try to apply this knowledge in a meaningful and effective way to the individual who has taken the time to visit us. The prevailing model of health sees the doctor and patient as separate entities, two closed, isolated structures, with the former trying to figure out a way of altering the latter's insides for his or her ultimate benefit. With this in mind, he has a number of tools available to penetrate his patient: pills through one end, suppositories through the other, hypodermic needles and scalpels through the skin.

Another approach involves talking the problem through to see if there is anything patients can do themselves to alleviate their problem. Although this approach is encouraged by all academic colleges in general practice, most family doctors find they are too busy to do this effectively. Counsellors, psychologists and complementary practitioners have built their lives and practices around longer consultation times so they can listen empathetically to their clients in a peaceful, relaxed space.

And it was this space that I was determined to develop in my practice. My aim was that the consultation served as a brief but meaningful retreat from the pressures in people's lives, allowing a complete focus on their healing. The acupuncture I was giving was to be a two way process, with myself being in harmony with the person seeking my help.

I was aware that it takes a certain amount of time for us to unwind during the day. Most deep meditation sessions are 20 minutes or longer. If I was to truly listen, and understand what changes were required to heal, I knew that this was the very minimum time we needed.

Unlike the 'ships that pass in the night' biomedical model, I became aware that it usually takes several minutes for two people to feel comfortable with each other, allowing each to share a common place of respect and trust. As we develop a friendly rapport, our bodies harmonize with each other; our shared body language is a telltale sign of this. Laughter can help seal this harmonic state, as we tune in to each other's wavelength.

As people were by-and-large coming to me on referral by another doctor, they had usually been fully investigated in a formal medical way, and I was free to start delving more deeply into their problems. I became conscious of how important it was for us to share this special place of harmony; but also I needed to protect myself from absorbing their pain.

I was also becoming aware how, within this shared space, there was a real potential for the therapist to be dangerously controlling and disempowering. In a sense we were so close that a vulnerable subject could be at risk of being controlled. I somehow needed to step aside so the healing could be owned by the healee.

As I was figuring out how on earth to do this, a book I was browsing through fell open at a page with an illustration dating back to 1852. The diagram illustrated the 'Four Steps of the Magnetic Blending of Minds'; it was step four that commanded my attention.

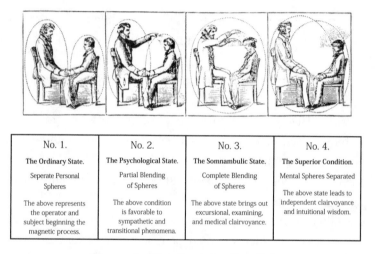

No. 1.	No. 2.	No. 3.	No. 4.
The Ordinary State.	The Psychological State.	The Somnambulic State.	The Superior Condition.
Seperate Personal Spheres	Partial Blending of Spheres	Complete Blending of Spheres	Mental Spheres Separated
The above represents the operator and subject beginning the magnetic process.	The above condition is favorable to sympathetic and transitional phenomena.	The above state brings out excursional, examining, and medical clairvoyance.	The above state leads to independent clairvoyance and intuitional wisdom.

Figure 1. The Superior Condition
Four Steps of the Magnetic Blending of the Minds (19th Century)

As the operator somehow withdraws from the subject, shown here as separating magnetic field 'bubbles', a superior state of *independent clairvoyance and intuitional wisdom* is induced in the subject. Above this poor blindfolded lad's head appears a curious halo of wavy lines, representing a connection to this source of wisdom.

I was not a hypnotist; this is an art I have learned but decided not to practise because of my concerns (just outlined) regarding control. Also I was not about to blindfold all my patients! However I could instantly relate to the symbolism this sketch expressed. I continue to show this ancient picture to many people and have found that it truly paints a thousand words.

It demonstrates not only a magnetic blending of minds, but also the vital stages of engagement in a healing encounter.

Over the years I have tried to develop a deeper understanding of this process. If I am to facilitate a profound state of self-healing in another person, I must follow certain steps:

- Allow a sharing of each other's 'sacred' space through the normal friendly greeting process.
- Foster within myself a true compassionate intent to promote healing.
- Detach myself from the outcome.

As acupuncture rather than hypnotism was my healing tool, I was intrigued by the entry/exit site of this young man's intuitive wisdom, as shown in the diagram.

One remarkable acupuncture point we were taught early in our training is right at the top of our heads – known in China as Baihui; the Point of a Hundred Meetings. People frequently ask me to put in their 'antenna' (acupuncture needle), as it has a remarkable calming effect. I am often reminded of the star of an old TV series, called *My Favorite Martian,* who had two small antennas sticking out of his head, allowing contact with his home planet.

A needle placed at this point is also the most likely to be mistakenly left in someone as they leave a busy acupuncturist's rooms, especially if they have a fine head of bushy silver hair.

In the early hours of one morning, I answered a distressed call from the wife of a stressed businessman I had seen the previous day. She had discovered a needle sticking out of the top his head and she dared not wake him. Somewhat embarrassed by my mistake, I reassured her that no harm had been done. Calming down, she then remarked that he had in fact been in a strangely wonderful mood all evening and had even volunteered to do the dishes. I told her how to remove it without waking him; she phoned me early the next day saying he awoke in his usual foul mood, and could I please tell her how to stick it back in.

Many a time since, I have rushed out of my office and lovingly patted someone's head, unable to remember whether I have extracted this needle or not.

But it was not only this acupuncture point that had a remarkably soothing effect on people. Most would leave my rooms with a sense of inner calm, wherever the needles had been placed. One lady remarked that it was as if she was sitting under a willow beside a tranquil lake.

Nature thrives on our planet because of a unique set of environmental factors. As a result of lightning strikes over the equatorial rain forests, our atmosphere is filled with just the right electromagnetic frequencies that allow growth and repair of our plant life. These are known as the Schumann resonances (7–10Hz), and they are as vital to all animal life as plant life.

Acupuncture needles are made of either steel or copper, and are literally conducting wires. Our bodies conduct electricity too; we jump and recoil after receiving a nasty electrical shock. Electrocardiograph machines use this conductivity to detect electrical impulses conducted from our heart to electrodes on our wrists and ankles.

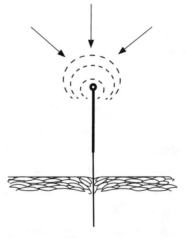

Figure 2. The Metal Antenna
An inserted acupuncture needle or conducting antenna.

Our living tissue, particularly our connective tissue, has the property of being a semi-conductor: a state somewhere between a conducting wire and the insulating earth. The Chinese meridians that appear on wall charts like an electrical grid map are now known to represent concentrated planes of connective tissue; part of an intricate network of branches that divides into smaller and smaller branches like leaves on a tree. These tiny branches end up inside every cell of the body.

Because doctors have been trained to view the body as a mechanical object, we have come to regard our body's connective tissue (collagen is a component of this) simply as a firm internal binding structure; unfortunately as we age this becomes weaker and we sag in embarrassing places. But it is far more than this; it is the very tissue that transmits these healing vibrations to every part of our body. An acupuncture needle acts as a conducting antenna for these Schumann resonances; the acupuncture points are like sockets near the surface of our body connecting to this semi-conducting electrical circuit within.

The skill of the acupuncturist is to work out the best combination of sites to be used. Usually a treatment firstly involves placing one or two needles close to the area that needs treatment (eg a sore foot), and then spreading some symmetrically around the body for an even absorption of these calming rays.

Because every cell in our body is part of this network, some balance can occur even if the correct point is missed, but it is not ideal – akin to the poor reception received by a television where the antenna is placed in the wrong spot.

Performing acupuncture in a peaceful setting helped me appreciate the importance of this other dimension of being – our electromagnetic selves. It helped me think not only of structure, but also of energy. But deeply fascinating though it was, and continues to be, it was to prove merely a stepping stone towards unearthing further mysteries.

Although it helped explain why people felt peaceful and balanced after a treatment, I remained curious about how a few people seemed to have dramatic results from one or two treatments, while others took far longer. Then there was one young man whose watch stopped whenever I gave him acupuncture.

One lady returned home in a state of bliss, and informed her family, 'I heard the angels sing.' Later I was to ask her what precisely she had experienced; was she talking metaphorically? 'In fact,' she explained, 'I heard nothing, but the metaphor of song best conveyed the experience. I felt a joyful harmony, a sense that I was resonating with the universe and was part of a divine song. The joy lingered for an hour or two then faded. It came unasked and unexpectedly, as a blessing, but in that moment I was both the dancer and the dance.'

I seemed to be dealing with a phenomenon that defied logic, but I was beginning to learn that maybe in time, if I were patient, answers would begin to surface. The need to report and explain observations in a rational and scientific way was deeply imbedded in me. Although I was avidly reading enlightened authors who were exploring the margins of science, whose scholarly works both explained and forged links between art, science and spirituality, I felt the distance between the majority of my medical colleagues and myself widening.

On one occasion, I was invited by a group of interested hospice workers to speak on the role of gentle acupuncture in the care of the dying. At the end of the talk, the specialist medical director of one of the hospices stood up and proclaimed; 'There is no role for acupuncture in a hospice.' An embarrassed silence engulfed the room, but I felt strangely comfortable in its midst; I was already learning that it was not my role to battle conditioned dogma. Quite apart from my hard- earned awareness that the negativity of others could drain me of energy, I was finding that no amount of scientific evidence could persuade someone who was not ready to learn.

The Baby in the Ear

For many years, I had been treating people with acute neck and back pain by placing tiny needles in specific tender points on their ears. In many, the relief was so rapid after a single needle that it appeared instantaneous. I followed the map charted by the famous French doctor Paul Nogier, who had started to treat thousands of patients with this method in the 1950s. Remarkably, all the information held by the body was being portrayed within the few square centimeters of a human ear.

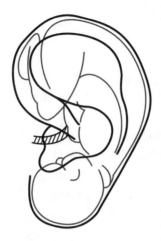

Figure 3. The Baby in the Ear

The points are very specific, and are found by using a small blunt probe over the area of the ear that corresponds to the painful part of the body. The correct point, no bigger than a pinhead, is acutely tender. The electrical resistance of the skin is reduced at the precise point, so the acupuncturist may also use an electrical detector as a guide.

Such was the simplicity and safety of this procedure that I had been using it every day in my practice. Not only was the method relieving a lot of suffering, it was also cutting thousands of dollars off the country's annual drug bill. I was curious to research the science behind such a strange and wonderful healing technique, but for several years any logical explanation alluded me.

Then one Saturday I attended an exhibition of holographic images in Auckland. These weird, ghost-like 3D images of everyday objects fascinated me. Beneath one of the displays – a transparent apple – was a detailed explanation of how a hologram came to be formed. Apparently a laser beam was first split into two, with one half rebounding off the apple and the other deflected by a mirror. The two beams met up again and blended like ripples on a pond. This was recorded onto a special flat photographic plate.

When another laser beam was shone on this plate, a three-dimensional matrix of the apple appeared on the other side. Somehow, human beings had discovered how to reduce a three-dimensional object into a two-dimensional form, only to convert it back again into a three-dimensional, but weightless form.

If this wasn't startling enough, the best was yet to come. A scientist, Dennis Gabor, had won a Nobel Prize in 1971 for discovering that if a tiny corner was cut from the plate, and subjected to another laser beam, the image of the whole apple appeared again. And if another small corner was cut from this sample, the same thing happened. And so on and so on.

The penny began to drop. Here at the frontiers of science was a glimmer of an explanation for my observed effects of ear acupuncture. Here was proof that information conveying the three-dimensional form of a structure could be stored within the tiniest fragment of that structure. Of course this shouldn't have seemed so revolutionary – we had known for fifty years that all our genetic information is encoded within microscopic strands of DNA. And that for centuries Chinese doctors have gained information about the whole body by observing its map on the surface of the tongue, and by gently palpating the character of the arterial pulse at the wrist.

In the *Auguries of Innocence* William Blake invites us:

> *To see the world in a grain of sand*
>
> *And heaven in a wild flower*
>
> *Hold infinity in the palm of your hand*
>
> *And eternity in an hour.*

Somehow, one-and-a-half centuries before Dennis Gabor's remarkable discovery, William Blake had decided we lived in a holographic universe, within a world of patterns whose origins existed beyond the reach of our five senses.

Veering from the Prescribed Path

Throughout the nineties, along with others in the Medical Acupuncture Society, I became increasingly involved in teaching acupuncture to doctors and physiotherapists. Our intimate group of friends, who had been so keen to explore the holistic basis of acupuncture in the eighties, had now become teachers of others. There was, by this time, vast experience within the group; several had studied extensively in China and other countries, and we had formed strong links with like-minded doctors in Australia, the United States and Canada. I had worked for a short time in a hospital in Shanghai in 1995.

We were invited to run a weekend's introductory course in acupuncture for qualified doctors at the Auckland School of Medicine. We were excited at this opportunity to present our experiences to doctors curious to learn more about a growing trend in health care. We demonstrated points, persuaded them to have a go at needling the doctor sitting beside them, and introduced them to the science behind acupuncture.

On the Sunday afternoon, our two most experienced and well-travelled doctors explained the art of Chinese tongue and pulse diagnosis, with a balanced view of its relevance to their own practice of medicine. The audience found this fascinating, and there followed much hearty and healthy debate. We were delighted to receive a warm reception at the end of the course, and several doctors showed real interest in committing themselves to the several years of study and supervision needed to become a Registered Medical Acupuncturist.

The following day I received a call from the medical school. The Dean had apparently heard that we had conducted a session on Chinese medicine, and was displeased. We were told that we could only use the premises again if we omitted references to 'unscientific' Chinese Medicine. We had entered the era of scientific Evidence Based Medicine, and we were evidently basing our medicine well outside the prescribed patch.

Two questions came to my mind: were the pioneers of the modern scientific model (widely known as Newtonian science) really so convinced we lived in a purely mechanical universe? And, how come the mechanical model of health was still so dominant?

I remembered studying Newton's Laws of Gravity at school, with fond memories of dropping apples from the window of our second floor classroom to watch them smash satisfyingly on the asphalt playground below. I had even belonged to Newton House in my first school in London. So I decided it was high time I renewed my acquaintance with Sir Isaac; I was to find the experience enlightening.

Out of the Darkness

"Just as the world was created from dark chaos through the bringing forth of the light and through the separation of the aery firmament and of the waters from the earth, so our work brings forth the beginning out of black chaos and its first matter through the separation of the elements and the illumination of matter."

–Sir Isaac Newton

Sir Isaac Newton, the 17th century expounder of the Laws of Gravity, was an alchemist. Alchemy is not simply the mystical process of extracting gold from base metals: it literally means, 'out of the darkness'. So the one man most strongly attributed with setting the Western world on a course of mechanical materialism seems to have been as much aware of levity, as he was of gravity. Newton's Laws explained how we are all bound to this earth, and why the moon is bound to the earth in orbit as the earth is to the sun. Yet it appears that Sir Isaac knew that this was only part of the story.

One of Newton's influences was Robert Fludd who died five years prior to Sir Isaac's birth. Fludd was a doctor, a philosopher and scholar whose seminal work had been based on the concept that the workings of our bodies somehow reflected those of the universe itself – a unifying theory in line with Eastern Taoist thought – *as above, so below.* In the 20th century, this understanding of the basic nature of our selves and our universe was rediscovered by physicist Dennis Gabor, who first demonstrated the nature of holograms, and neuroscientist Karl Pribham who then applied these principles to the nature of our human brain.

Others influenced by Fludd were his friend Sir William Harvey, the physician who mapped the human circulatory system and Newton's contemporary, Sir Christopher Wren, the architect who designed St Paul's Cathedral and many other magnificent buildings within whose sturdy walls, and upon whose solid foundations, generations have continued to experience the divine.

So when William Blake, the visionary poet, somewhat despairingly exclaimed in 1802 in a letter to his friend Thomas Butt: *'May God us keep,*

from single vision and Newton's sleep' he may well have been paying Sir
Isaac a gross disservice.

We'll never know whether Newton envisaged how great an influence
his discoveries were to have on the history of the Western world. How
they would help spawn the Age of Reason, the Industrial Revolution and
a deep understanding of the mechanical workings of our bodies and our
world. Their influence was to be to such an overwhelming extent that,
by the end of the nineteenth century, many Western scientists confi-
dently exclaimed that they had learned everything that could be learned
about science.

And then along came Albert Einstein. Fifteen generations after
Newton, Einstein's Laws of Relativity added subjectivity to the laws of
nature. He declared that just what we observe may depend on us, the
observers, and that our mass, our physical being (in fact all 'things'), could
be regarded equally as energy.

Then, one single generation later, came the startling theories of
quantum physics: Heisenberg's theory that all matter exists fundamentally
as probabilities, only coming into existence when we observe it. And like
light itself, all matter can also be viewed as wave forms. Thus the reality
conveyed to us by our senses may only be part of the story. That all
we touch, see and hear is in fact an apparently chaotic kaleidoscope of
interfering fields of information, converted into our space/time model
by our very selves. It is not surprising that even Einstein himself initially
found this all rather too much.

But what exactly are the implications of this new quantum awareness
– a state where, as Buddha was to declare, *'all is illusion'?*

How, for instance, does it affect our understanding of life itself? . . .
of love? . . . of healing? . . . of death?

But it is also important to remember that the mechanistic world
of gravity is as real as it ever was for us – it is responsible for our days,
our nights and our months. It secures each and every one of us to our
home, Mother Earth, allowing us to see the light by day, and reach for
the stars at night.

So maybe only now that we have been so thoroughly grounded, we
are ready to share the true glory of Sir Isaac Newton's vivid alchemic
vision – the light emerging from the dark – a state of levity from gravity.

And I am beginning to suspect that if, as William Blake implied, Sir Isaac had fallen asleep, one of his eyes remained firmly open.

At times, I am convinced it continues to watch over us.

A Journey into Inner Space

Our 50 trillion cells are made up of molecules; our molecules are made up of atoms. Each of us has 7 billion billion billion atoms in our body. About two thirds of these are hydrogen atoms. About 90 percent of all atoms in the universe are hydrogen atoms, but as yet no one has been able or patient enough to count them!

The wonderful thing about a hydrogen atom, for those of us who struggle with math, is that it has no more than one of anything – a nucleus of one proton being orbited by a tiny solitary electron. The ubiquitous presence of hydrogen atoms in our bodies is the reason why MRI (Magnetic Resonance Imaging) works. This wonder of modern medicine measures the way different concentrations of positively charged hydrogen protons in our body vibrate after being subjected to a very strong rotating magnetic field.

I am about to use this simplest of all atoms as an example of how all atoms 'talk' to each other. Although atoms are incredibly tiny, they are in reality filled with a vast wasteland of space. To give some idea of proportions, if the central proton were the size of a tennis ball we would have to travel 300 km outwards before we met our circulating electron. Even then we would have trouble catching it, as it has a tendency to flash in and out of existence.

Luckily it flashes conveniently into view as soon as we look at it. It can be regarded as a ball-like particle if we want, but it prefers to be known as a wavy blur; it is aware we make it into a particle, rather than a blur of probabilities as we find bits easier to understand. However the really weird part is of course that we are actually talking about ourselves – a huge bunch of atoms trying to look in the mirror at ourselves. Our electrons come from somewhere else. Because they are really wavy lines they come from bigger wavy lines – known rather unimaginatively as *superstrings*. At this point in my talks, someone always asks where the superstrings come from. Well I don't think we know, but I suspect it is the place one half of every pair of my socks goes after I carefully place them in the laundry basket.

It is humbling indeed to become aware that we are in essence, made up of vast amounts of nothingness; that it is consciousness rather than structured form that underlies all things and us. For three hundred years we have examined the workings of our body in more and more intricate detail, reducing our field of vision to smaller and smaller areas, only to discover that our inner space is remarkably like outer space.

Just how atoms 'talk' to each other was initially dismissed by scientists as being preposterous. Albert Einstein said it was 'spooky'. But over the past thirty years the process of 'entanglement' has become more and more accepted by the scientific community.

So what is 'entanglement'? As we observe an electron it settles into spinning around the atomic nucleus in one direction. It appears to choose its spin randomly. Entanglement occurs when a twin atom's electron instantaneously spins in the other direction – i.e. when one is clockwise, the other is anticlockwise. I am careful to say here that one electron doesn't cause the other to spin in an opposite way, because that would imply a time delay. Entanglement happens instantly, together in unison outside our known dimension of time.

Initially scientists were excited to see this phenomenon happening with two electrons in the same laboratory. Over recent years this instant effect has been tested over longer and longer distances, leading them to conclude that entanglement occurs not only outside our known understanding of time, but it is also independent of distance – now referred to as a non-local event. This means 'entangled' electrons can exist anywhere in the universe, and yet the entanglement happening is not weakened by distance.

There are many who say that the sub-microscopic world of electron behaviour lends little support to the debate whether humans can communicate telepathically. Some would argue that at best it is a metaphor for events on a larger scale. However, alongside my learning about these fascinating scientific observations, I was becoming increasingly aware of spontaneous non-local happenings in my everyday working life.

In the early nineties I was the medical director of the North Shore Hospice, Auckland, and became aware of how family members often needed to 'let go' of their dying loved one to allow a peaceful transition. Often I had to talk to a relative either in another room, or make a phone call to their home, before the dying person could relax and die in peace. In some cases this appeared instantaneous.

On one occasion, I talked by phone to Scotland to the sister of a dying patient, trying my best to guide her through this process. Her brother had been very restless for a number of hours, but was completely at peace as I returned to the room after I had made the call out of earshot. It appeared to me that this special form of instant communication came to the fore at the times people dropped their barriers – when egos dissolved – i.e. in the very young, the intellectually impaired and the dying. And it occurred by and large between people who were in close loving relationships. In fact I began to understand that these special connections travelled on the wings of love – between a mother and her child, and of course between animal lovers and their pets.

It is common knowledge that identical twins can often experience each other's pain. This is one example of what is known as *telesomatic* communication. On one occasion, Anne, a woman in her later forties, came to see me in Auckland with a painful stiff neck that had come on suddenly the day before. Two hours after the onset of pain, she had received a phone call from her identical twin sister living in Brisbane, Australia, who told her she had been in an accident. Luckily there had been no serious injury, but she was developing pain in her neck from the whip-lashing movement of her head during the accident. Anne had already felt something was wrong, and had tried to contact her sister on her cell phone, only to get her answer message.

Both sisters were developing pain in the same part of their neck, and another phone call to her sister that morning confirmed that their pains were worsening. I found the sore spot on Anne's ear that corresponded to the painful area in her neck, and stuck a small acupuncture needle into it. Her pain was considerably relieved. A minute later, her phone rang. It was her sister in Brisbane, who told Anne excitedly that her own pain had just 'magically' disappeared. Anne then gave me a wink as she asked me whether I could split the medical bill between them!

This experience could be classed as anecdotal, and would be unlikely to convince a hardened skeptic of the existence of telepathic communication. However, telesomatic experiences between identical twins are now becoming more accepted within the scientific community, with well-documented studies appearing in peer-reviewed journals.

Over recent years, many patients have opened up to me about their own non-local experiences. I found Eva's story particularly powerful:

Eva's Story

Eva had been particularly busy that evening – her two small children were bathed and settled, the housework finished and at last she had some time to herself. Since moving to New Zealand from Romania four years previously, Eva had had little time to rest. A part time job, her children and now a distance-learning business course had given her little time to reflect on her new life.

Her husband was working late that night. As she sat alone on the side of her bed, she became aware of a vision – a strange feeling as real as the familiar surroundings of her comfortable bedroom. To describe it makes the episode sound sinister, but Eva felt a wonderful calmness come over her. This was surprising as the vision was of a fatal car crash all played out in slow motion; and then, a feeling she could only describe as absolute love – as if a warm blanket of deep compassion surrounded her while the vision changed into a beautiful luminescent orb of bright blue light.

Slowly the experience faded, leaving Eva in a rather confused, mixed-up state; she started to panic, fearing her husband might have been involved in an accident. She phoned him immediately – it was 10.30 pm – and he was on his way home. She pleaded with him to drive carefully, and was overjoyed to hear the garage door open. She found it difficult to explain the sensations to her husband, who did his best to console her, reassuring her that everyone was safe. That morning, the warm loving blanket returned – and Eva was conscious of a sensation like a guiding hand on her left shoulder. Later that afternoon came the news that both her parents had been killed in a car crash in Romania at 5 am New Zealand time.

Another piece of the jigsaw, and it is a particularly large piece, has been put firmly in place by the British evolutionary biologist Rupert

Sheldrake. Sheldrake talks of *morphic fields* – invisible fields of information that are fundamental to all living matter. As in our entanglement scenario these fields exist in a dimension apart from our known concepts of space and time. According to the theory of *morphic resonance,* the fields are the reason why flocks of birds fly and turn in perfect unison, why hundreds of fish within a massive shoal turn together spontaneously.

His theories extend to explaining both human and animal behaviour patterns, with these fields having their presence in the past, present and future. He hypothesizes that they form the very template – or matrix – upon which our physical bodies are formed. Rupert Sheldrake is a leading light in the field of non-material sciences. His work is viewed as controversial by many scientists, but for me it continues to be truly inspirational.

The Mystery of the Caduceus

I have grown up with the caduceus. The staff supporting a curled snake was part of the emblem on my father's Royal Army Medical Corps brass badge. It is the major feature in both the British and New Zealand Medical Associations' logos. The prominent medical research and development company, The Wellcome Trust, and the US Army Medical Corps use the image of twin serpents entwined on the staff, climbing towards open wings signifying the Greek god Hermes (Mercury according to the Romans) the winged messenger. The emblem of the caduceus appears on many logos in the medical and air travel business.

The caduceus has meant many things to many people over the years. It was the emblem of Enki, the Sumerian god known as the Lord of the Sacred Eye (c2000BC). The Greek physician, and later god of healing, Asklepios, held a staff with a single serpent coiled around it (c1200BC). Several centuries later Hippocrates literally took up the same baton. The twin serpented staff, regarded by many as the 'true' caduceus, (Figure 4) has become the symbol of alchemists or practitioners of the hermetic arts such as Sir Isaac Newton. As we have already shown, alchemy is the craft that brings light out of the dark – often depicted as transforming a base metal (mercury) into gold.

Figure 4. The Double-serpent Caduceus of Hermes

During the nineties, my overriding goal was to practise medicine in a style that honored both Western and Eastern thought. I became increasingly interested in the traditional Hindu concept of the
chakras. The major *chakras,* Sanskrit for wheels, are the seven energetic
planes of the body and are depicted as spinning vortices of energy. In
traditional texts, they appear in illustrations as beautiful multi-colored
lotus flowers. Our health depends on a balance of forces – harmony –
within each chakra, as well as a state of balance between every level. Each
chakra also acts as a connection of the physical body to outer layers of
subtle energy.

I was to discover that many diagrams of the chakras incorporated
the model of the caduceus, as shown in Figure 5 on the next page. Here,
deeply etched within ancient Hindu culture, was a symbol used as a
proud logo for our most prominent Western medical institutions. This
excited me.

The twin serpents of the caduceus wrap around the chakras
controlling the entry and exit of energy. They are referred to as the female
energies providing balance to the 'male' central spinal cord, depicted in
the caduceus as a stiff staff. This central column is the channel for the
universal life force, or *kundilini* that in Vedic tradition enters the body
through our familiar point at the top of our head to rest at the base of our
spine. The *kundilini* rises up the body throughout our life, accompanied
by a transforming growth in consciousness, to eventually depart from
the same point at death. On reaching the sixth and seventh *chakras*, the

person approaches an enlightened state – a state of oneness with the universe. The transformation is precisely that envisaged by the Hermetic alchemists, whose craft embraced the occult traditions of the West.

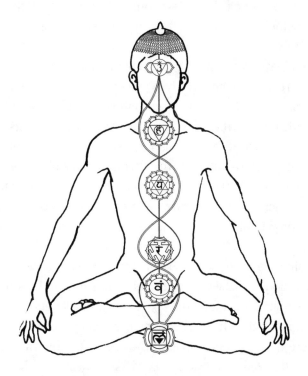

Figure 5. A Diagram of the Chakras Incorporating
the Model of Caduceus

I was attracted to the *chakras* because I found them very 'user friendly'. Whereas patients would struggle to understand the intricacies of the Chinese meridians (it was alright for me as I was using them every day), they had no problem knowing that their heart was within the heart *chakra,* or their thyroid gland was within their throat *chakra.*

There is much common ground shared by the Chinese and Indian Ayurvedic systems; combining these models allowed me to help initiate healing using acupuncture, and then involving the person so that they developed a deep understanding of their healing journey through an appreciation of their own *chakras.*

I have found many insights from this ancient Hindu model that have helped patients in their quest for healing. As in traditional Chinese medicine, it is important not to be put off by the mystical language. Rather than accepting these descriptions literally, I have tried to regard them as metaphors and colorful myths carrying within them many valuable truths.

The chakras were not the product of rational scientific thought. Rather they were recognised intuitively by Vedic seers who were experienced meditators. Using their own model, their *kundilini* would have risen to the sixth chakra, the third eye, allowing them insights into hidden realms. Paradoxically, the one man whose very name signifies Cartesian reductionist Western thought, the French philosopher, Rene Descartes (1596–1650), meditated for three hours every morning, and attributed the development of his theories – the most famous of which is 'Cogito, ergo sum' or ' I think, therefore I am' – to a combination of rationality and intuition.

Helping me make sense too of the chakras was the understanding that in addition to the seven major chakras, there are hundreds of minor charkas scattered all around the body. These smaller energetic whirlpools correspond with the Chinese acupuncture points and are regarded as the sites where there is interchange of the body's energy with the energy of nature. So the Vedic description of chakras was very close to my own conclusions about the nature of acupuncture points. The symmetrical twin serpents of the caduceus represented the balancing energies at different levels of the body; the goal of the acupuncturist was to help the patient achieve an ideal balanced state by easing the exchange of energy between the body and nature. Our acupuncture training encouraged a symmetrical placement of these conducting needles around the body if one was giving a treatment for general well-being. In the chakra model, perfect balance allowed the body to open up to another dimension in healing – the universal life force or kundilini. As this rose in the body, the consciousness of the person would grow eventually, and hopefully, to a superior state of enlightened bliss.

As this force had initially entered the baby through the soft spot on top of the head, and would exit from this very point at death, I wondered if this was a fair description of the human soul.

In Chapter 3, *The Growth of the Human Antenna,* I will describe my experiences with working with this model, and what relevance I believe the chakras have to our present and future health.

Superconducting DNA

Fascinated though I was by the chakra model, I felt the need to explore modern scientific models that might support the presence of these new dimensions of healing. It did not escape me that the twin serpented caduceus and the molecular structure of DNA shared the same double-helix pattern. What was to really catch my eye were the reports that were appearing in the popular scientific journals in 1996 that DNA, under certain conditions, behaved as a *superconductor.* As I am about to explain some cutting edge science, I appreciate I risk turning some readers off. Please stay with me, though, as I'll try to make it as painless as possible!

Figure 6. Superconducting DNA

Briefly, a superconductor is a substance that conducts electrical energy incredibly quickly as it has little or no resistance. In 1911, a Dutch physicist named Onnes discovered that mercury lost all its electrical resistance and became a superconductor when he froze it to 269 degrees C below zero. Other superconductors were discovered: tin, aluminium, titanium, tungsten and zinc – but they too only acted this way at these ridiculously cold temperatures.

The hunt then started for superconductors that functioned at warmer temperatures. The research was spearheaded by the computer giants as the IT revolution gained pace in the eighties and nineties. If they could discover materials, or combinations of materials, that worked at room temperature they could incorporate them into specialized and personal computers making them faster and more efficient.

In 1995, the *Scientific American* reported an experiment that in the presence of the superconductor ruthenium, a strand of DNA became 10,000 times more conductive. Further reports followed, including the discovery in 2001 that a combination of DNA and another superconductor (carbon coated rhenium) achieved this state at room temperature.

Superconductors are used in computer equipment, often suspended in compounds that keep them cold. Because these materials conduct electricity so efficiently, the magnetic fields generated around them are huge. This has led to the development of MRI scanners, which exert these large fields on the body causing hydrogen atoms to vibrate. Other examples include superfast switches in modern computers, and long distance electrical cables. The MagLev train in Japan travels at high speed on two opposing magnetic fields generated by superconductors. As a result there is absolutely none of the friction found between wheels and rails, as passengers ride in a state of levitation.

So superconducting technology, and our thirst for speed and efficiency, is driving us beyond the world of restrictive electrical currents, to a dimension where things happen comfortably and instantly. When DNA is extracted from a living being, dried and added to a superconducting compound in the laboratory it appears to enhance that compound's superconductivity at the temperature nature prefers. This raises the, as yet unanswered question about whether DNA, when nestled cosily in its friendly environment within the nucleus of a cell, behaves in this extraordinary way. Could its coiled double-helix shape in any way be behaving as a balancer of opposing magnetic forces, like the caduceus, allowing another dimension of energy to enter into its midst?

As I was asking myself this question, I discovered reports from physicists 'disproving' that DNA had superconducting properties.

I e-mailed one of these researchers at Princeton University asking for details of his scientific method, and he very courteously replied. He explained that his experiments that disproved that DNA was a good conductor were carried out on dried strands of DNA, and that the intrinsic conductivity of DNA in the body (in vivo) is 'virtually impossible to measure' as the molecule in its natural state is always in a solution of salt and water. His focus, and that of the vast majority of researchers, was on the properties of dried DNA as they were, 'mindful of possible nano-electronics applications'. This is understandable as funding for such cutting edge research comes from the computer companies, eyeing the massive profits to be made from potential discoveries. However, working on 'dead' DNA adds little to our understanding of its healing role nestled cosily in a harmonious, interconnected state within the living body.

I was reminded yet again of a fish, struggling and gasping, out of water.

There are yet other dissenting voices. Some scientists have scoffed at the possibility of living DNA being a superconductor, basing their opinion on the massive electromagnetic fields that would be generated inside and outside the body. They say that this would mean we would walk into our kitchen to be greeted by flying cutlery and saucepans hurtling towards us at great speed (even if we hadn't upset our spouse). One reason why this skepticism could eventually prove to be unfounded lies deep within spiralling strands of the DNA molecule itself.

The DNA Antenna

Only 10 percent of our DNA is directly involved in setting the genetic structure of our bodies. The remaining 90 per cent has been rather unfairly labelled 'junk DNA' – the researchers have been unable to match it up with any particular processing function. There were great hopes in the eighties and nineties that the Human Genome Project, the unravelling of the genetic code, would be the major step in understanding the nature of living things. This pioneering landmark has certainly taught us much about the human body and has opened up the exciting and life-saving field of gene therapy. However, the limitations of seeing the genetic process as a linear code of fixed molecules has left many questions unanswered. We are slowly beginning to see beyond the chemistry of the DNA to its mathematical coding, its geometric design and even its poetry.

There are only 26 letters in the Western alphabet, and only eight major notes in an octave. But from these simple constructs all the great literary and symphonic works in history have been created – from the complete works of William Shakespeare, to all of Beethoven's symphonies.

There is a huge step we need to take from learning the alphabet to writing our first masterpiece; the step mankind has to make from the decoding of the genome to a deep understanding of the new science of life is by comparison a quantum leap. As long as our primary focus is on how DNA can best enhance our IT industry, we will be held back from making this leap.

Russian scientists have had a long history of looking at DNA in a far more holistic fashion. Rather than just regarding it as a chemical structure, they have researched its vibrational and electrical qualities. Understanding that light is vital to life, they have discovered that the DNA molecule responds to photons of light. They claim it actually receives, harmonises, stores and transmits light – mainly in the blue part of the colored spectrum that we see in a rainbow. It is, perhaps, no coincidence that this is the same shade of blue we have over us in the sky.

Light and color therapy have been used as mainstream forms of treatment for years in Russia, whereas the view of color therapy in most orthodox medical circles is that it is quackery. My own understanding of light is still in its infancy. For many years I have used a soft, low-powered laser over acupuncture points for young children and for those who are scared of needles. This painless device emits an infrared laser beam (remote controls produce the same frequencies) that penetrates several centimeters beneath the skin. Over the years I have been amazed that a number of people, especially young children, can actually feel the laser 'light' as a faint tickle

Light is a strange concept; its smallest 'particles' or quanta can also be considered to be waves and travel literally at the speed of light. Stranger still is the whole issue of color.

Many of us still think of color as a surface phenomenon; it is as if a rose is red and the grass is green because, like our cars, it is painted that way. But living color is far more wonderful than this, and reflects the total involvement of the organism. When light shines on a green leaf, some of the colors of the rainbow are absorbed and used by the plant, whilst others like green are deflected. On a hot day a white cotton shirt is cooler than a black shirt because it reflects back all the colors of the rainbow together, in the form of white light.

Light, like all the information received by the body, is put to good work providing energy, and enhancing healing. It appears from the Russian research that our DNA is involved in this process to a major degree, acting as a true receiving and transmitting *antenna*. In their projects, linguistic experts were selected to work alongside the scientists in an attempt to unravel the language of the code.

Astoundingly, they have discovered that the pattern of the 'junk DNA' is constructed in precisely the same way we construct our own languages, with syntax and grammar. It is perhaps more accurate to say that the blueprint of our world's languages started life encoded within our DNA, and has been somehow transmitted into human consciousness over many generations.

DNA resonates with sound as well as light. It will be interesting to discover whether the sacred chants of all religions have aligned themselves to these healing frequencies through the intuition of generations of holy women and men. Also, through this research, we may gain deeper insights into the soothing healing effects of all forms of music, and the spoken word.

There is mounting evidence that it is the kindness and loving intent behind our words that heals. In a dramatic and beautiful area of research, a Japanese scientist, Dr Masaru Emoto, has noticed that water crystals change their shape when exposed to different words and music. Even words written on paper suspended on the water produce effects. Kind and loving words and music in general produce beautiful crystalline shapes, no matter which language they are spoken in. Angry words and gangster rap produce bizarre images. He has even experimented with exactly how words are meant – are they well meaning or simply flippant? – and found that the water 'knows' the good intent behind the words. Maybe this research will lead us to a deeper understanding of the affects of prayer, counseling, and good old-fashioned tender loving care.

DNA – The Link between Dimensions

It has been calculated that if we were to unwind the DNA in each of our cells and stretch it out on the floor it would measure over 5 feet. So it is obviously in its coiled shape for packaging reasons – but as I have already hinted, maybe there are other secrets held deep within the double helix, our ubiquitous micro-caduceus.

Let us step back – just briefly I promise – into the world of secondary school physics. The standard electrical coil we find in our electric kettle consists of conducting cable through which passes an electrical current. Around the coil, an electromagnetic field is produced, heating our water (Figure 7A). By doubling the coil, or by wrapping the coil in tight circles around a ring, some North and South electromagnetic fields cancel each other out (Figures 7B and 7C). When the coil forms the figure-of-eight shape seen in Figure 7D, the Möbius Coil – you can play around with a rubber band to get this shape – all the magnetic fields cancel each other out, leaving a magnetic vacuum. This is a space beyond magnetism, like the space between the magnetic fields produced under the MagLev train. This space, like the entangled space connecting electrons of opposing spin, is the opening to another dimension; an energy that exists outside our concepts of space and time, known variously as free, zero-point and scalar energy.

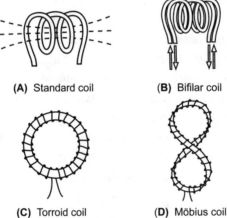

(A) Standard coil   (B) Bifilar coil

(C) Torroid coil   (D) Möbius coil

Figure 7. Coils

Coils used to emit fields and potentials:

    Coil (A) produces a standard magnetic field.
    Coil (B) produces electrical scalar and magnetic vector waves.
    Coil (C) has the same effect.
    Coil (D) produces only scalar waves.

Adapted from Abraham (1998) and Oschman (2000).

Scalar energy is non-local and non-temporal. Information does not travel from 'here' to 'there'; it coexists in both places simultaneously.

The double helical DNA is constructed of many tiny, but powerful Möbius coils laid end on end. We are beginning to understand that every molecule of DNA within every 50 trillion cells is continuously transmitting this non-local scalar energy to receptors all around the body. It works rather like an old-fashioned slide projector converting the image held in a tiny transparency onto a large screen. Only DNA is not projecting simple rays of light, but this other-dimensional scalar energy, instantly and holographically. And not in one direction onto a flat screen but everywhere as the matrix of our three-dimensional body. To use the analogy of a hologram where the smallest part holds all the information of the whole, the DNA molecule holds within its field the information of the total body. The microscopic double helix of the DNA therefore leaves its imprint within the matrix of the whole body.

There is, however, a subtle difference between the 3-dimensional 'apple' hologram and the DNA model. Some scientists speculate that the DNA acts as a projector for a 4-dimensional state, as time itself is processed by this remarkable molecule.

So it appears that our DNA, in addition to coordinating the building of our physical structure, dynamically and continuously constructs a map of our body in the form of a holographic matrix, so that the building blocks know where to go. It is interesting to ponder that many centuries before Watson and Crick won their Nobel Prize for discovering the double-helix structure of DNA, Vedic seers had already envisioned the twin serpents of the caduceus uncoiling within the essence of our body, thereby conveying a fundamental truth about our physical and spiritual growth.

Just how the matrix converts to the tangible reality of our body is a question presently only answered in science fiction movie scripts (see Endnote at end of this chapter). At present, de-materialising then re-mataterialising (or teleporting) on a human scale is observed by most of us only in re-runs of *Star Trek*. But without a doubt this is the very drama played out within every corner of your being as you read this. (For further insights, see Appendix 1: Shedding New Light.)

It is complex, outside our wildest imaginings, as trillions of information fields projected by our DNA interact with each other, as countless ripples on a lake.

It is even more mind boggling to realize that these fields are also in direct contact with morphic fields 'outside' our body – from our society, nature and the boundless cosmos. Fuelling this incredible frenzy are the more recognizable sources of our earth's energy: light, sound, and the Schumman resonances, all gratefully received by these tiny micro computers. Our understanding of DNA deepens, as we perceive it as a vital link between our earth-bound mortal/physical body and the more ethereal realms of our immortal, timeless soul.

It is perhaps no coincidence that the shape of the Möbius coil is the classical sign of infinity. (See Figure 7D, p. 58.)

Figure 8. Infinity Symbol Reflected in Double Helix

The DNA molecule is an exceptional generator of energy. It is proposed that it functions as a relay station, connecting our inner and outer worlds. It appears that the fundamental nature of reality is contained within fields of information. Our perceived real world 'collapses' down from these realms.

Into the Eye of the Storm

If we were to view the DNA molecule from either of its ends, it would appear as a donut-shaped ring – like the torroidal coil in Figure 7C. In the central hole, the magnetic fields are cancelled out, opening our window to another dimension. If we were to shrink ourselves down enough to sit inside this hole, it is likely we would experience a wonderful state of peace while all around us we would see this fierce electrical storm raging.

Those who find themselves in the eye of a hurricane often experience an eerie calm, while the storm forms a formidable whirling wall around them. I have often used this as an analogy for meditation – finding a still point in one's day even though all around there is chaos and tension. Deep healing frequently involves finding a central core of peace within a body and a world wracked with pain and suffering.

I was recently keen to discover whether others had explored this metaphor, and so I searched the Internet to help deepen my understanding of this process. I found that Father John Dunne, a pastoral counsellor at the University of Notre Dame, Indiana, had taken the hurricane visualization one further step. He remarked that if we were to stay still within the eye of the storm, the swirling winds would quickly engulf us, sending us spinning in turmoil. The trick was to keep moving with the storm, as this still point was also continuously on the move. His underlying message was that we needed to keep vigilant with our meditations, practising every day, as life's challenges never let up. I was graphically reminded of this powerful mix of grace and discipline while watching a surfing championship on the television recently. The surfers were riding waves whose giant walls all but totally encircled them. They somehow managed to maintain their balance within the rapidly moving 'eye of the wave', keeping just ahead of the waves breaking powerfully behind them. Their skill had been acquired after years of practice, allowing them to respond intuitively and spontaneously while remaining fully alert in the present.

As I started to appreciate the holographic nature of the universe, I became more aware of the significance of patterns, shapes and proportions. What appeared before to be visual metaphors now began to convey more profound meanings. I started to consider whether the hole in the DNA, the eye of the hurricane and the way my bathwater disappeared down the plughole were more closely linked. I was seeing whirls everywhere, from the cute swirls of hair on the top of my son's head, to Steven Hawking's vivid descriptions of Black Holes. The chakra openings were described as whirling vortices, as were the acupuncture points. Physicist John Wheeler theorised that space itself comprised an infinite number of tiny spiral wormholes; he named this phenomenon 'the quantum foam' (Appendix 1).

By expanding our awareness to realms outside our comfortable parameters of space and time, we begin to grasp that a pure form of information is fundamental to our universe.

Another word for this pure form of information is *consciousness*.

Fibonacci's Rabbits

Leonardo Fibonacci (b. 1170 in Pisa, Italy), perhaps the most influential mathematician of all time, spent much of his early life as a merchant, working for his father. While stationed in Algeria, he traveled to many countries in the Middle East and Europe, where he became interested in each country's differing currencies and mathematical techniques. Fibonacci has been credited for introducing the Hindu-Arabic numbering system to Europe, 1 through 9, which the Europeans were to find much less cumbersome than the Roman numerals.

On returning to Pisa in 1200, he became a full-time mathematician, writing four books. His work was the first documented record of simple math equations using today's numbers. He also set himself many practical problems, which he then attempted to solve. The answer to one, involving the breeding pattern of rabbits, proved to have a profound effect on generations of artists, architects and scientists for centuries to come.

Figure 9. Fibonacci's Rabbits

Fibonacci tried to estimate how quickly a rabbit population would grow in ideal circumstances. As in all math problems, certain assumptions were made. Firstly none of the rabbits would die; secondly that each pair of rabbits did not produce more than one pair of offspring each month. Finally, it was assumed that each rabbit only reached sexual maturity in their second month.

Thus, the Fibonacci sequence was born. As we have all observed, a rabbit population grows exceedingly rapidly, with the number of pairs per month being shown in the following sequence: 1, 1, 2, 3, 5, 8, 13, 21, 34, 55, 89, 144, 233, 377, 610, 987, 1597 etc.

Each number is the sum of the preceding two numbers; as the number becomes larger, the ratio of the last number to the one before approaches 1.618 – known as the Golden Ratio. As we achieve adulthood, 1.618 to 1 is the ratio of the length of our body below our navel to that above.

This of course could be regarded as an irrelevant isolated coincidence – was it not for the Golden Ratio or Mean, and Fibonacci's series, revealing themselves within every corner of the natural world from the smallest microscopic structure to the largest mammal, from the simplest algae to the largest tree. A nautilus shell grows, and a fern unfurls, 'mindful' of the blueprint first observed by Fibonacci. Note that each line is divided below according to the Golden Ratio of 1.618.

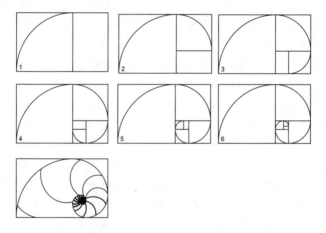

Figure 10. The Golden Ratio

The distribution of seeds in the sunflower is governed by this spiral, based in turn on the Golden Ratio. The daisy family will also only have a number of petals from the Fibonacci series. The branching of shrubs, trees and even the bronchial tree in our own lungs also follows these 'divine' rules.

Leonardo da Vinci (1452–1519) used the proportions of the Golden Ratio in his masterpiece the Mona Lisa. His Vetruvian man displays the sacred geometry of the human form based on the proportions and divisions demonstrated three centuries earlier by his fellow countryman and namesake Leonardo Fibonacci. The relationship between the length of bones in the human finger, hand and arm are examples that are easily demonstrated on any medical student's skeleton. On the microscopic level, every double-helix spiral of DNA measures 34 angstroms long by 21 angstroms wide. You can see these numbers in the Fibonacci series page 62, Figure 9; their ratio is 1.619.

The Renaissance artists introduced perspective to art. They observed that all of nature followed the same rules of form; the Golden Ratio was a measurement of proportion that linked the smallest simplest life form with the most complex.

Architects such as Sir Christopher Wren incorporated these universal proportions into their churches not only for aesthetic and religious reasons. They were also aware that they contributed to excellent acoustics. The harmonics of sound and music are also based on this sacred geometry.

I can only give you a taste of this extraordinary subject, as it could easily fill a lifetime of study. It represents a measurable link between many times and cultures, between art, science and spirituality. It touches on everything from the mundane to the mystical, from labyrinths to whirling Dervishes, from DNA to black holes and even galaxies. Spiral dynamics, a new discipline arising from this living geometry, is applied increasingly in the business world to predict financial markets and help direct sustained growth within companies. Evolutionary and sociological trends are now plotted in spiral form, suggesting a collective morphic field effect – similar to the concept of Carl Jung's 'collective unconscious'.

For my part, I began to realize that the numbers themselves weren't so important; for me this was all to do with proportions and relationships. Describing this geometry as sacred seemed to me to be no rash overstatement. It was not only strong confirmation of the holographic nature of the universe. It also suggested that everything within this universe shared something very special at the most fundamental level – an unseen, organizing, interconnected intelligence that gave birth to energy and form – a benign pure consciousness that for many would be the very essence of God.

In Leonardo da Vinci's day, openly expressing this abstract view of a divine force would have been nothing short of heresy. He was wise to keep his secrets locked securely away within his work in code form; sacred secrets concealed within the knowing smile on the face of the beautiful Mona Lisa.

We Are Connective Tissue

Many people presenting themselves to me have conditions under the collective label of connective tissue diseases. Under this banner lie illnesses such as multiple sclerosis (MS), and lupus (SLE), as well as many that defy an accurate formal diagnosis. Although these conditions are rarely fatal, sufferers often feel isolated and misunderstood, as their debilitating symptoms tend to be so haphazard and difficult to describe. A complex network of connective tissue is present throughout our body. As well as holding us together, it acts as a semiconductor of electricity.

Planes of connective tissue called fascia run between our muscles – the white skin we find between the meat in a prime steak – and these are comprised of thousands of strands of collagen molecules arranged in a triple helical pattern.

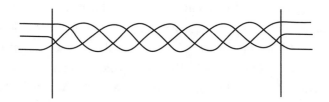

Figure 11. A Triple Helical Pattern

As in our DNA molecule, collagen molecules have water molecules bound to their surface, and conduct electricity as liquid crystals. The fascial layers, made up of this collagen, are now recognized as the ancient Chinese acupuncture meridians conducting energy in and out of the body. The collagen fibres connect with a complex array of filaments and tubules on the surface and within the cells – known as the cytoskeleton – forming an interconnecting web reaching every muscle, bone and organ.

Inside the cells, we find tiny hollow tubes called *microtubules,* whose walls comprise of tightly wound spirals of protein molecules.

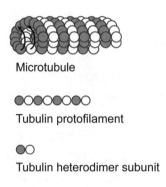

Microtubule

Tubulin protofilament

Tubulin heterodimer subunit

Figure 12. Microtubules

Our brain has many more of these microtubules in its cells than other organs. Before we explore why this is important, we need to pay attention to the vital organ that joins forces with our brain to create a powerful healing partnership.

Our heart generates a far more powerful magnetic field than our brain, and it is the harmonic connection between our heart and brain that lies at the root of deep healing. So many of us live 'in our heads', desperately trying to sort things out logically and rationally, that we forget that it is through our hearts that we make the most profound connections.

According to the Chinese meridians, and the Vedic chakras, our healing hands are the extensions of our hearts. During my time in Shanghai, my very patient teachers used to laugh at the way I pondered studiously over a patient, trying to work out the correct acupuncture points I should use. After a time, I asked our interpreter what exactly it was that I was doing that so amused them. There followed a lengthy exchange between them in Mandarin, ending in more raucous laughter.

Eventually she turned to me and said: 'They say you look so serious, so worried you will make a mistake. If you smile more, the treatment will come from your heart.'

Most complementary therapies seek to heal the body through its connective tissue. The therapists – be they osteopaths, chiropractors, massage therapists or Reiki practitioners – work to achieve energetic balance within this cytoskeletal network which is known to be a conductor of energy. As this energy becomes balanced, we again become connected to society and the world around us, and even beyond.

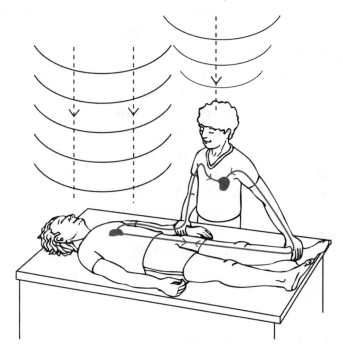

Figure 13. The Healer and the Healee in a Connected State

However a healing encounter also involves the healer. When relaxed, balanced and smiling, the healer's connective tissue is in the perfect state to be a receiver and transmitter of subtle energy – the ideal *human antenna*. The healer and healee may then, in an instant, achieve a harmonic state of oneness, as joint antennas, tuning in to a universal source.

As I was treating the lady who 'heard the angels sing', I too was aware of pleasant sensations. Over the years, the acupuncture I give has become gentler, much to the relief of patients seeking my help. In more complex cases, I allow the end of the needle to barely penetrate the skin, using only two points – one on the wrist and one around the ankle. These are access points to what the Chinese refer to as the extra meridians, and represent meeting points of many other meridians. As I touch these points, I turn myself into an effective *human antenna,* transmitting – channelling – information to the patient. In fact we work in tandem, receiving and passing on these healing frequencies to each other. I recognize a tuning-in by experiencing a pleasant feeling in a line between my heart and my stomach. As I have learned to recognize this, I can sometimes feel it before the patient becomes aware of the connection. In the case I have described, we both 'heard the angels' sing together.

Recently, it occurred to me that our bodies were first and foremost connective tissue. After all, a purposeful, meaningful life is rarely lived in isolation. We all live in an interconnected state with each other, and with nature. Our connective tissue infiltrates every cell and every organ; rather than viewing this as merely the scaffolding that prevents us from turning into a blobby, squelchy mess, it deserves at the very least to share equal billing with our vital organs. In truth, it is the food from our contracting guts, oxygen from our inflating lungs and blood from our beating heart, that nourish our connective tissue, allowing us to live our unique interconnected lives.

PCs in Every Cell

Early in the 1980s Microsoft's founder Bill Gates surprised the world by declaring publicly his aim of equipping every family home of the future with its own personal computer. Few at that time realized that 540 million years previously, a far more impressive plan was being implemented by a still unidentified computer giant. This was the time that the first single-celled, mobile organisms appeared on the earth. One example of these, the amoeba-like Paramecium, is still around today, wending its way to and fro in freshwater ponds. Inside these primitive creatures, helping them decide where to go and what to do, are the very microtubules we have within our own cells. There are some who believe that these hollow structures represent our on-board computers.

In the early 1990s a British physicist, Sir Roger Penrose joined forces with an American anaesthetist, Dr Stuart Hameroff, as both were intrigued by these microtubules. Sir Roger was naturally drawn to the spiral structure and wondered if he could be looking at a sophisticated *quantum computer;* a processor of information gleaned from the quantum world. To Dr Hameroff, the microtubules resembled a computer switch.

As a student, I was fascinated by the way living cells divided. Our DNA is tightly packed within chromosomes in the central nucleus of each of our cells. As each cell splits, these chromosomes are prized apart by strong tentacle-like spindles. I remember wondering how it was that these spindles knew exactly what to do; what intelligence was guiding them? Of course, I kept the question (and my ignorance) to myself. I recently discovered that Dr Hameroff asked precisely the same question, and unable to come up with a satisfactory explanation, has dedicated much of his life to providing an answer.

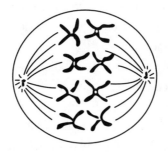

Figure 14. The Dividing Cell
Diagram showing how chromosomes are prised apart by strong tentacles like spindles.

Early on, he observed that these spindles were hollow microtubules, and that this structure was replicated within the skeleton of each cell of our body. Our brain cells were exceptional in that they appeared crammed with microtubule structures. Together with Sir Roger Penrose, he developed the hypothesis that these hollow tubes were our body's link with consciousness – an environment where the timeless quantum world was allowed to 'collapse' down to our recognizable physical world of space and time. Hameroff postulated that the reason patients lose all track of time and space under general anaesthetic was because these microprocessors are unable to work. Time literally stands still, as it does when we slip into the realm of our dreams while we sleep naturally.

This revolutionary theory suggests that a timeless quantum consciousness lies at the root of our very being, and that we have an intricately linked Internet of trillions of computers downloading this information from a boundless cosmic cyberspace.

The Penrose-Hameroff theory poses some startling questions:

Could the spiral shape of the microtubules, as in our DNA, create a balance of opposing electrical forces allowing access to these quantum fields?

Do these structures, like trillions of minute antennas, communicate instantly and coherently with each other, and with our DNA, to regulate the growth and regeneration of our cells with the ever-present input of the cosmos as a whole?

Do they play a major role in converting the weird quantum world of probabilities and boundless fields, into the familiar physical world we can see, smell, taste, hear and touch?

And doesn't this suggest that our bodies are tangible representations of a vast fundamental consciousness shared by all life forms?

Microtubules are found in all animals and plants, regulating the function and growth of cells. This suggests all living cells have a degree of consciousness, although a state of *self-awareness* seems to come only when a huge number work together in a synchronized fashion. It is thought that certain states – meditation and prayer – enhance this coherent state. When people join together in prayer groups, all their microtubules may cooperate with each other, effecting change at a distance. There are now many scientific studies supporting the effects of intercessory prayer and distance healing. We'll examine these later in this chapter.

The microtubule hypothesis is still regarded as being highly controversial within the orthodox scientific community. The prevailing view of consciousness, though paradoxically never proven scientifically, is that it is purely a by-product of our brains; our brains create our conscious state. The Penrose-Hameroff model challenges this by suggesting that consciousness exists somewhere 'beyond the brain'. Our brains are merely converters of this primal entity, receivers and transmitters at the same time. In traditional Chinese medicine, the brain is referred to as 'The Hollow Organ'.

This model also gives credence to the presence of other dimensions of being that may be accessed in states of 'altered consciousness' – i.e. dreams and out-of-body experiences. Neuroscientists still prefer to use sophisticated scans to identify the part of the brain that 'lights up' during these experiences. Their interpretation is that this is where these events start – within the structure of our brain.

Like my two-year-old daughter years ago, they maybe need convincing that our world does not exist solely locked within the TV set of our brain.

Near Death and Out-of-Body Experiences

Perhaps the most significant sign that a paradigm is well and truly shifting is when two independent scientific papers appear in leading medical journals within the same year suggesting something that flies in the face of orthodox thinking. The first study published in the May 2001 edition of Resuscitation, researched the incidence of near-death experiences (NDEs) in 63 survivors of cardiac arrest in Southampton General Hospital in England. The researchers were respected medical doctors Sam Parnia and Peter Fenwick. This, together with a second, larger study published in the Lancet in December 2001 from Holland by heart specialist Dr Pim van Lommel, suggests that about 10% of people who have cardiac arrest have near death or out-of-body experiences (OBE). In a cardiac arrest, the heart stops and within 10 seconds our brain waves also 'flatline'. The heart is then given an electric shock and often drugs are injected to help restart the heart, together with ventilation techniques using an oxygen mask, or mouth-to-mouth resuscitation. The studies challenge conventional medical thinking by documenting that these NDEs occurred when the brain was clinically not functioning, and presumably – under the existing model – while thoughts were unable to be processed.

The experiences recorded in these and other studies are remarkably consistent, depending on how long people are 'dead'.

Firstly, they have an awareness of floating outside their body, often looking down to see medical staff working on them. They have no pain, and feel happy.

Then they see a spiral tunnel forming around them, and are drawn to the light at the end. In the tunnel they may meet loved ones that have died, or spirit guides.

At the end of the tunnel they emerge into a beautiful, loving state of light and lightness, often in the presence of a spiritual being.

They experience a complete life review. This includes every instance of their time on earth – including the feelings of all those they helped or harmed. Most describe no external judgment by the 'beings of light', although some have reported their own judgment of themselves to be harsh.

Finally, they return to their earthbound state, often experiencing the searing pain of their medical condition, and from the emergency procedures being performed. But, perhaps the most significant effects occur later. They report feeling more spiritually connected, more focused on helping and healing others, more environmentally aware, and less fearful of death. Many are truly transformed.

One of the most remarkable and publicized cases is that of American Dannion Brinkley who has been clinically dead three times. Brinkley describes himself as a bully as a child, who because of his fondness for violence, went on to work for covert military organizations involved in political assassinations. His first experience followed being struck by lightning, after which, despite attempts to resuscitate him, he was declared dead. He was on his way to the morgue, under a sheet, when he 'awoke'. He had been 'dead' for 28 minutes.

Brinkley described a sequence of events in his NDEs exactly as we have described, together with his own soul-searching. He has since had two further near-death experiences. Understandably, he is now a reformed character, dedicating his life to helping others, founding a national hospice organization, 'Compassion in Action'.

It is fair to say that not all NDEs are perceived of as pleasant. In his autobiography, the extroverted Australian entrepreneur, the late Kerry Packer, describes his brush with death following a cardiac arrest.

'I've been to the other side – and there's nothing f . . . g there!'

It seems that even in these realms, beauty is very much in the eye of the beholder.

Although I have not had a NDE, I meet many patients who have, but remain wary of telling others, particularly doctors, of their experiences for fear of being judged as being crazy. This is a shame, as recounting a NDE always has a beneficial effect on someone's future health. Our taboo on talking about death has led to the fears we still see within our profession and our society as a whole.

My wife, Trish, describes her experiences at the time when our youngest child was born in 1996. Soon after the birth, while I left to get a takeaway with my oldest daughter, Trish bled profusely from the womb losing about 3 pints of blood. From the overwhelming joy of seeing, and holding my new son only a few minutes before, I entered the delivery suite to see a bed full of blood and the midwife inserting a drip into her arm.

In Trish's words:

I had just given birth to Toby. As I lay on my bed exhausted with a tiny bundle in my arms, my husband said he would drive my thirteen-year-old daughter to the local takeaway, as she was hungry. I think he was too!

As they left, other relatives arrived and I noticed blood seeping onto the sheets. I covered this up, only to notice more was coming. I reached for the blanket and counterpane, but the seep had now become a gush. I remember my sister calling out for a nurse; then all went black for a moment.

Then I was looking down at myself from the ceiling; nurses were rushing around and the doctor appeared. The feeling I had was lovely – the most fantastic feeling I have ever had. I had no worries. A warmth enveloped me, and I experienced an overwhelming feeling of peace. I didn't feel the pain of the needles, or hear any noises, but saw myself on the bed and Toby in his crib. I didn't want this feeling to end.

Then suddenly everything changed, and I experienced the pain of a doctor's hand deep inside me, with another hard on my abdomen. I saw my daughter at the door with my ashen husband.

'Please don't die, Mum,' she said.

Prayer and Intent

In an operating theater of the Duke University Medical Center, USA, Dr. Mitchell Krucoff, a prominent cardiologist, bows his head and leads a short, 60-second prayer for the patient on whom he is about to perform catheterization of the heart. The theater staff, no matter what their individual religious beliefs, joins him in this act of goodwill and healing. This ritual is repeated on each and every one of Dr Krucoff's patients undergoing this specialized procedure. There is now open discussion in the medical journals about the effects of prayer on healing. As with the landmark studies on NDEs, the new millennium has heralded much healthy debate about distance healing and prayer. Large scientific studies have confirmed both prayer and distance healing to have an effect greater than chance, and several remarkable studies have made even hardened skeptics take notice.

One such study, published in 2001 in a leading journal of reproductive medicine, showed that prayers directed from great distances to a fertility unit in Korea resulted in a doubling of successful in vitro fertilization transfer rates (from 26% to 50%.) Prayer groups were organized in three different countries, the USA, Canada and Australia, and included people from all nationalities and religions. One group prayed for the mothers and fetuses, while the second prayed for the first group and the mothers and foetuses, and the third for all the groups and everyone in the clinic. The mothers were divided into two groups – one group was prayed for, and the other wasn't. None of the mothers, or the staff, was told of this until after the study had been completed. This has led to some criticism of this study on ethical grounds.

However this is one of many studies that collectively suggest prayer at a distance can have healing effects. In an even more startling study, a cautiously skeptical doctor, Professor Leonard Leibovici in Israel, prayed for a group of patients with blood poisoning ten years after they had left hospital. He divided old hospital notes randomly into two, and prayed for one pile while ignoring the other.

Remarkably, when the two groups were analyzed, the prayed-for group did better, showing reduced mortality, shorter hospital stays and duration of fever. This article provoked a flurry of debate after it appeared in the British Medical Journal in 2001, as it added the weird concept that we could pray backwards in time to influence an event that had already happened – retroactive prayer!

But can science really effectively evaluate something so ill defined as prayer?

The word *pray* is derived from the Latin verb *precari,* to *implore,* and commonly means asking God, or an anonymous higher power, to help out in areas beyond our worldly control. It is worth noting that after over a thousand scientific studies on prayer, no one religion has been shown to produce a more effective outcome than any other.

It also appears there are right and wrong ways to pray. Praying for a big win in the national lottery, or for the All Blacks to win the rugby world cup, doesn't seem to work – I know this as I have tried. The consensus appears to be that our prayers are better directed to a reduction of suffering, and an enhancement of peace, either on a personal or a global level. It may be at times more effective to pray in a healing way so that a dying person has a peaceful transition, rather than praying that the person undergoes a miraculous cure. Over the years, I have observed much healing within the dying process, although the disease itself may prove to be incurable. It appears that within the essence of a prayer is a loving intent to heal, and a profound humility as we surrender our egos to a higher universal presence.

So it is all the more remarkable that so many of these scientific studies are showing measurable physical changes in those being prayed for. However, the current method of designing medical trials seems to me to be a far from ideal way to evaluate prayer, and I am not inclined to wait till there is incontrovertible proof. I try to spend time in silence at the beginning of my day, sending good wishes to all those who are about to come for my help. I know of many others in the healing arts who have similar rituals. I also try to consciously direct my good wishes to somebody as I greet them in the street with a 'gidday' (Kiwi for 'Have a nice day!'), and as I sign my e-mails, 'cheers'.

It may be a long time before there is overwhelming scientific proof that this is having a definite healing effect, but for me it contains three very valuable ingredients.

It is completely safe, it keeps me happy and it is absolutely free.

Something in the Air

Over the past twenty years, Professor Robert Jahn and Dr Brenda Dunne of Princeton University have conducted research showing that humans can, by their very intent, change the workings of machines. The machines used in the study are called Random Event Generators (REGs), and are like sophisticated lottery machines designed to produce completely random numbers all day long. The human participants were asked to try to influence these results through their own mind power.

The experiments have been repeated thousands of times with thousands of different subjects. Small but statistically significant results have been consistently obtained showing that the output of these REGs can change in response to acts of human intention. Remarkably, significant interactions occurred when the humans and machines were separated by great distances and even while the machines were turned off, and restarted several days later!

These results are described as being *anomalous,* as there is as yet no obvious explanation for what is happening. However, hopefully by now you are aware of an underlying trend developing in this cutting edge area of research that strongly suggests that we are touching on new, non-local dimensions. Although the fact that machines may be able to detect and respond to human mind-power is fascinating enough, it is the power of human intent and concentration that to me is more compelling. The effects were increased when two people joined together to direct their thoughts to a machine, and increased further if these two people were romantically attached. Larger groups have also been shown to produce even more significant results. This synchronised group effect is known as *coherence.*

In 1996, the respected psi researcher, Dean Radin, wondered whether these machines (REGs) could act as measuring devices for coherent group consciousness. He was keen to know whether, when many people focused on a particular event, there was any deviation from this pattern of randomness. He knew that the Academy Awards Ceremony had a huge US television audience monitored in thousands of Nielson families, who had boxes on their TVs measuring their viewing habits minute by minute. He compared these readings on Oscar night with the output of two of these REGs located 12 miles apart. The results tallied significantly. Radin repeated the test with more REGs during the OJ Simpson trial in 1997. The machines recorded marked changes at the moment of verdict – a time when Reuters estimated there were half a billion people glued to their TVs or radios.

As a result of these preliminary studies, Radin, together with Dr Roger Nelson, has pioneered the Global Consciousness Project, setting up over 50 REGs around the world. It appears that these machines are able to detect a background level of consciousness for reasons yet to be discovered. The events of September 11 2001, when terrorist planes destroyed the Twin Towers in New York and part of the Pentagon in Washington DC were 'recorded' by the 37 REGs that had been set up at this time. Given the huge emotional impact of 9/11 on the world, the researchers were not surprised to see major changes in the output of their machines that correlated exactly with the time of the attack at 8.45 am, and again when the towers collapsed. What they were not prepared for was the fact that definite 'shifts' were being recorded from 6 am that morning suggesting a precognitive element to group consciousness!

These results are the subject of much speculation and scrutiny. Analysing them is extremely complex, and skeptics have poured over the data at length, suggesting possible flaws. However, if this is examined within the context of the other information I have presented in this chapter and accepted as 'work in progress', as the researchers themselves see it, then it provides valuable evidence for the existence of a background human 'consciousness'. If this phenomenon continues to be repeatable, it is possible we could have an effective early-warning system for large terrorist acts, that potentially could save thousands of lives. In my own work, I have for many years been aware of the possible connection between a global consciousness and the symptoms many patients experience. Eckhart Tolle in his impressive book *The Power of Now,* talks of the collective *pain body,* and how it relates in particular to women's gynaecological illnesses – how their individual bodies reflect the pain women have held for centuries around the world. This concept again is one other way of expressing the holographic nature of our being. Dr Patch Adams, the revolutionary doctor and clown, talks of the *pain society* reflected constantly in our sensationalist news media. Many people I see, especially the sensitive sufferers of chronic fatigue, pain and eating disorders are easily affected by this negativity.

I recently saw a young student whose severe chronic fatigue started on 11 September 2001. It is my impression that those with this debilitating condition are particularly sensitive to levels of consciousness not detected by our five senses, possibly in a similar way to that by which certain animals detect changes before humans can – like canaries in the mines who lay their lives on the line to protect miners from toxic gases, and the precognitive sixth sense of animals that know when an earthquake is about to strike.

In an interesting aside, the REGs responded in a different way to the 2004 Boxing Day Tsunami. In this case there were no warning shifts recorded prior to the earthquake activity. We can speculate that global consciousness possibly differentiates between events that reflect man's inhumanity to man, and natural events that – though devastating – carry with them no ill will.

Tuning into the Dead

Over the years I have been intrigued by the skill of those who act as mediums, accessing the souls of loved ones who have died. My interest in this area has lead to many people telling me how those with psychic ability have helped them; in turn this has opened up areas we can explore together, clearing unresolved blocks to healing. This is especially so when a loved one dies, when a great deal has still to be said. The natural process of grief can be delayed in such a situation, and a skilled and humble psychic may be valuable in unlocking this position of stalemate.

I also have the privilege of seeing many gifted psychics as patients, and one afternoon two booked in for consecutive appointments. The first was an elderly, retired naval captain in his eighties whose wife had died several years before. I had looked after her when I was in full-time general practice; she had suffered several severe strokes over the years, and always referred to me as 'the boy'. As we fondly reminisced about her, he remarked she was 'here with us, checking that 'the boy' is treating her husband ok'. He told me he always knew when she was coming, as he could smell the expensive perfume, Chanel #5, she loved so much and that 'cost me so much!'.

After he left, I greeted the next lady whom I knew had worked from time to time as a medium, but had never met the previous gentleman. Politely sniffing the air, she said, 'I just love Chanel #5!' They had been the first two patients of the afternoon session, and Trish who was in attendance at the reception can't wear Chanel, as she is allergic to it. Unfortunately neither Trish nor I could detect this heavenly fragrance.

Soon after this experience, I received a visit from another lady whom I had known for years. Carol had organized spiritual meetings for years, and on this occasion she asked me to help reduce the severity of her migraines with acupuncture. The session included using two points in the way I described on page 68, with me resting a finger of each hand gently over a pair of acupuncture needles on Carol's wrist and ankle. A medium is already a walking *human antenna,* and as I focused on the points I experienced the connected feeling between my heart and stomach.

'Your father is here,' she said calmly. 'Are you OK about this?'

My father had died the previous year in England, and I had had the privilege of being with him during his final illness. He had died peacefully, and with the greatest of dignity. She went on to repeat the very words he had spoken to me before he had died. He added that all was fine, and that had he known then what he knew now, he wouldn't have worried so much.

Although this was really my one and only 'afterlife' contact with him, I felt very calm and reassured by the experience. Moreover, it has carried with it a peaceful sense of completeness, enough for me to encourage others to explore these realms if they so wish.

Recently, a woman, Sarah came to see me after she had received some distressing and unexpected news about her state of health.

Sarah's Story

Sarah, a registered nurse and mother of three teenage children, had been a blood donor for years. Her world had been turned upside down after her doctor had phoned out of the blue for her to come to see him after a routine blood test conducted on all donors. Despite feeling well, he told her that she had a cancer within her bloodstream – multiple myeloma. She knew of this condition only too well – she had nursed her mother with this same disease three years previously – she had subsequently died.

Also her younger sister Debbie, a fun loving, high achiever in the business world, had been diagnosed with another type of cancer at the age of 30, ten years previously. She had undergone chemotherapy but had died within 18 months of receiving the news. Sarah supported her unfailingly through this overwhelmingly difficult time.

Despite this Debbie was to die in a very agitated way – unable to come to terms with her own impending death, becoming very uncomfortable and restless in the final days. Debbie's illness and death proved to have a profound effect on her own family doctor Brett. Despite being only in his mid thirties, he had begun to question whether he could continue to practise medicine.

Two years after Debbie's death, Sarah, who describes herself as open-minded but healthily skeptical, visited a psychic medium. She didn't know what would happen. To her surprise, the medium did make contact with someone – named Debsie – a pet name Sarah had used since Debbie was a toddler. Sarah was intrigued, but even more so as Debbie proceeded to tell her to reassure Brett that he was a good doctor and that he "shouldn't give it all away".

To help convince Brett that this message was indeed from Debbie, she asked Sarah, through the medium, to tell him about the clutch repair he had just had done on his car, and about that new pink shirt he had bought – the one his wife had taken such a dislike to.

Debbie, Sarah told me, had always been mischievous.

Before the session with the medium ended, Debbie again stressed that "Dr Brett" should not give up, and that his skills and compassion were very special. She also reassured Sarah that her own (Debbie's) "cancer had gone," and that she was "truly at peace."

The following day, Sarah phoned Brett, who was confounded by the information she gave him. His car had indeed just come back from the auto repair shop with a brand new clutch. He could only imagine that Sarah had been talking to his wife about this and the pink shirt – the very shirt only a few days before she had described as being "Just awful!".

Sarah then passed on Debbie's message of encouragement – and it was then that Brett admitted at the time of Debbie's illness he had indeed toyed with the idea of giving up general practice, feeling dispirited and inadequate.

Sarah wasn't exactly sure just how Brett had eventually responded to all this information – but is delighted that eight years later he is continuing to run a thriving practice.

"So what difference has this experience made to you, and in particular on how you are dealing with your illness?" I asked Sarah keenly.

Without a hesitation she replied, "Well, I no longer fear dying."

She went on: "My sister's agitation while she was dying was about her losing everything – the fun-packed, exciting material world she had so thrived in was slipping from her grasp, out of her control."

On receiving the news that she herself had cancer, Sarah visited her doctor and then a blood cancer specialist. After a bone marrow biopsy, the specialist had been insistent that she started chemotherapy immediately, but Sarah wanted space to think it over. Her specialist told her he feared she was "not taking it seriously enough", a remark that upset Sarah greatly.

Sarah sought my help as she had found it difficult to explain to the doctors how she had felt. She had identified within the doctors the very pattern of fear that she herself had resolved, but was keen not to alienate herself from a medical system she may need to call upon. She sensed that if she was to give away her 'power to heal on her terms', her healing would be compromised. She was indeed taking her treatment "very seriously".

By sharing the remarkable story of her 'afterlife' communication with her sister Debbie, Sarah regained her self-confidence. And we both gained valuable, new insights on how we, as patients or health professionals, should release any unhealthy fear of dying, and live joyful, productive lives.

It also appears that those who have had NDEs and OBEs gain a healthy new perspective on their earthly lives. Somehow, stepping outside the confines of the purely 'physical' brings with it a peaceful reassurance that they are more than flesh and blood. It is interesting that they always describe how 'they' are looking down on 'their' bodies. A body is something they own, but is not the essence of who they are. Their comfort in knowing that the physical world is only one perspective of a greater reality doesn't ever seem to make them 'flippant' about everyday life. In fact, they are more likely to see their physical lives, and the whole of nature, as true on-going miracles. They are more likely to make a strong personal commitment to conserving and protecting the environment for future generations of all sentient beings.

Their stepping outside of our worldly time frame often acts as a catalyst for living in the 'now' as they become more aware that this is where reality dwells. Those who have made contact with departed loved ones with the help of a skilled medium also tend to gain this new perspective on life. Many become aware of letting them go, releasing them unconditionally, till they meet again; *au revoir* rather than *goodbye* forever. I have not encountered anybody who wishes to actively end his or her own life as a result of contact with a departed loved one.

The Gift of Mediumship

My understanding of heaven is in a perpetual state of flux.

I no longer envisage a heaven packed with pleasant folk sitting on clouds, smiling benignly at one another, playing harps and watching endless re-runs of *The Waltons*. Not even an updated version of this, where each celestial inhabitant carries their own translucent mobile phone eagerly awaiting their chiming ring tone – inevitably something from the *Sound of Music* – that would mean contact with someone below.

I am now more inclined to perceive another timeless level of being that can, given the right circumstances, be tapped into by us from time to time, often with a 'little help from our friends'. It would appear that genuine mediums possess a special innate talent that they then carefully hone during their lives. This gift enables them, somehow, to tune into the information (or morphic field) of their client – into that very portion of their soul in which their loved ones reside.

It is important to perceive that the medium is not working alone. Indeed the word medium, like midwife, implies she or he acts as an intermediary in the process. Both the medium and her client are *human antennas* of equal importance, acting together in a coherent state. The vital ingredient that binds the process together is that four-lettered word, love. Love is truly 'non-local'; we don't love our husband or wife any less if they are away on business on the other side of the world. And love is timeless; absence, it is said, makes the heart grow fonder.

So it could be said that access is gained to this other dimension 'on the wings of love'. I recently watched how a popular medium interacted with his TV audience, skillfully engaging them in a charming and friendly way. He cracked a few jokes, easing any tension they might be holding; their laughter resonated through the studio, helping them all to become coherent antennas. As he scanned the audience, he intuitively picked up on where 'messages' were beginning to be received.

His first encounter involved a mother and daughter sitting together, both keen to contact the same person – their husband and father respectively. Here therefore was an example of a wonderful entangled love-bond; mother with daughter, wife with husband, daughter with father, all further sealed by a truly compassionate medium, and a tuned-in, 'entrained' audience.

The stage is well and truly set for access into what some would call the 'spirit' world, and others would refer to as an underlying field of quantum consciousness. The medium's talent involves both 'hearing' and interpreting the message jointly received, but somehow hidden within the audience member's 'hard drive'. This code-breaking talent does not make the medium any more spiritually advanced than others, just as clairvoyants who read auras are in no way 'further up the spiritual ladder'. Genuine mediums tend to be modest about their gifts.

Remote Viewing – Connecting Beyond Space

Since the end of the nineteenth century, there have been many experiments exploring the phenomenon of remote viewing. This is the term commonly given to the ability to perceive objects and places from a distance. The Princeton University PEAR project has conducted thousands of these studies, involving pairs of people separated by great distances. In each pair, one member acts as a viewer, absorbed in the environment she finds herself in, while the other tunes into her, recording the messages she receives.

Similar studies have been performed since the early 1970s under physicists Drs Russell Targ and Hal Puthoff at Stanford University. The US government has funded many projects, as the possibilities of using this phenomenon as an espionage tool are far reaching.

The overall results show a remarkable consistency. It appears that within the human population, positive 'hits' occur in a way, although not dramatic, that is significantly better than chance. Targ and Puthoff continue to run Remote Viewing courses, attended by a significant number of frontline police. They claim that this is an art everyone can learn. The Princeton group showed the effect was statistically better between human subjects who had close personal bonds.

However, about 1% of the population proves to be extremely talented remote viewers, able to tune into this process with consistency and great clarity. This, as for the mediums we have mentioned, appears to be an innate gift.

One notable remote viewer was retired businessman and Californian Police Commissioner, Pat Price, who successfully used his skills to solve police cases (most notably the Patricia Hearst kidnapping). In 1973, under the guidance of Targ and Puthoff, Price was asked by the CIA to help lo-cate a secret Russian facility they suspected was being used for military purposes. They gave him only the map coordinates. He went into a trance, quietening his mind, and was able to 'go inside' the plant, and describe in detail complex machinery, and even a type of welding equipment not known in the West.

His findings, including scaled drawings, were subsequently con-firmed by other intelligence sources. It was later discovered that this was a manufacturing site for anti-ballistic missiles. The Stanford research program received US government funding for a further 23 years before it was eventually disbanded in the mid-nineties. The researchers cite two main reasons for this. Firstly the Berlin Wall had fallen and the Cold War was coming to an end. Secondly, growing numbers within congress and within the CIA itself, held fundamental Christian beliefs that psychic ability was the work of the devil.

In an equally impressive experiment by the same team, Pat Price again confined in a Faraday shielded room, tried to envisage where two laboratory scientists ended up as they travelled by car in the city. They had no prior knowledge where they were going, making the same turns as the car that happened to be in front of them at intersections. Price was supposed to decide where their journey ended up after 30 minutes of travel. After ten minutes, Price was able to describe to Russell Targ, who had remained with him in the laboratory, the precise location the two scientists were yet to visit. This was 20 minutes before they themselves knew where they would finish up. Price's psychic ability not only cut through space, it also reached into the future defying our concept of time.

However, there is evidence that Pat Price's ability to predict future events is likely to be an extreme manifestation of a natural process held, but rarely recognized, by us all. Dean Radin recorded this phenomenon on 11 September 2001, when the REGs indicated a raising of global consciousness prior to the catastrophic terrorist attacks. In his groundbreaking book, *The Conscious Universe,* he documents a remarkably similar pattern of *precognition* occurring consistently in individual subjects, strongly suggesting every one of us is armed with our very own early warning system.

Precognition – Connecting Beyond Time

In his laboratory in the University of Nevada, Radin attached measuring devices to the left hand of subjects, leaving their right hand free to use a computer mouse. One pair of devices measured the electrical activity in the skin, while another recorded the pulse rate and amount of blood in the fingertip. These are all measurements of the subjects' autonomic, or involuntary nervous system.

Under controlled conditions, they used the mouse to view target photos on the computer screen programed to appear in a completely randomized way. The photos fell into two categories: calm and emotional. The calm images were of natural landscapes and smiling faces whereas the emotional categories included shocking and erotic images. The images would always appear five seconds after clicking the mouse.

As one would predict, the body responded in opposite ways to these categories and the changes recorded following exposure to the pictures reflected this. On examining the recordings taken during the five seconds between clicking the mouse and the appearance of the photo, Radin noticed an anticipatory response for all photos. This in itself was unsurprising.

But what did surprise him was the fact that the responses were consistently more marked before the 'emotional' images appeared, even though the subjects were not consciously aware of what was to come. In fact, the recordings appear as mini-mirror images of the reactions to come.

So although their bodies were wise to these events before they happened, this was not recognized by their rational mind. This pre-event alertness obviously could have an evolutionary significance, as a sophisticated kick start of our fight or flight responses. It may also give us some understanding of how animals can respond, and warn us of natural disasters that are about to happen. This has profound implications for healing.

Firstly, it adds some scientific credence to the whole area of intuition, suggesting a natural sixth sense, independent of time and space that is available to all. Together with the remote viewing studies, it begins to clarify the mechanisms at work when gifted intuitives, such as Carolyn Myss and the late Edgar Cayce, can know so much about a client in an instance and often at a great distance.

But for me the most powerful message is what it tells us about ourselves. It tells us our bodily symptoms themselves are part of our intuitive network, our special link to an underlying, interconnected field of consciousness, constantly informing us and pre-warning us of potential hazards to our health.

The following chapter plots the growth of our intuition literally from our tail to our top. We'll examine how our body and the world around us work in harmony as catalysts for change at each chakra level, guiding us to a state where we can each become aware of our unique role in such a vast and varied production.

For most of us our journey is a struggle; at times the challenges seem insurmountable, and the path a lonely one. But as the *human antenna* grows, we become more and more convinced that we are not alone, and that the barriers that separate us are mere illusions.

Summary – Science and the Soul

I have presented in this chapter several models and theories that support the concept of a timeless field of consciousness, a universal soul reflected uniquely within each of us.

We will not find our soul with a microscope. Our soul is not locked somewhere in our body waiting to be opened. The fascinating world of DNA and microtubules simply allows us to glimpse possible ways that our bodies manifest themselves; how we are continuously formed and reformed from the yet-to-be manifested. It is maybe more accurate to say our body resides within the framework of our soul. I explore the emerging scientific theories that suppport this profound concept in Appendix 1: Shedding New Light.

We are privy, however, to strong circumstantial evidence concerning both the existence and nature of our timeless soul. Our sub-atomic model suggests a state of 'entanglement' at our most fundamental level, which exists outside the confines of time and space. The Big Bang theory, now accepted as fact by scientists, describes how the universe exploded into existence from an infinitesimally small 'space' from which it continues to expand at increasing speed. So each particle in the universe can be seen to have a shared ancestry and continues to be linked in a synchronized entangled state.

Rupert Sheldrake's theory of *morphic resonance* carries this concept into the wider domain of shared, non-local fields that carry with them the presence of the past. And the new studies on DNA and microtubules give us some understanding on how we convert these fields of quantum information into the miraculous living, breathing, growing reality of our bodies.

Our DNA is responsible for processing and coordinating this quantum information, projecting a four-dimensional holographic matrix upon which our physical body grows and regenerates. It is at the same time connected to our ancestral past through our genetic code and our current environment, receiving vibrational messages of light and sound.

Meanwhile, many trillions of microtubule antennas are involved in 'downloading' timeless quantum fields (the consciousness of the cosmos) into data we recognize as our physical reality. The microtubules are in constant non-local communication with our DNA, and all the other intracellular antennas. The universal nature of our soul is also illustrated by the discovery that the smallest, humblest organisms share with us this same microscopic hardware, designed to 'download' consciousness. And every one of these structures is composed of molecules that are in turn composed of atoms whose particles are really wave forms that wink in and out of existence.

Sacred geometry reveals holographic patterns of form, common to all in the universe, arising from realms beyond, and fundamental to physical structure. The underlying mathematical rules are consistent from the tiniest subatomic state to the largest galaxy. The divine beauty of this natural graphic design serves as a perennial reminder of just how wonderful a process this is. It serves as a constant reminder that the physical universe we detect with our senses is nothing short of a dazzling, on-going miracle unravelling continuously before us.

I find it helpful to consider that between humans and other living beings, there are three levels of communication – all intricately linked.

- Firstly, we use our five senses to respond to the world around us.
- Secondly, we are continuously responding to the electrical frequencies in our environment, via our web of connective tissue that conducts energy in and out of our body.
- Thirdly, we have continuous communication with realms outside our time space model. This 'sixth' sense reaches our everyday consciousness when attention to the dominating, 'interfering' information from our senses is released, as in meditation, sleep, and during a general anaesthetic. We achieve energetic balance in a harmonic, coherent state with nature, with loved ones, in groups, healing circles etc.

The scientific studies of prayer, remote viewing and precognition all support the everyday existence of non-locality, while our acceptance of the reality of near-death experiences helps us to envisage that consciousness exists outside our brains, and survives the death of our body.

There are some with highly developed innate psychic skills of mediumship and remote viewing, who are able to tune into specific realms with consistency and accuracy.

However, the precognitive and global consciousness research suggests that we all communicate in a non-local way, even though this is still not apparent to many.

As we try to fathom all this out, it is perhaps reassuring, and sobering, to consider that 'all this' is really just *us looking at ourselves*. For my part, the science of the soul is both colorful and comforting. Its vast mysteries do not force me to lie awake at night pondering endlessly over the ultimate meaning of life.

They simply allow me to sit back, close my eyes, and smile.

ENDNOTE:

    Real answers may not be too far away. Experiments are soon to resume in Geneva, Switzerland, with the intention of creating, and capturing, particles of mass formed as a result of the high-speed collision of protons within vast underground tunnels. The whole complex is known as the Large Hadron Collider, and the units of mass the physicists hope to create have been preliminarily nicknamed 'God' particles. If they are successful, who knows what insights we may then gain about the origins not only of our universe, but also of our very own living tissue?

3: The Growth of the Human Antenna – The Chakras

*"The whole body of spiritual consciousness progresses without pause;
the whole body of material substance suffers decay without intermission."*

–Chinese saying

Most of us become wiser with age. We may move about less freely, see less sharply, hear less acutely and experience frequent 'senior moments'; but what we have more of is *nous* (pronounced *nowce*).

I often hear: 'If only I knew then what I know now.'

By the time we reach our middle years, our accumulated challenges and successes have guided us into an awareness of just how hard we need to strive to achieve our goals, and how much we have to wait patiently and vigilantly for the right opportunities to present themselves. If in the past we have had a tendency to control situations and people around us, we become more laid back. If we have allowed situations and people to control us, we become more assertive. The more aggressive may mellow; the passive may find their voice.

I am perplexed by many futuristic science fiction movies. The world of the future is often portrayed as being filled with fantastic labour-saving machines – robots that anticipate our future generations' every need by performing the dreary tasks that supposedly make our present day lives so tedious and miserable. But the characters portrayed by the movie stars seldom seem to have 'moved on' from their present day counterparts; they still struggle with the same frustrations while playing out the same petty dramas in their co-dependent relationships. Even though, in this imagined future, traffic congestion seems to have been eased by the invention of airborne cars, the drivers/pilots still exhibit all the telltale signs of road rage. Only now it is termed 'hover' rage, an updated version whose only redeeming feature is that there is less chance the perpetrator will get out of his car and punch you on the nose.

I prefer to carry a more optimistic vision of the future. This chapter sees a return to the model that gives me such hope – that of Spiral Dynamics. We have now learned that a spiral growth pattern infiltrates all dimensions of our natural life; it applies as much to the growth of a seashell as it does to the unfolding of consciousness on our planet. The spiritual growth that each one of us undergoes in the course of our life is an intimate reflection of this unfolding process.

In the mid 1960s, psychologist Clare Graves pioneered the theory of a spiral growth of human consciousness that has been applied successfully to both individuals and populations. Graves' model has been widely recognized by sociologists as playing a vital role in ending apartheid in South Africa. Rather than using the term *chakras,* the stages of growth are referred to as *memes* (*meme* is the French word for 'same'). Each *meme* is represented by a segment of the spiral, which unfolds progressively upwards as each meme is transcended by the next. This is not a classical hierarchical pattern that sees that each evolving meme reject the values of its predecessor. Rather, it values and incorporates its roots, progressing ever upwards to a state of increasing conscious awareness. This is an example of a *holarchy,* retaining the holographic principle that each part contains the essence of the whole.

In this chapter we will examine the ways that conscious patterns or memes in our society correspond *holographically* within our bodies as our seven chakras. These patterns exist all around us, in all aspects of our lives, even within the architecture of our buildings.

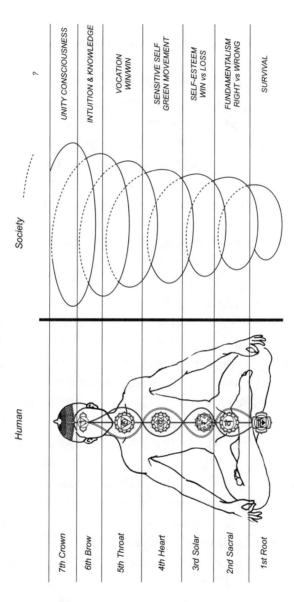

THE SPIRAL GROWTH OF HUMAN CONSCIOUSNESS
(Adapted from the work of Don Beck, Chris Cowan and Ken Wilber)

Human   Society   ?

Chakra	Consciousness
7th Crown	UNITY CONSCIOUSNESS
6th Brow	INTUITION & KNOWLEDGE
5th Throat	VOCATION WIN/WIN
4th Heart	SENSITIVE SELF GREEN MOVEMENT
3rd Solar	SELF-ESTEEM WIN vs LOSS
2nd Sacral	FUNDAMENTALISM RIGHT vs WRONG
1st Root	SURVIVAL

Figure 15. The Chakras and the Spiral of Development

Patterns Everywhere –
A Tale of Two Buildings

In the Chandrakirti Buddhist Center outside Nelson in the South Island of New Zealand stands a magnificent *Stupa,* a sacred manmade monument that was blessed by the Dalai Lama in 2002. Stupas (Sanskrit word for 'a tuft of hair') were originally built over sacred relics of the historical Buddha, or on the spots he had performed sacred acts. Enclosed within the Chandrakirti Stupa are artifacts such as artworks and paintings; the uppermost part contains the most sacred revered relics. The broad square base, though, in many contemporary stupas is packed with modern everyday items, such as computer parts, that some may regard as being far from spiritual in nature. However, Buddhism honors the sacred in all aspects of life, including the realities of the material world. The foundations of a building are as vital to the structure as a more dramatic or aesthetic feature such as a tower housing priceless treasure.

If we travel north to Auckland, we can hardly fail to notice another dramatic tower. At 328 meters tall, the Sky Tower dominates the Auckland skyline, with magnificent views to be had from the revolving restaurant near the top. It finally comes to an end at the tip of a transmitting mast perched like a giant knitting needle protruding high over the circular viewing decks. The base of this building, blending in with the central city bustle, comprises of a huge casino complex where fortunes are won and lost every day. If we spend too much time on this floor, it is likely that we would miss out on much of the rich and varied tapestry of life. In extreme cases, the addicted gambler can even lose the shirt off his back.

But there is a more balanced and enjoyable way to enjoy the Sky Tower. Those who venture higher up the tower are rewarded by a view that stretches for miles around them, allowing them to ponder on the beauty and diversity of nature. This all-embracing perspective from the top stands them in good stead, if on getting out of the elevator they find themselves tempted to have 'a bit of a flutter on the pokies'. The wise visitor will enjoy the challenge, only gambling with small change, and in the words of Kenny Rogers, will know when to walk away.

And so when we refer to the lower memes or chakras, we do not necessarily imply these are totally inferior levels of energy. The problems come if one is solely locked into this state of awareness as in the case of our addictive gambler. Addiction means the elimination of life-enriching choices. An addict is unable to say no to the chance of immediate material or emotional gain. Those who have accumulated wisdom throughout their lives are able to deal in the material world without having their fingers burned in the process. The truly integral human being can step in and out of all levels of consciousness at will.

Over several years, I have come to embrace the concept of the chakras in my work. Every patient who comes to see me brings with them a problem residing in one or more of their chakras, so I have been fortunate to have had plenty of opportunities to examine the validity, and practical usefulness, of this system. In the majority of cases, I have relayed any insight I may have gained back to the person, who as often as not, has returned the favour by enlightening me further about the intricate workings of the bodymind.

Acknowledging the chakras allows a dialog to open up on the meaning of symptoms and disease, as it so often places the physical problems within the context of what has been happening in the person's life. It often gives an indication of previously unresolved issues arising in childhood, which are now given the opportunity to resolve permanently. In more dramatic cases this may apply to problems that have been stuck within families for generations.

The aim of this section is to illustrate examples of common conditions that present to me, so that you can identify areas in yourself that may represent unresolved problems. For each chakra, I will run through an exercise that will help you achieve the necessary balance, allowing a smooth transition to the next level. I am grateful to many enlightened teachers over the years, each of whom has given me a fresh perspective on the chakras. The texts I still refer to constantly are by British psychiatrist and healer Dr Brenda Davies *(The Rainbow Journey)*, American medical intuitive Carolyn Myss *(The Anatomy of the Spirit)*, and neurologist and intuitive Dr Mona Lisa Schulz *(Awakening Intuition)*. My friend and mentor, Dr Steven Aung, from Edmonton, Canada, is an ever-present influence on the meditative and visualization exercises I describe here. And it is the focused vision of one of the foremost thinkers of our time, Ken Wilber, which gives so many of us who work in these areas the confidence to apply these principles in a truly integral fashion.

All these wise beings are remarkable *human antennas* – perceptive, intuitive and rational, yet with their feet planted securely on this earth. As you will see, for most of us, reaching these heights without becoming dizzy involves a seemingly endless series of checks and balances – an arduous journey filled with unexpected turns, blunders and triumphs.

For this is the stuff that makes up our lives.

An Overview of the Chakras

By our late teens, most of us have grown as tall as we will ever be. Our spiritual growth, however, continues unabated throughout our lives. The map over which our body tissue forms is holographic in both time and space. I'll try to explain this.

The quantum information fundamental to the universe exists outside time and space – a timeless non-local field whose unified nature is revealed to us visually by the consistent patterns of sacred geometry. But there are also patterns for us to recognize within our dimension of time – cycles of growth common not only to humans, animals and plants, but also to seasons, societies, cultures and corporations. This 'circle of life' lies at the heart of all indigenous holistic wisdom; a philosophy common to the Hopi in North America, the Aborigine in Australia and the Maori in New Zealand. At the root of traditional Chinese medicine lies the understanding of how five elements – wood, fire, earth, air and water – nurture each other in a cyclical fashion. This sequence is then applied to all natural phenomena from the change of seasons to the functioning of our bodily organs. We recognize these associations when we say someone is in 'the autumn of their life', or has 'given birth to a new venture'. I have been involved at the birth of many committees; initially there is a huge amount of childlike enthusiasm fired by imaginative creative thought and youthful energy; this is followed by a rocky adolescence where restless members clash, often resulting in rebellion and mutiny. Some may jump ship. A maturity then sets in with the remaining members driving the amended ideals with enthusiasm in a democratic manner until middle age spread slows them down. Hopefully by this time, the committee has recruited younger blood to support this sag in energy, allowing the founder members to grow old gracefully as wise and trusted advisers.

This natural growth pattern can be equally applied to all businesses and organizations. The process sees a balance of activity and passivity, control and surrender. An organization that harbours a dominant 'control freak' is less likely to survive, as also is one whose leader, or committee, is too submissive.

My interest in the chakras, and the unwinding of the *kundilini,* was initially centerd on the regional mindbody connections; for instance, someone who had a chronic pain in his stomach area (third or solar chakra) would often have a perception that others were controlling his life. I could then adopt the role of an interpreter of the body's language, and relay the message back to that person. Hopefully the insights gained would help the person move on and resolve these issues. If I were to just prescribe a medication that might relieve the symptoms without addressing the underlying problem, I would risk joining the gang of controlling influences at work on this person's body and soul.

The body 'within' the soul then would have one of two options; either it would come up with some other message, or symptom, that would have to be louder and more dramatic than the first so it could be heard. Alternatively it would give up altogether.

This dilemma lies at the root of my disquiet about a purely mechanical, allopathic approach to health. Symptom control, drugs and surgery are all rightly prominent in modern medical care, but it has been their overall dominance that has proved unhealthy. Prescribing a drug that exhibits control over every one of our fifty trillion cells should only be done after deep consideration of what the underlying symptoms mean. In chronic cases where symptoms are persisting, there should literally be much *soul searching* first.

So a knowledge of our own chakras empowers us to interpret these important messages, and make the changes needed to get our lives back on track. These messages inform us where are bodies and our lives are out of balance – where there is either too much control or too much submission.

- The first root chakra informs us of external control and expectations from family members and our bloodline.
- The second sacral chakra deals with issues of financial security, relationships and peer pressure.
- The third solar chakra talks to us when our own individuality is being undermined, and reflects self-esteem issues.
- The fourth heart chakra introduces aspects of love and nurturing, and can be seen as the gateway to deeper insights – often referred to as second-tier consciousness.
- The fifth throat chakra plays a part in guiding our vocation – finding our voice.
- The sixth brow chakra just above and between our eyes helps provide insight with a balanced mix of intuition and intellect.
- The seventh crown chakra allows us to experience our unique role in a unified, interconnected universe. It is here, after the arduous climb to the top of our head, that we reach our potential as fully aware, living receivers and transmitters – true *human antennas*.

In scaling the highest and toughest peaks, experienced mountaineers wend their way painstakingly across the terrain, sometimes traversing to and fro and sometimes climbing vertically up sheer rock faces. They work in teams, often alongside trusted guides (as with Sir Edmund Hillary and his faithful companion Sherpa Tenzing Norgay). The exhilaration on reaching the top is a true reflection on the difficulty of the climb. The view that greets them at the top of the world is both humbling and life changing.

In each of our lives, we are perpetually climbing through our chakras. In 2002 I attended a workshop run by Dr Brenda Davies, a medically trained psychiatrist from the north of England, who had been aware of her healing gifts since she was a child. Like Dr Anita Cignolini who over ten years previously had enlightened me about the traditional Chinese mindbody connections, Brenda started to fill the gaps in my knowledge of the chakras. Most important of these was a fascinating insight into just when and how the chakras were involved in our spiritual development.

Brenda explained that over the first thirty or so years of our life we experience our first climb through our chakras. From our early years when we have no voice, and are dependent on the love of parents and guardians, to beginning to know who we are, how to love and be loved and to recognize our true vocation in our lives. Some of us have an easy passage through this first thirty years, as we are nurtured and encouraged by those close to us along the way. Others may have had their vulnerability exploited, even abused, as children and the climb has been particularly rocky.

Having completed the first climb, whether it has proved easy or hard, we are given a second chance. In our thirties and forties we can gain insights about our childhood, and resolve issues that remain from this time without self-blame and recognizing that forgiveness lies at the root of our well-being. It may be that our own children, nephews and nieces become our most profound teachers at this time.

These cycles repeat throughout our lives, as each time we are given the opportunity to revisit and heal past wounds. If we are lucky enough to live to 120 years old, we will have had at least four bites of this juicy cherry!

Over the past three years, I have now had the opportunity of applying this time map to a large number of people coming to me for help. As with all holistic principles, these insights are best used as an overall guide; for instance if I say that the fourth chakra opens between the ages of 12 and 16 years it is important to know that this is a 'ball park' range. This is one of the challenges that presents as we try to explain holographic concepts within the limitations of our linear, Western vocabulary. It is also important to realise that within each chakra lies the holographic imprint of all the chakras, as all portions contain aspects of the whole.

I have already explained how the double-helical spiral pattern of our DNA allows a balancing of electrical fields, thereby creating a vacuum at its core, providing access to non-local fields. I have found it helpful to extend this model to the larger scale of the chakras, with each completed cycle representing a state of balance of opposite forces. In classical Chinese terms, this means the balance between yin and yang. It appears that there is still progression 'upwards' even if perfect balance is not achieved in the chakra 'below'. However the flow does not seem to be as smooth, and so ingrained imbalances in the base chakras tend to cause a 'drag' in the progress of all subsequent higher chakras. This is not all bad, as too rapid a rise in the *kundilini* is extremely hazardous, and can literally prove to be a mind-blowing experience. This phenomenon has been variously described as a psycho–spiritual crisis, or the *physio–kundilini syndrome,* and could result in the sufferer being escorted off for an enforced stay in a psychiatric hospital.

Despite all these potentially complicating issues, I have discovered I have been able to adapt Brenda's teaching in a simple way to the wide range of problems and illnesses that people present to me. So many people blame themselves for events in the past, and an understanding of how their lives have been influenced as vulnerable children acts as a potent catalyst for deep healing. They are then able to stop blaming themselves, and even to see the perpetrator of this control or abuse in the light of his or her own spiritual journey.

Many then discover that forgiveness lies at the heart of their healing.

The 1st Chakra – Our Tribal Roots

I was not a particularly brave nine-year-old. It wouldn't have been so bad if I had been taller, as this would have allowed me to become a fully signed-up member of my school's notorious Sycamore Gang. In the summer, after lunch, the eight-to ten-year-olds were set loose to 'play' on a large grassed field around which grew several magnificent large sycamore trees. A sycamore seed has as part of its design a double-leafed propeller, known as a samara, which on becoming detached from the tree floats gently towards the ground while rotating on its axis. The idea is for these seeds to be caught by the breeze to be transported far and wide like tiny green helicopters.

Members of the Sycamore Gang were unfortunately not interested in reflecting on such diverse wonders of nature. Their founding member, a tall, heavily built ten-year-old called Daryl, had impressed his peers by splitting one of these seeds longitudinally, and placing it on his nose so that the propellers stuck up vertically to the sky. A few of his most ardent admirers followed his lead, and the Sycamore Gang was duly formed. To protect the gang's exclusivity, the members decided to restrict membership on a height and weight basis. They then decided on an agenda, which basically consisted of terrorizing all those not lucky enough to meet their membership criteria. Non-members would be captured and taken to areas beneath trees, by now strictly designated as Gang Headquarters. Once kidnapped, one could only pray for the bell that heralded the afternoon's lessons. Even math was better than this.

So it was inside a hedge that I met up with my best friend Johnny. Like me, he had realized he was ineligible for membership, by about a foot, and suggested, given the gravity of our situation, it was high time we sealed our bond of friendship. He took out his brand new Swiss Army knife, a birthday present from his uncle, and to my alarm made a sizable gash in the palm of his hand.

'Blood brothers!' he said, looking me firmly in the eye.

I gulped, and vainly suggested an alternative bonding ritual – maybe a special code, a secret handshake? Unfortunately, a full 16 years was to pass before baseballer Glenn Burke held up his hand at home base to greet Dusty Baker as he completed his 30th home run for the Dodgers, thereby introducing the world to the far more sensible 'high five'.

But Johnny's gaze only hardened. Succumbing to his intense peer pressure, I shakily took the knife from him and made the tiniest of scratches on the palm of my own hand. After squeezing the skin around it, and much to my relief, a tiny drop of blood appeared. By now blood was gushing from Johnny's hand, and our hands gripped together in a squelchy and painful mess.

'Blood brothers!' we declared triumphantly in unison. By now Johnny was looking very pale, and I thought I was going to faint. Thankfully, the bell rang for math, and we staggered inside, clutching our hands that were bound up with grubby handkerchiefs. When we accept friends as family, we are allowing them into our most profound inner circle, where blood is thicker than water. To appease a tearful mother who fears losing her marrying daughter, we may remind her she is also gaining a son. The first chakra is associated with our roots, our family and our bloodline. Through our DNA, we inherit the traits of our ancestors, and from conception through to our early childhood we are totally dependent on our family; and in ancient times, our tribe. This is when our bodies and souls are the most vulnerable. Bonds are formed that will effect our health and how we interact with the world, over our entire life.

The Early Years – From Conception to Four

In our early years we are active and indiscriminate receiving antennas. Our skin and bones are thin. As babies we have open fontanelles (soft spots in our head) before our skull bones have fused. Our sense of self, and the protective shell of our ego, has yet to form, leaving us vulnerable, at the whim of our parents and close family members. The children who are held lovingly as small babies, and who are breast fed, grow to have stronger immune systems than those who, for whatever reasons, miss out on this intimate contact. These are the years we find difficult to recall. Yet those who are mistreated or abused in these early years may sub-consciously carry deep scars within them for the rest of their lives.

The Sanskrit name for the first chakra is *Muladhara (mula*=root; *hara*=base/foundation). It is represented by the earth element and the color *red*, the color given to our blood by the iron content of our haemoglobin. The element of the first chakra is the *earth*. It is from the red earth that we derive the basic minerals to live; we are as one with the earth. With our every breath, the earth and the air meet, as iron from the core of our mother earth bonds with oxygen inhaled into our lungs. Using the now familiar holographic model, our blood is manufactured deep within our own core – within the marrow of our bones. Imbalances associated with this chakra often show up with disorders of the blood and bones.

Bloodline Pressure – Terry's Story

(Note: A recent 2007 trial in the peer reviewed medical journal, *Cirulation,* examined the effectiveness of acupuncture in lowering blood pressure. The authors, doctors from Germany and China, concluded that acupuncture was as effective as medication in lowering blood pressure during the six weeks of treatment. However, the effect disappeared once the treatment stopped. I have found it is important, in addition to interventions such as acupuncture or medication, to address deeper underlying reasons for medical conditions such as high blood pressure. If these are understood, and owned, by the patient, truly sustainable results are more likely to be achieved. In the allopathic medical model, raised blood pressure that is not associated with an identifiable pathological cause, is referred to as essential hypertension.)

Recently, Terry, a man in his early forties, came to see me, as his doctor was having difficulty lowering his blood pressure with medication. Terry, like many in his situation, felt confused that no cause had been found, as this left him powerless to address any problems personally. His doctor had asked whether there were any stresses in his personal and work life, but in many ways his life had never been better. He then admitted to feeling some resentment at having to start long-term medication, and was further frustrated when increasing doses of medication failed to lower his blood pressure.

During our first meeting, we acknowledged this sense of frustration, which Terry likened to some of the feelings he had as a child as a response to his strict father.

His father, a successful lawyer, had always acted as if Terry was a disappointment to him, expecting him to excel in the classroom and on the soccer field, just as he himself had done as a young man. He felt his father was trying to groom him in his own image, and this had come to a head when Terry had dropped out of law school. Up until then the plan had been for Terry to join his father's law firm as a junior partner.

Instead, Terry pursued his love of the outdoors, eventually becoming a successful and award-winning landscape designer. Despite being happily married with two gorgeous children, he still harboured an inner sense of failure, of not living up to the expectations of his father. His father had died suddenly of a heart condition three years before Terry consulted me, and he regretted not having had the opportunity to resolve this deep source of discontent in his life by 'having it out with Dad'.

I suggested to him that it appeared that he was really suffering from 'bloodline pressure' and his eyes filled with tears. He went on to explain that he couldn't remember his father ever saying he loved him, or even giving him a hug.

'I make a point of hugging my own son every night at bedtime,' he stated.

(There is now strong evidence that our perception of how much love and caring we receive as young children from our parents can be a major influence on our health later in our life. One famous study has followed the health of Harvard graduates from the 1950s to the present day, and has found an increased incidence of hypertension, coronary heart disease, duodenal ulcers and alcoholism in those who, as students, used few positive, loving words to describe their parents.)

Terry admitted he still found it difficult to forgive his father. Despite loving and respecting him, he was unable to grieve deeply for him. He decided to talk to his family about this, and as a result he began to understand that his father himself had endured a strict upbringing. In fact, it became clear that this 'bloodline pressure' had been passed down from generation to generation, and it was now Terry who had the opportunity to break this cycle, by not treating his own son as simply a 'chip off the old block'.

I decided to delay giving any acupuncture, sensing it was important for Terry to be a master of his own destiny in this matter. I advised him to buy his own blood pressure monitoring machine, as this encourages people to fully own their condition. He acted upon my suggestion of writing a letter to his late father, expressing his predicament and his new understanding of their relationship.

Over the following month, Terry's blood pressure began to settle. He was still taking his medication, and we cautiously reduced this until eventually stopping it altogether. During this time, Terry also enlisted the help of a qualified regression hypnotherapist, who took him back to his early childhood, giving him a valuable insight into the time before his conscious memory took over.

Terry, who is now drug free, continues to monitor his own blood pressure. He no longer has a deep inner sense of discontent, and remembers his father with a fondness he never truly experienced when he was alive.

Keeping Our Feet on the Ground

Over the past half a century, it has become clear that we are far more than the sum of our parents. Our genetic skeleton, our DNA, comes from our mother and father, but how these genes respond depends not only on our environment but also on how we perceive it.

Our DNA and our microtubules within each of our 50 trillion cells are constantly exposed to free, quantum information from a universal source; even the spindles pulling our chromosomes apart every time our cells divide are perpetually on-line.

Parents who love their children unconditionally, for who they are, create the perfect environment for their physical, emotional and spiritual growth. The cells of their children are able to divide and grow throughout their lives, unburdened, free from the unbalanced conditioning of guilt and worry. It would appear from the accumulated evidence I have already relayed in this book, that it is the intent behind this love that truly 'hits home' with children – even Dr Masura Emoto's water crystals are able to recognize loving words that are said with sincerity.

Balance in the first chakra causes us to feel truly earthed. We are at home here on the earth, protected and nurtured, but not controlled by our parents. We are guided through their firm example to live safely, to keep away from the hotplate; we are encouraged to take our first steps, but are allowed to fall over occasionally. We learn that a temper tantrum will not always gain us our parents' undivided attention.

The time from conception to the age of four is when our earth-bound roots take hold. We toddle around eventually learning to stand on our own two feet. But if we are neglected, we may not learn to seek help when we slip down. The first chakra in balance promotes our sense of stability and resilience but without the fear of isolation.

The songs of Simon and Garfunkel have always moved me. In the lyrics of *I am a Rock,* Paul Simon likens his character to a rock and an island because, 'a rock feels no pain, and an island never cries'. If we become too independent, we risk alienating ourselves from what is important. When Buddha remarked that 'Life is Pain' he was not being unduly pessimistic. A fully lived life involves pain and tears, as well as joy and happiness. These are our early lessons in life.

As we grow as *human antennas,* we learn that we are continuously receiving and transmitting messages. In these early years we are more vulnerable receivers, as we are yet to learn the lessons from the higher chakras. We have not yet developed a conscious awareness of exactly who we are, and how we fit into the world. Even when we begin to gain this awareness, we have to be diligent about remaining earthed. Once we start to realize that our bodies are mainly space, that we live in a world of infinite possibilities and so on, it is easy to start living with our head in the clouds. Our friends may remark that we are 'away with the fairies'. I recently saw a wonderful and colorful middle-aged woman, Clarissa, who was blessed with the gift of clairvoyance, and gave readings from her home and at the local spiritualist church. She had been aware of her healing touch since she was a small child, yet her early childhood was not happy.

Her father was alcoholic, leaving home when she was a small child. Her mother couldn't cope, and Clarissa was adopted out to an uncle and aunt who were kind, but emotionally distant. Despite being highly intuitive, she admitted her life had always been a mess. She was unable to form close lasting relationships. A believer in reincarnation, she had come to the conclusion that her present life was being lived to learn about the need for close, loving relationships.

I have noticed that those spiritual teachers who are most at peace, somehow rise above the pressures that weigh most of us down. They commonly are diligent with their meditation, which serves to enrich their higher consciousness and intuitive skills, but at the same time they are perfectly grounded. My Qi Gong master, Steven Aung, is such a person who literally settles in to the earth that surrounds him as he starts to teach a session of this ancient art of energy balancing. I remember my first lesson with Steven, who instructed me to stand in the *horse-riding position,* with my feet wide apart and my legs partially bent at the hips and knees, around the back of an imaginary horse. My first thoughts were that there was no way I could keep in this position, and I groaned as every muscle in my legs ached. But to my surprise the aches faded, and I was able to remain comfortably rooted to the ground for nearly an hour.

For those whose life is 'in a whirl', who are feeling dizzy or light-headed, the following Qi Gong exercise is a quick, easy and effective way to feel grounded again. People from all indigenous cultures honor the sacredness of the earth, and so I have learned to include in this ritual a vote of thanks for its unending generosity.

Earthing Exercise

- Find any small area of lawn or beach, and slip off your shoes and socks.
- Begin by offering a simple blessing to the earth, thanking it for helping you.
- Smile.
- Breathe in gently, and on the out-breath consciously become aware of discharging unwanted energy into the earth through the soles of your feet.
- Visualize this energy descending down your legs from all parts of your body.

- Repeat this exercise three times.
- Next, take a couple of steps forward, and again send thanks to the earth.
- Now, focus on the in-breath, at the same time drawing in the earth's energy through the soles of your feet.
- On each repeat in-breath, visualize the energy reaching and revitalizing every part of your body.
- By now you will probably have a sense of calm, deep within.
- Again, thank the earth – and gently re-engage with the world   all around you.

The 2nd Chakra - Sex, Security and Seduction

By the age of five, our son Toby had become Albany Primary School's definitive authority on all matters dinosaurian. Even given that all five-year-old boys are obsessed by Tyrannosaurs, and all fathers think their boys are extraordinarily bright for their age, Toby's ability to respond instantly and accurately to any inquiry from his peers was a wonder to behold. Nothing seemed to ruffle him, and no question was too obscure whether it concerned the mating habits of the Allosaurus or the eating habits of the Parasaurolophus. On the rare occasion he was stumped, he would refer to his vast library of books that adorned his bedroom wall, or diligently surf his favorite sites on the Internet.

Dinosaurs, you will now have realized, were very much 1st chakra creatures. Despite being the likely primitive ancestors of birds, many, like the Brontosaurus, were land loving, with low centers of gravity and huge bones. They lived in herds, doing their best to avoid the attention of the blood-loving carnivorous Tyrannosaurus Rex. It seems unlikely, however, that dinosaurs ever wrestled with relationship issues – outside of Disney movies.

Unfortunately, Toby's world of dinosaurs was to end about as abruptly as did the dinosaurs some 65 million years previously (according to Toby.) On the eve of his sixth birthday, the magnificent Triceratops that stood proudly on top of his bookcase disappeared, to be replaced by the noble sword waving Aragorn, valiantly defending Middle Earth from the corrupt army of Orcs. All of a sudden there were goodies and baddies, issues of right and wrong and frequent blood curdling yells coming from his bedroom. He began adopting the persona of characters from his favorite movies, role-playing in dramatic productions with his friends, and even, on rare occasions, lending them one of his treasured plastic warriors. The second chakra evolves between the ages of five and eight, and is involved in defining our personal boundaries. Adult symptoms in this area – in our low back and sex organs – inform us of imbalances in our relationships with other humans, and our security in the material world. Any conflicts that exist between our work and family life are relayed back to us via messages from this part of our body. The Sanskrit name for the 2nd chakra is *Svadhistthana* (*sva* = self, *shthana* = place). Its color is the color of the sunrise – orange – signifying the dawning of personal consciousness and creativity.

A large number of people present to me, and to all general practitioners, with symptoms that reflect imbalances in this chakra. Financial or relationship insecurities, particularly in young and middle aged men, frequently show up as low back pain or sciatica. I see this pattern every week in my practice, and it often allows me to open up a discussion into the underlying causes. Sometimes this is their first introduction to the links between their body and their mind, and once they realize this, they are able to make the necessary changes that ensure healing. For men, this often opens the door to a deeper understanding of their health needs, which serves them well for the rest of their lives.

The need for women to achieve a healthy balance between work and family is highlighted by another 2nd chakra condition – that of infertility. Many women now earn considerable success in their careers only to find it extremely difficult to fall pregnant in their thirties. They may feel a profound sense of failure as they struggle to achieve something many women seem to find so easy to accomplish. They are then submitted to the emotional and financial stresses of a drawn-out fertility program, surrendering their futures to what can appear to be a mysterious and highly technical game of potluck. So alongside the high-tech approach, and preferably before, it is ideal that the woman asks herself certain questions about the balance in her own, and her partner's, lives. I ask each hopeful mother-to-be to look at their lives through the eyes of her future baby's soul; what would be the checklist she would go through before entering into this world under their care.

In many cases it is the partner that has to make the changes, cutting down on his work schedule, even at the expense of earning less money. It may be important for him to realize his responsibilities in helping his partner to become pregnant do not end with producing a satisfactory semen sample.

If, in her frustration, she despairs at the number of children that seem to be born into far-from-perfect homes, I suggest that her baby is an extremely choosy soul, satisfied only in traveling first class, and staying exclusively in luxury, five-star accommodation!

Our second chakra talks to us about our relationship with others, and may reveal the truth on how much trust we place in a sexual partner. For instance, the incidence of cancer of the cervix of the womb, a second chakra organ, increases if the partner is promiscuous. I often see women with on-going symptoms of pain, abnormal bleeding and vaginal discharges, whose symptoms only resolve when they are helped to confront their partners about their fidelity. These are extremely difficult issues to deal with, as leaving a relationship often leaves a woman financially the poorer. However, by choosing to stay in an abusive relationship, especially if her symptoms are suppressed by drugs and alcohol, she sets the scene for serious ill-health in the future. These are the risks that we take if we ignore our body's and our soul's wake up call.

The years between five and eight are also important for our under-standing of our personal boundaries with others. It is well known that sexual abuse of children at this age, and younger, can have a devastating effect on their future health, and ability to form trusting adult relationships. Young children have not yet had the time to build any protection to the negativity of others or to the world around them.

Their bodies and souls are often violated by the unbalanced power of someone who had also been similarly damaged at this age; and so the generational cycle of abuse continues. With great care, and extensive counseling, abused children can indeed recover to lead normal happy lives. Those who do, break a cycle of abuse that has continued unabated for centuries, possibly millennia. The next generation may play a huge role in their healing, as the abused are given the chance, in their thirties and forties, to form wonderful balanced relationships with their own children. Forgiveness of the perpetrator of this abuse, often a close family member or friend, may come from an understanding that he himself was a victim of this system. Although by no means excusing him for his actions, the healed, abused-person now has insights into this conditioned behaviour, ensuring that future generations achieve balance in their lives and in their second chakra. The sun can truly rise on a new era in their family.

Addictions

Imbalances in the second chakra also show up as addictions. We all struggle with addictions. Even if we are not overtly addicted to alcohol, drugs, tobacco, sex, money or power, we are likely to be addicted in some way to our past, our expectations, our relationships, our emotions or our work. One simple definition of an addiction is that it is something we can't stop doing.

We all know people who are addicted to negativity. For them the weather is either too hot or too cold, too wet or too dry. As so much of my work involves resonating with a patient, I sometimes find myself in a never-ending battle with someone exhibiting this line of conversation. Unfortunately, this is a battle I seldom win:

'Lovely day,' I say.

'You haven't been out in the wind,' they reply.

'Ah but the sailors will be happy.'

'Don't talk to me about sailing – I get sick just looking at a boat.'

'So how are you feeling today? . . .'

On the odd occasion though, misery can have a positive therapeutic effect. One of my close friends at medical school used to cheer up the sickest patients in a hospital ward, by letting them know that none of their symptoms were nearly as severe as his own. He had the knack of making each of them feel amongst the luckiest people alive, even though the next day they could be facing serious life-threatening surgery.

Of course, addictive behaviour can be changed, and addicts can reform. The difficulty resides in the depth of its roots within the second chakra. If we are exposed to addictive behaviour as a sensitive child, we may grow up only to imagine that happiness can come from an instant 'hit'. If the dominant male figure in our early life is addicted to gambling and alcohol, we are trapped within the vice of control this brings to our parents' relationship. Not only is this a highly destructive role model in itself, further damage ensues with the abusive behaviour and financial destitution that inevitably compounds the scene. All this negativity infuses within us, as we are yet to learn how to protect ourselves – this is handled by the next chakra that deals with our individual rights.

As a low sense of self-worth remains unmanifested, many children brought up in these circumstances perpetuate the cycle by forming relationships with addictive partners on reaching their late teens and early twenties.

We are, however, given opportunities to heal from the effects of addictive behaviour. Addicts have to exert self-discipline and willpower to say no to the substance or behaviour that has controlled their lives, and the lives of many of those around them. Unfortunately for many, this only happens once their lives are in tatters.

We are in the midst of a devastating epidemic of methamphetamine (or 'P') addiction. Methamphetamine addiction turns a human being who is aware of the value of nurturing relationships with others, into an uncaring, selfish and dangerous liability. Ancient Sanskrit texts illustrate the second chakra with a six-petalled lotus flower. Each petal represents a negative quality that we need to overcome – anger, hatred, jealousy, cruelty, desire and pride. In this case, 'P' addicts usually exhibit all of these negative traits.

Recently I had the opportunity of treating a young lawyer addicted to methamphetamines. His mother was dying of cancer of the stomach, and she confided in me that her biggest stress was her son's addiction. As if to emphasize the importance of this, two other women in their fifties, both mothers of 'P' addicts, presented to me with similar stories within the next fortnight. One had bowel cancer, and the other a severe form of arthritis.

Each woman said that she was the only meaningful person left in her son's life. Yet their sons' actions, including their inability to return their mothers' unconditional love, were draining them of their life's energy. The young men only mixed with other addicts and all relationships were conditional on getting their next fix.

So I asked the young lawyer, an articulate and intelligent man in his mid-thirties, just how he had come to be hooked on 'P.' He surprised me by saying that the only feeling he had on first taking it was that of gentle elation. It was almost innocuous, but he noticed too a sense of being 'bullet-proof'. Somehow the outside world posed no threats.

During the Second World War, methamphetamines (branded as Pervitin) were distributed widely to German soldiers to give energy and reduce human empathy for the opposition. Adolf Hitler's own behaviour later in the war was perhaps history's most chilling example of 'P' addiction. I was interested to see a TV documentary detailing the day the Nazi generals plotted to kill Hitler in July 1944. By that time, Hitler was receiving a cocktail of intravenous drugs every morning from his physician, Dr Theodor Morell. Included in this brew was methamphetamine. As we know, the assassination attempt failed. At a critical moment, the briefcase housing the bomb was moved a few feet away from Hitler, allowing him to be shielded from the blast by the table top. Three others died.

Rather than destroy Hitler's confidence in his generals' support, this dramatically close brush with death apparently only further convinced Hitler that he was truly invincible. At the end of the war, the Nazi Governor General of Poland, Hans Frank (1900–46) explained to a prison psychologist the effect Hitler had on him and the German people. Like the young man describing to me his initial seduction by the innocuous 'P', Frank described how easy it had been to fall prey to the man and his ideals:

It is not with horns or a forked tail that the devil comes to us, you know. He comes with a captivating smile, spouting idealistic sentiments, winning one's loyalty. We cannot say that Adolf Hitler violated the German people. He seduced us.

It is during our early years, before we are 10 years old, that we learn right from wrong. If we are lucky our parents teach us through their good example, with consistent messages of support and warning. If we are unlucky enough to have addictive, abusive parents, the messages become blurred, and tainted with fear. We may never develop the self-esteem necessary to rise above this cycle of abuse. As no one in our formative years has given us cause to trust them, we will struggle to develop the skills to know exactly when to follow advice, and when to query orders.

The rise of Nazi Germany has taught us to be ever vigilant of blindly following orders. The charismatic leaders of fundamental groups offer the disaffected glory and salvation, often spouting their 'idealistic sentiments' alongside their messages of fear and bigotry. One only has to remember those massacred at Jonesville and Waco, and those terrorists that boarded the planes on 9/11 believing their mission was a straightforward hijacking, to realize how these 2nd chakra imbalances have dominated our recent history in a horrific way.

Meanwhile, the world's major entertainment companies continue to expose the children of the world to increasingly life-like computer games in which they are encouraged to perform sadistic and graphic acts of violence. It is cold comfort to me, as a parent, to be told that most children from 'good' homes are unaffected by these games.

The vast majority of the victims of Nazi Germany, of 9/11, and from Columbine High School, also came from 'good' homes.

It is perhaps appropriate that the dawn of human consciousness emerges from its darkest hour. Balance within our 2nd chakra allows us to form harmonious relationships, in which we neither overpower nor give our power away. We learn how to juggle the demands of our personal life with those of living in the material world. And we learn how and just who to trust.

From this firm platform, we can start to define our own special role in the world, as our sun begins to rise and shine.

Summary and Exercise

I have found it difficult to talk about the second chakra without absorbing some of the negativity that surrounds this level of consciousness. So how do we remain concerned and vigilant about the destructive power held within an imbalanced second chakra, while not holding on to resentment and anger? Similarly how can someone, abused as a child, ever forgive the abuser? How can we fail to be outraged by witnessing the terrible consequences of substance abuse, or the inhumane terrorist acts carried out by fundamentalist zealots?

In a recent song about the tragedy of 9/11, Leonard Cohen asks us if we went crazy or 'did we report' on the day they 'wounded New York'. The sleeve notes on the CD include a definition of the verb 'report' from The American Heritage Dictionary: 'To present oneself: report for duty.'

We were all deeply affected by the events of 9/11; many of us were changed forever. Leonard Cohen asks each of us to do something useful in the wake of this tragedy. Just how we *report,* and what our duties are, will vary from person to person – but any tragic circumstance creates an opportunity for us to use our special gifts to make a real change in the world.

Mother Theresa, when asked what one individual could do to help heal the planet, and to create peace, suggested that each of us look deeply at our own lives. Her advice echoes the old saying, 'Charity begins at home'. If we are to prevent prejudice, and an 'eye-for-an-eye' mindset, we must first act by forgiving those in our own past, and by recognizing our own imperfections. Everyone in the world has a neighbour he can start to tolerate, appreciate and even love.

The Dalai Lama gives a useful tip about forgiveness. He explains that deep down we all share our own, personal wish to avoid suffering. This even lies at the root of those seduced by methamphetamines, and of those who have yet to develop the self-esteem necessary to escape the trap of fundamentalism. It could be said that their course in life has been misguided.

Most of you who read this book will have already realized that to heal the outside world, we each have to heal the world within. The Christian ethic of loving one's neighbour as oneself gains new meaning as we realize that there are no true barriers between people. We love our neighbour, as he or she is part of ourself.

So we can report (in Leonard Cohen's terms) by ensuring that we are living our lives according to these heart-centered principles. Although some of us may have special skills with words, it is our actions that will speak louder. Our vulnerable children, and those adults who have been misguided in the past, will then have the opportunity to be guided by our deeds.

Exercise 2

So I suggest as a simple 2nd chakra exercise, that you create for yourself a special affirmation or prayer, freeing you from any fears conditioned into you by misguided individuals, past and present. This can then be used whenever it is needed.

The 3rd Chakra – Solar Power

Between the ages of eight- and twelve-years-old, we learn to understand we are unique and special. We learn to make judgment calls, when to go with the flow and when to act. The Sanskrit name is *Manipura (mani = jewel; pura = place)* as it is here we gain clarity in our lives. The chakra is centered around and above the navel, and its color is golden yellow. Like the midday sun, this is our energy center providing us with vitality and strength.

Disorders of this center show up as dis-ease in our stomach, intestines and pancreas. If our personal power is being undermined or controlled, messages in the form of symptoms are relayed back to us from here. This is also where we have our *gut feelings,* intuitive messages that a balanced 3rd chakra helps us 'hear' and trust.

But it is also a place we can store our worries, and literally have a *guts-full* of our problems. A sudden insult can be *a kick in the guts,* while asserting ourself requires self-confidence and a lot of *guts.* The lining of intestines are teeming with receptor sites for the chemicals Professor Candace Pert calls our *molecules of emotion.* These spiral-shaped peptide molecules, induced by our emotions, attach to the lining of our cells, and start vibrating, passing messages into each cell's insides. These messages can be passed on each time the cell divides, so emotional memories, good and bad, can persist within us for years.

The navel is the focal point of many energy-enhancing exercises. It is here we have all received our energy and nutrition while in our mothers' wombs. It is to here that we direct our inspired breath at rest when we are breathing correctly. And it is the navel that divides our adult standing body into the precise dimensions of the Golden Ratio. Ayurvedic teaching, itself based on intuitive awareness, explains that Prana, or life force, is attracted like a magnet through the *Manipura* chakra from the cosmos. On the microscopic level, this area is a frantic hive of emotional activity. It is perhaps no coincidence that our molecules of emotions are spiral shaped, perfect for downloading quantum information, in the form of timeless wisdom, through a 'direct' line to our guts. Meditation and relaxation exercises involve focused breathing to this area, so that only the present moment is savoured. This effectively reduces all interference from past worries that may block clear reception on this direct line. By learning to follow our gut feelings, we learn to become more efficient, wasting less time in useless worrying.

An open door through our 3rd chakra may also let in unwelcome guests. Through this area, we can take on the negativity of others, and can have our own personal power taken away. We sometimes have to have the self-esteem to walk away, or to say 'no'. We have to learn how to win, but also how to lose gracefully without harbouring resentment. And as this chakra helps to define us as personalities, it is important that our egos are kept in tow.

Imbalances in this 3rd chakra, as with the 2nd, produce addictive behaviour. It is here that we could become addicted to power and to controlling others. If our egos become over-inflated, and our self-esteem unchecked by humility, we may become a leader of those locked and imprisoned within their 2nd chakras. Because we have not yet experienced an opening of our heart chakra, we may assume that we have reached the top of the tree, and that we hold the secrets of right and wrong. Many cult leaders function in this way and the consequences, as I have already explained, can be dire.

Our 3rd chakra lets us know whenever we are trapped in the middle of controlling forces. We all exist between generations, and many women I see are caught between the demands of their children and the needs of their own parents whose health may be failing. Occasionally more sinister stories are relayed by 3rd chakra symptoms.

Cathy's Story

I was recently consulted by Cathy, a 23-year-old solo mother, who had debilitating stomach pains and fatigue. She was extremely pale and close examination revealed a severe anaemia. I suspected that she had a bleeding stomach ulcer and arranged for an ambulance to take her to hospital. While she was waiting for this, I asked her about the stresses in her life and she explained that she lived with her six-year-old daughter who, she had recently discovered, had been abused by a close family member. She had had to go through the courts to protect her daughter, and as a result her own mother had 'disowned' her, claiming Cathy's story was a complete lie. I suggested we talk about this after she left hospital.

Cathy's role of protecting her daughter had alienated her from her own family support. When she returned from hospital, Cathy talked about a cycle of abuse that had existed in her family for generations; she herself had been sexually abused by her own teenage step-brother, and strongly suspected her mother had suffered similarly during her own childhood. It was seemingly more painful for her mother to confront these memories, than to cut ties with her own daughter.

I asked Cathy if she had told anyone in the hospital about this story. She hadn't. Nobody asked, and she said she would be wary of telling them anyway.

I explained that I fully understood, but secretly felt concern at how the root cause of illness is so frequently by-passed by our hospital system.

I was reminded of an article that appeared in a medical magazine in the early nineties under the headline, 'Bacteria, not Stress, proved to cause Peptic Ulcers'. It detailed convincing research that many ulcers were formed by an overgrowth of the bacterium *Helicobacter pylori* in the stomach. This important work led to a dramatic change in the management and treatment of peptic ulcers, which now includes tests for this bacterium and, if detected, antibiotic treatment. However, what concerned me was the assumption that a medical condition was either the result of a 'bug' or stress; that somehow these two causes existed in isolation from one another. It even suggested that there was no longer a need to search for 'psychological' causes. In reality, *H.pylori* exists in all healthy stomachs, but only overgrows and becomes a problem when the body's immunity is affected – in Cathy's case, by the extreme stress of her predicament. The trapped situation that Cathy found herself in caused her bodymind to give her a powerful message within her solar chakra. The fact that her ulcer was also *bleeding* severely, points to the ingrained generational *bloodline* issues expressed by imbalance of the 1st chakra.

Classically, people who feel stuck in unfulfilling jobs, where their initiative and intuition is undermined, have been candidates for peptic ulcers. Initially, their 3rd chakra starts to talk to them by producing more acid, and then together with an overgrowth of H.Pylori, the condition progresses as the messages go unheeded. People handling public complaints for a company without the caring support of management staff are particularly at risk.

I see many people in well paid but unsatisfying corporate jobs whose active, irritable bowels and stomachs are busy informing them to break free. The symptoms only settle when they move to a company with a heart, or break free completely to follow their own unique dreams.

So balance in the 3rd chakra is achieved when one has esteem for oneself, but not at the expense of others.

Global Shifts

The shift from 2nd to 3rd chakra consciousness has been witnessed on a global scale with the collapse of communism, and the falling of the Berlin Wall in November 1989. Totalitarian states of the extreme left or right give the individual little personal power. Democracy, a 3rd chakra ideal, acknowledges the right of every mature human to decide who governs her or his country. Constitutions are set up to ensure the democratic process is protected and allowed to evolve and thrive. Whilst democracy is far from perfect, it is actively being developed as our societies learn to create successful structures within it, to better care for the needs of all, and it is a great deal better than the cruel, controlling 'I win/you lose', dictator-run regimes we have seen in countries such as Iraq.

Much democratic, political philosophy and argument is based within the 3rd chakra, and its corresponding meme. Left-wing politicians argue that if too much power is given to too few, the majority will be overpowered and disadvantaged. Meanwhile right-wingers say that if personal enterprise and the competitive marketplace are over-controlled, no one – rich or poor – will benefit. In the ideal democratic environment these yin and yang viewpoints are endlessly debated and a balanced compromise found.

In the wake of the US invasion of Iraq, international debate and concern now focuses on the moral rights and wrongs of reaching a democratic solution through aggressive force. The Cold War has now been replaced by the War on Terror, protecting the personal freedom of the democratic world. By replacing one war with another, it could be said that the world is still to evolve out of the first tier of consciousness. The first three chakras house this level of consciousness within each of us. If they are allowed to operate without input from our higher centers, other solutions will remain obscure. A balanced 3rd chakra sets the scene for the opening and balancing of our 4th heart chakra, allowing us to progress past the old rules of 'I win/ you lose'.

For many of us in the West, the door opened in the sixties with flower power and hippie-dom. These baby-boomers, who embraced the joys of free love and peace in their early twenties, found it less easy, however, to convert those principles into practice as they forged successful lives in an increasingly materialistic world.

Many had experienced other dimensions of consciousness through the use of psychedelic drugs, only to find that they had to break free from their destructive power. Some used this experience in a positive way as the start of a journey exploring spiritual dimensions without the need of addictive substances. One notable example is Brazilian writer Paulo Coelho (author of *The Alchemist*) who admits to using drugs in his more rebellious youth, only to become a leading advocate of following one's own special inner journey.

Other prominent figures involved in researching the effects of psychedelic drugs such as LSD in the sixties, now teach safer, more intrinsic ways to explore deeper levels of consciousness. Examples are the transpersonal psychologist Stanislav Grof, who pioneered holotropic breathwork, and philosopher Ram Dass (formerly Richard Alpert).

Simple Exercise for the 3rd Chakra

- Lie down on a soft, comfortable bed.
- Close your eyes.
- Breathe in gently and slowly through your nose, while your abdomen expands.
- Visualize the breath reaching your navel, bringing new energy to your very core.
- Gently breathe out through your mouth as your abdomen flattens.
- Repeat this exercise about 10 times.
- Keep a smile on your face.

The 4th (Heart) Chakra – Love and Devotion

As a medical student in London, I was lucky enough to sit in on consultations conducted by one of the country's leading heart specialists. A highly distinguished, silver-haired man in his early sixties, he wore impeccable, pinstriped, Saville Row suits that were always adorned with a fresh carnation in the buttonhole. He embarked on the same elaborate routine with every new patient. If the patient happened to be a woman, he would rest his hand gently on hers, look her in the eye and say softly – in a Harley Street version of an Irish brogue – 'You see, my dear, your heart is a pump . . .'.

With his other hand he would then simulate the rhythmic contractions of a healthy human heart. If the patient was unfortunate enough to have an irregular fluttering heartbeat, he would then demonstrate this with more frantic jerky spasms. He then described how he would prescribe a special medication that would allow her heart to resume beating precisely as nature intended. His hand movements then became silky smooth again.

Male patients received the same patter, only without the handholding and the 'my dear'.

Although scientists over the past thirty years have never disputed the fact that the human heart is indeed a pump, they have also discovered it to be much more besides. It is now known to be a hormone-secreting gland responsible for producing chemicals that balance the autonomic (or involuntary) nervous system. It is also an organ littered with receptor sites for molecules of emotion. When it is in a loving, caring environment it is more likely to beat in a coherent, silky-smooth way. When there is conflict and anger, it is more likely to beat in an irritable, haphazard way as opposing forces battle within. So science is beginning to rediscover that our heart is indeed the 'seat' of our emotions. At medical school in the early seventies, we were advised to avoid becoming 'emotionally involved' with patients; unfortunately this distancing was also responsible for many of us over-prescribing drugs. As doctors, we were trained to bury our own emotions. Prescribing tranquillisers was deemed to be perfectly good medicine. It also avoided the need for us to delve too deeply into patients' problems – something that is impossible to do in five or ten minutes.

The older traditional doctors of that time, however, also understood the calming effects of touch. But with less and less time being allowed for consultations, this unrecognized feature within modern medicine may be fast losing ground.

Taking a pulse at the wrist is a two-way process, with subtle energy being exchanged between two concerned beings. In the eighties I learned the art of Chinese pulse diagnosis which involves palpating the wrist pulses with three fingers at three different depths. I became aware that this was not only an effective way to find out about the background energy in the body, it was also part of the treatment.

I learned to center my attention on my own heart, while at the same time feeling the quality of the patient's pulse through the tips of my fingers. I also try to do this when I am checking a pulse in the traditional Western way, when my principal focus is on analyzing the heart's rhythm.

For those skeptics who feel this is an unnecessary and dangerously distracting waste of time, I can reassure them that, in my own case at least, I eliminate such practice during a life-threatening emergency; for example when I am feeling for a pulse in someone whose heart has stopped after a heart attack. Then I find myself switching into my trained, conditioned, rescue mode; we all have the capacity to function at a level that is appropriate to the occasion.

The HeartMath Institute in Boulder Creek, California, has focused its research on the link between our emotions and our heart. The heart is our body's energetic center, with an electromagnetic field five thousand times stronger than our brain. In one of their experiments, researchers measured the heart wave signal (ECG) of one person, and the brainwaves (EEG) of another sitting four feet away. When the subjects held hands, the heartbeat signal of one showed up in the other person's brainwaves. Further studies have also revealed that brainwaves can be affected subtly when two people are less than five feet apart, even if they are not touching.

I am sure the Harley Street heart specialist of my student days knew that medicine was not only a science, but also an art. Although his methods now appear old fashioned and a tad patronizing, it seems likely that his patients' hearts were responding not only to his drugs, but also to his charming bedside manner; something that also helped pay for the gas in his glistening Silver Cloud Rolls Royce.

The HeartMath Institute's research work bridges the gap between the art and the science of medicine, giving us insights into the science of healing. It provides recorded proof that in close contact, we all function as *human antennas,* passing on and receiving electromagnetic signals. When we begin to understand that our heart transmits calm, balancing messages within our own bodies, and within the bodies of those we touch, we also begin to appreciate the value of touch in healing.

A close, loving bond between individuals also facilitates non-local connections, as demonstrated by the studies on remote perception, telepathy and telesomatic experiences. Mediums allow loved ones to communicate with their relatives who have 'passed on', by forming a non-threatening, empathetic bond with their clients. Our body's chemistry is at its most balanced when we are in a relaxed, trusting state. In Western terms, this means our sympathetic system is balanced by our parasympathetic system. In Eastern terms it means our yang with our yin. Then we allow another dimension to present itself. Love is timeless and non-local. We do not love someone any less because they have died, or have gone to the other side of the world on a business trip.

So as we move up to the 4th chakra, we progress from being conditionally self-centered, to being unconditionally heart-centered. To love truly, we have to release control.

By giving out love in this way, we also find we benefit and feel better ourselves.

The Gateway to Higher Consciousness

The center of the heart chakra (the *Anahata* chakra) is represented in Ayurvedic philosophy as two triangles superimposed on each other, one pointing upwards and the other downwards. This symbolizes how our emotions may either rise up as feelings of pure love and devotion, or else our heart can literally sink to a despairing state, as we become immersed in the overwhelming conflicts of the lower chakras. The latter is the pattern of depression. Surrounding these triangles are twelve petals of a lotus flower, each one representing a divine quality of the heart – love, understanding, peace, harmony, empathy, bliss, clarity, unity, compassion, kindness, purity and forgiveness.

The meridian, in Chinese medicine, known as the Heart Protector is said to clothe and nurture the heart; it runs from the center of the chest, down the inside of each arm to the palm of the hand, ending at the tip of our middle finger. We access this meridian when we hold hands, or touch someone in a healing way.

If, however, the touch does not carry this good intent, as in the case of the inappropriate touching of sexual abuse, the victim may suffer ongoing internal confusion, being unable to trust and receive the benefits of loving touch. Not only will touch then represent a whole raft of negative emotions within, but the person may also be denied access to a vital pathway to self-healing.

I begin every acupuncture treatment with a heart-centering exercise, allowing a patient to gain access to this pathway. One effective way is to warm a point in the inside of the wrist whose Chinese name *Neiguan* is translated as the *Inner Gate*. I use a lighted cigar-shaped stick of the Chinese herb, moxa, which provides a soothing dry heat to this area. Beneath this point lies the median nerve, and the sensations are transmitted by this nerve back to the spine, and to the autonomic (involuntary) nervous system.

Another point, this time on the heart meridian, lies on the inner corner of the inside of the wrist. This point is very effective in reducing anxiety and helping sleep. Its Chinese name is *Shen Men* or *Heaven's Gate*.

Of course, as effective as this, is a heart-felt hug once our trust is gained. As a popular substitute, we have a heart-shaped teddy bear named

Bob. He first spends a minute warming in the microwave (his insides are wheat) and then lies quietly over the person's chest, warming up the heart chakra.

Feeling Love

Although love is difficult to define in scientific terms, there is now much medical evidence supporting the importance to our health of 'feeling loved'.

One study at Yale University by heart specialist Dean Ornish, showed that men and women who felt loved and supported had substantially fewer blockages in their heart arteries, as demonstrated by coronary angiography. Another large study examined the perceived effect of marital love on 10,000 men with angina. All had equally high risk factors for heart disease, such as high blood pressure, diabetes and high cholesterol. Those who felt their wives were not showing them love had almost twice the incidence of angina.

Other studies have shown that the effects of aging can be reduced by giving out love and social support. The love that appears to be the most beneficial in these studies is not the dramatic, crazy and exciting phase we experience when we fall head over heels 'in' love. It relates far more to a deeper, less selfish commitment of trust and support. Close unconditional relationships with friends, and in particular pets, have a profound effect on our lives and healing. Evolving through the 4th chakra sets aside the control and judgment of others and ourselves that we have encountered as conditions in the lower chakras. It is where we learn to share our hearts, and not take advantage of another living being. And where we learn to give and receive unconditionally.

The heart chakra is said to develop between the ages of 12 and 16 years, once our personality and our egos have started to strengthen. It is then that we might begin to experience the early signs of adult love, often expressed as a sexual attraction, or crush for another. Despite the temptations heightened by their rampant teenage hormones, those who have grown up in homes where there has been open expression of love and support are less likely to become promiscuous in their early and mid teens. They are less likely to become addicted to the short-term pleasures of sex, at the expense of developing meaningful, lasting relationships.

The heart chakra also houses the lungs and breasts. It is our lungs that are confused if we try to ease our grief and tension by smoking. When we stop, our whole body grieves as if we have lost an intimate friend. Cigarettes are far from being loving, unconditional friends though. If they continue to be part of our lives, they eventually rob us of our life force, our breath.

Women with breast cancer who attend support groups have been shown to heal more quickly, and survive longer than those who are socially isolated. Recent large studies have shown that women live longer, healthier lives if they have true, meaningful, women friends. One possible reason for this is that their friends see them for exactly who they are; they do not have to adopt a role of mother, wife or daughter, all of which can prove draining, even in the best of families. Someone who is a practical, faithful and non-judgmental friend is exhibiting the precise version of love that both frees and heals.

It is precisely this profound level of friendship that can grow within a relationship or marriage, resulting in a deepening of true love. Candace Pert, the research professor at Georgetown University and author of the excellent *Molecules of Emotion,* acknowledges the presence of many stimulating chemicals that flood our body as we fall in love. However she encourages us to celebrate old love, suspecting that as love becomes richer and deeper, the effects on our body are more balanced and healing.

Nurturing and the Breast

Many women come to see me soon after receiving the diagnosis of breast cancer. Often they are already embarking on a course of chemotherapy, followed by radiotherapy, and some have had extensive surgery. Just because someone is suffering from an illness within their 4th chakra, it doesn't necessarily mean that they have an unhappy marriage or relationship.

Indeed, many have husbands and partners who are able to show the depth of their love in a new and profound way at this difficult time. However, most women who find themselves in this situation carefully re-examine the relationships in their lives, and particularly the relationship they have with themselves. The breast is the organ through which a woman nurtures others; she begins to ask whether this nurturing-out has been balanced by a self-nurturing within.

Sometimes this means that a partner has to change and give more in a relationship; at other times it is up to the woman to allow herself to receive more, as she identifies a self-sacrificing role dating back to her own childhood.

A patient, for example, may have been the oldest child, who, as her father died when she was 13-years old, may then have dedicated her teenage years to lending support to her grieving mother, helping her raise her own younger brothers and sisters. She then might have gone on to marry young, and to produce a family of her own, caring also for a husband working long hours at his job.

As her children grew up, she may have found that any 'spare' time was spent attending to the needs of her ailing mother, who had never really recovered from the sudden death of her husband years ago. She may begin to realize too that she has been holding her mother's grief too, for all those years.

Her diagnosis of breast cancer makes her look deeply at the meaning of her own life. Has all this 'giving out' created an imbalance that needs to be addressed? The reaction of her friends and family to the news of her illness may give her a sense of clarity about who loves her. She may well identify that she needs to follow her heart, and do that university course she never had the chance to do as a young mother. She may decide to be a rock climber, an artist or a poet.

For some, very painful decisions have to be faced.

Claire's Story

Claire had recently returned to New Zealand from Los Angeles, where her husband, David, was a hugely successful lawyer. They lived in a mansion in Beverly Hills. Many of her husband's clients were well-known movie stars and directors.

Although she had many acquaintances in L.A., most of them knew David and Claire as a couple. Six months before her diagnosis of breast cancer, Claire had found out that her husband was being unfaithful. She had confronted him with the facts and he agreed to stop the other relationship. Three months later, however, she discovered he was having another affair.

Just as they were arguing about filing for divorce and who would gain custody of their two children aged 5 and 7, she found a breast lump and her world was sent into turmoil. David took control, organizing for her to see the best surgeon that money could buy. Her diagnosis took center-stage, and Claire was forced to put aside all immediate thoughts of divorce.

After the surgery, David again promised he would behave himself, but Claire felt alone and frightened. Despite his help with arranging the surgery, she felt deeply hurt by David's unfaithfulness. The day her husband picked her up from hospital, she waited for him to leave for work and, via the Internet, booked three one-way tickets to New Zealand. She arrived in Auckland three days later with her two young children, having left a note for her husband on the kitchen table.

By the time Claire reached my rooms, she had already started a course of chemotherapy at the oncology department of the local hospital. She was keen for my overall help, and for acupuncture to reduce the nausea arising from her treatment. As Claire's story unfolded it was clear that she had suspected David of having affairs for years; there was even an incident while she was pregnant for the second time, which he had denied adamantly at the time.

She regarded her illness as a warning sign; a confirmation of her strongly held intuition about his ongoing unfaithfulness. However she knew he would battle hard for custody if they divorced, and despite the conclusive evidence of his actions, she knew he had access to California's best lawyers. In short, she felt if she stayed with him, she wouldn't survive the cancer; if she filed for divorce she risked losing one or both of her children.

As the weeks passed, her resolve hardened as she shared her story with close friends and family. She decided to stay in New Zealand in a small rented home with her children, taking a job as a relief teacher.

She says she will file for divorce once she has re-covered fully from the effects of her treatment. Meanwhile, David has agreed to offer Claire financial support.

Balance in the Heart Center

For many of us, balance in our heart center is achieved by expressing our emotions freely in a relationship that is truly a partnership. For Anglo–Saxon men like myself who have been conditioned to keep their feelings close to their chest, this means acknowledging and expressing our emotions regularly to our partners. However it also means taking time to listen to their needs.

Our emotions are a truthful record of what is happening to us. Burying them only makes the body come up with other ways to teach us the direction we should take. Our emotions may then become our symptoms and, if unheeded, our symptoms become our diseases. Our body takes on the role of our inner tutor, helping us graduate in the art of in(ner)-tuition.

A balanced heart chakra allows us to experience our emotions fully, and to understand our role as givers and receivers of love. In the ancient Vedic texts, its corresponding element is air, signifying freedom and expansion. It guides us to an appreciation that life can be joyful; it gives us permission to see the light.

We become light-hearted rather than heavy-hearted. We learn to laugh at ourselves without judgment, to allow ourselves to smile and project joy. Comedians and joyful people help us stand outside, and rise above, the struggles we all have battling the human imperfections seated within our lower chakras. The great comic partnerships of Laurel and Hardy, Abbott and Costello, and Morecambe and Wise cleverly pitched two adults locked in childlike competitive combat. The world responded by loving each of these gifted men. Their comedy is timeless, as it carries no malice, just a simple intent to lighten our load.

The other partnership forged within the human heart chakra is between each of us and nature. Appropriately the color associated with this level is green, and this color has become the symbol for global environmental concern. The green meme in Beck's spiral model of human conscious growth represents the sentiments of many in Western society born since World War II, the baby boomers.

Developed as a movement from the naïve flower-power slogans of the sixties' hippy generation, the Green movement has developed into a sophisticated international political force, holding the balance of power in many countries. Global warming, the depletion of equatorial rain forests, and the excessive burning of fossil fuels are now seen by most mainstream democracies as issues that threaten our planet's survival.

The Green movement's message, and that of deep ecology, is that we are in partnership with our earth. Our material growth and successes, with their roots in our lower chakras and memes, have given us the power to control the fate of our planet. The evolving heart chakra allows us to transcend our tendencies to control and prosper materially and selfishly from our earth.

Of course, 'greenies' have attracted a fair degree of criticism over the years. I still hear male callers to talkback radio deriding 'sandal-wearing, tree-hugging hippies' or 'touchy feely' New Age males. The Green movement itself may have to take some responsibility for this image, as there has been a tendency within the New Age movement towards its own versions of cultish exclusivity and judgmentalism. This, however, together with the extreme actions of eco-terrorists and violent protesters, represents an imbalance within the green, heart chakra. Rather, the heart chakra represents peaceful cooperation; resorting to violent protest for reasons such as 'the end justifies the means' represents a return to lower chakra imbalances.

Achieving balance within the heart chakra involves an understanding and forgiveness of our own, and other human beings' over-zealous competitive nature. Forgiveness lies at the heart of healing, and we have already used this heart chakra value as part of our exercise in resolving 2nd chakra imbalances. Another way to view this is by returning to our holographic model and an understanding that each chakra has a delicate point of balance within its own heart. This point holds within it all values dear to the heart chakra; it has been said that the greatest of these is *love,* the Christ consciousness of the Bible's New Testament.

Embracing Plants

To those who are convinced that reality only exists in the world if it is revealed to them via their five senses, the act of hugging a tree is a patently absurd pastime. In fact the term, 'tree hugger' is now often used in a derisory way to describe an aimless, alternative life-styler with wet, ineffective liberal views – someone who has taken leave of their senses. In my view, this is both unfortunate and unfair.

In the East, and in shamanic circles, tree hugging is understood to be a safe, effective form of meditation. I have always found it to be both calming and invigorating, and particularly helpful for those who have difficulty stilling their overactive minds. Trees of course are mostly taller, heavier and, if left to their own devices, longer living than human beings. Like us, their cells contain not only DNA but also microtubules, although these do not occur in the concentrations found in mammalian brains. Plants and trees, it can be argued, are not self aware. However it is now known that microtubules have a prominent role in plant growth patterns. In fact, sheets of these helical rods dictate the shape and size of the plant, receiving information from the plant's DNA. They are largely responsible for 'deciding' whether the plant looks like a daffodil or a sycamore tree.

I remember being fascinated by an episode of the BBC television series *The Private Life of Plants* that showed a speeded-up film of the growth of the roots of a large tree. David Attenborough commented that it appeared that the roots were moving consciously, feeling and plotting their way through the undergrowth much like large tentacles or fingers. Of course this 'movement' is somewhat of an illusion, as what is being portrayed is the speeded-up record of the growth of the roots, at the tips of which fresh plant cells are being continuously formed.

If we look inside these individual plant cells, we see something even more extraordinary. The microtubules themselves, each one 2,000 times narrower than a human hair, are busy moving around the cells in a curious manner known as 'tread-milling'. This describes the apparent 'movement' of microtubules as new molecules form at one end of the tube, while others die at the other end. Each molecule is like a person on a treadmill, marking time while not actually moving forward. This is also rather like watching a wave in the sea 'moving' towards the shore, whilst the seawater itself only rises and falls.

So we are beginning to understand that plant growth and regeneration is a consequence of this strange dance by these tiny spiral structures.

So what is it that guides the plant's microtubules?

In the previous section I described how it is proposed that our DNA molecules project a 4-dimensional holographic field throughout our body – a matrix, or map, upon which our cells regenerate and grow. Our microtubules, it is speculated, process this information (as well as other quantum information from the universe), and are then involved in the 'nuts and bolts' of cell growth. The presence of all these 'down-loading' structures in plants is further evidence that all living things are subtly, but profoundly connected, within a unifying entangled world wide web.

In a practical sense, the wonderfully intricate process of plant growth has provided human beings with the essential materials for sustainable living. The microtubules, under the direction of the plant's DNA, eventually arrange themselves within the cell walls in the helical pattern of cellulose (the water-resistant substance that is the major ingredient of paper, cotton and the fibre of a high-fibre diet).

There is yet another reason for us to be grateful to the microtubules in plants. And as in our own cells, microtubules form spindles that pull the plant's chromosomes apart when the cell is dividing. Several modern drugs such as *taxol* that are used to slow cancer growth in humans, are naturally occurring plant molecules that bind with microtubules to prevent a cell from dividing. It is the fundamental similarities between plants and ourselves that make this medical advance possible.

Plants as Antennas

Tangible proof of a remarkable non-local connection between humans and plants was uncovered by the lie-detector expert Cleve Backster in 1966. The lie-detecting machine, or Polygraph, measures small variations in skin voltage in the finger of a subject under emotional pressure. On a whim one night, he connected his lie detector, or Polygraph, to the pot plant in his office. He then watered it expecting the dial on the machine to reflect increased electrical activity in the plant. Instead the dial fell, precisely mimicking the pattern he had observed in humans who had been emotionally stimulated. When he burnt a leaf with a lighted match the plant also responded, this time in a stressed way.

Over the past thirty-five years many other operators have confirmed his findings. Backster's own experiments have been even more adventurous; for example plants have been shown to exhibit these reactions in response to other plants being harmed nearby. In one famous experiment, a plant reacted dramatically to the death of shrimps as they were dropped into boiling water in the same room.

Further experiments have shown the non-local nature of these reactions, as his pet plants tended to respond instantly when he himself was stressed; for example when he cut his finger. This would happen even if he were away on business, miles from his office. He has even shown that plants pick up on his level of intent at the precise time he makes a decision to do something. Solitary leaves detached from the plant respond in the same manner, as do minute samples of chopped up leaf. This suggests that the leaf is responding at the cellular level. Common to all the precognition and remote-viewing studies, a state of respect, even love, between the subjects plays an essential role in sealing these non-local bonds. It has long been observed that caring gardeners with 'green fingers' nurture healthier and more luxuriant plants. Backster has found that humans and plants can share a true affinity for each other.

His experiments strongly suggest that plants behave as wonderfully empathetic antennas, and this is reason enough for us to treat them well. We are also, of course, totally dependent on plants that provide us with the food we eat, the oxygenated air we breathe and the many herbal medicines that sustain and enhance our lives.

Magnificent old trees are amazing receivers, storers and transmitters of energy. It is easy to forget we see only a fraction of a tree above the forest floor; below our feet vast roots draw water and minerals from the depths of the earth. It is the stability and resilience of a tree that makes it such a perfect partner when our own energy is sagging. But way above us, it stands boldly as a highly impressive giant antenna, reaching high above the canopy of the forest while receiving and transmitting waves of light and unseen energy.

So a close encounter with a tree, whether we are touching it, sitting beneath it with our backs resting on its trunk, or passionately hugging it, not only earths us, but turns us into even more efficient *human antennas*.

Forging a relationship with the natural world into which we can retreat at will, helps us cope with our own relationships when they become strained and complicated. Animals and plants do not judge us, or harbor dark unforgiving thoughts. They engage us in true partnership, allowing our heart chakra to achieve a joyful balance.

As with all heart chakra exercises, tree hugging is a two-way process. We hug a tree in precisely the same way we hug a close friend, with the hugger and 'huggee' giving and receiving positive energy at the same time. It is an unconditional act. Shamans always make a point of offering the tree a gift (try something biodegradable like a potato) before imposing themselves, thus confirming their respect and noble intent.

Heart Chakra Exercise with a Tree

Over the years, I have frequently prescribed tree hugging in my practice. By and large, I have been amazed how many otherwise conservative folk have taken to it, overcoming their own conditioning, and the mocking jibes of others. I was particularly flattered when my street-smart fourteen-year-old niece, Joanna, allowed me to teach her the fundamentals of this ancient healing art while on vacation in New Zealand from London. Accepting the challenge, I first found a suitable tree just off the beaten track in an area of native bush, and I ran through the procedure outlined below. I left her in an unusually peaceful state with her arms wrapped around a beautiful old rimu tree, and returned to the path. After five minutes she emerged with a resigned look on her face.

I asked her how she had got on.

'Sorry,' she sighed, 'he's just not my type.'

That aside, here is what I suggest:

- Be choosy – first find a tree that ideally is old and with a reasonably thick trunk.
- Make sure the ground is firm and flat at the base of the tree – especially if you are wearing sandals!
- Then in an unhurried way, place your breastplate on the trunk with your arms encircling it, and with your legs astride. Gently rest your brow on the bark, and close your eyes.
- Breathe slowly using your stomach whilst focusing on your central chest area.
- Then turn your attention to your brow, or third eye. Gently alternate your attention between your chest and your third eye.
- Immerse yourself in the peace of the tree and its surroundings.

The 5th (Throat) Chakra – Freedom of Expression

Our throat chakra lies between our head and our heart, and represents how we present our true selves to the world. A balanced 5th chakra allows us to follow the passions of our heart while keeping a level head on our shoulders.

It houses our throat and our ears. When balanced it allows us to listen attentively without interrupting, yet also know when and how to express our views in appropriately forceful terms.

The important thyroid gland sits over the voice box. This regulates the speed that our body works. A balanced throat chakra allows us to act in a forthright, energetic way when needed, but then to chill out at other times. An underactive thyroid gland makes us sluggish, while an overactive gland makes us rush around at the rate of knots.

Traditionally this chakra is also viewed as housing the will. If someone feels repressed, or feels her voice isn't being heard, she may present with a thyroid condition – commonly, underactivity. I say 'she' as the majority of cases of underactive thyroid occur in women. If someone presents to me with a problem in this area, including the shoulders, neck and outside of the arms, I first allow her to talk at length about the frustrations she is experiencing about not being heard. Frequently this is a reflection of their male partner's 'selective deafness', and is usually an opening for a discussion about their relationship.

I run my practice at home with my wife, Trish, who as well as nursing, performs all the tasks of a receptionist, practice manager and of course wife and mother.

On one occasion recently I was involved in a lengthy consultation in my office with a fifty-year-old woman who was in considerable pain from a chronically frozen shoulder. Her children had left home, and she felt she needed more challenges in life. She was keen to enroll at university to study Fine Arts, but her husband was showing not the slightest interest in discussing it.

'He comes home grumpy every night, parks himself on the sofa in front of the TV, and refuses to talk about anything,' she told me despairingly. I tut-tutted quietly.

We discussed a plan of action, which included my offer to talk to him 'man to man', and I gave her an acupuncture treatment. As she left the consulting room, she told Trish about her painful shoulder.

'You know what,' said Trish, 'that's exactly the same pain that I have had in my shoulder for weeks. Robin has simply no idea how sore it is for me!'

I buried my head in the notes of my next patient.

The Sanskrit name for the throat chakra is *Vishuddhi* (from *visha* for *poison,* and *suddhi* for *purify*). This relates to how we tend to swallow the problems we have in life so they reside deep within us, and how we can purify our bodies with each new breath. Some texts talk about how balance in the throat chakra is achieved by forgiving those who have 'trespassed against us' in the past. Using our voice to forgive and to ask for forgiveness from others is always a powerful step for healing. It may be in the past we have exerted our will over others, been somewhat of a *dictator,* and we now have to 'eat humble-pie'. At other times we may have to simply 'swallow our pride'. The throat chakra is said to achieve maturity firstly between the ages of sixteen and twenty-one. Hopefully by then we have experienced a happy childhood, where our parents or guardians have guided us lovingly and firmly in our early childhood, and we have emerged relatively unscathed from the confusion of our early teenage years. We have fostered within us the appropriate level of self-esteem, and may have even experienced our first taste of adult love (teenage style). With any luck, we have learned how to be a valuable team member, either as a goalkeeper at soccer or a tuba player in the school orchestra. By our late teens we are beginning to learn that we are unique (just like anyone else!).

We are beginning to understand just where our talents lie, and to appreciate the hard work and humility needed to hone them into creating a life worth living; a life that best serves our own personal needs as well as the needs of others. This does not mean that our ambitions have to be grandiose – a mature understanding that a fulfilling life can be achieved through simple, sustainable means is in no way inferior to the driving ambition of an A-student determined to become a managing director of a multi-national company. It is our throat chakra that guides us towards achieving our *vocation,* or our *calling.*

Although some people are lucky enough to be drawn into their true calling in their late teens, there are now increasing opportunities throughout life to change course and follow one's passions. No longer is a woman who decides to have a family first, say in her early twenties, likely to restrict herself from achieving other goals in her life. Most men and women in modern society change their jobs, and their direction, several times during their lives, often involving themselves at higher academic levels in middle age. Alternatively it may be that a woman's true vocation is being fully present in the joys and complexities of family life. As a grandmother now, she may embrace this role with a growing passion and wisdom that sees her totally fulfilled. Chinese medicine is based on the meticulous observation of the human condition, handed down faithfully for generations. Every day in my practice, I find myself trying to pass on some precious pearl of wisdom from this wonderfully rich source. Time and again, someone responds that this is ' . . . just like my grandmother said'.

Spontaneity and Creativity

Can you remember the last time you heard someone speak to a crowd *from the heart?* Maybe it was your brother proudly giving away your niece at her wedding. It might have been someone with breast cancer sharing her healing journey with a roomful of caring health professionals attending a weekend seminar.

Those of you skilled in public speaking will, no doubt, have experienced the satisfaction of hearing words flow beautifully and eloquently from your own lips, while you remain somehow slightly removed, almost a distant observer – wondering at how easily and effectively they flow. It is likely that you have done some preparation, possibly scribbling a few rough notes on a napkin (that you can no longer see as you have vainly removed your reading glasses). But all is well nonetheless, as the emotion of the occasion, the goodwill of the audience and possibly a glass or two of champagne all conspire to create an environment that literally allows the words to flow through you.

At such times we are *in the zone.* Only the *now* matters, with worries and fears taking a back seat. I get the same feeling playing my harmonica, jamming with other musicians. Music is always in the present, although strangely it only works as we experience each note as part of the whole tune. We retain the memory of what we have just heard, and in the case of an old standard, we wait in anticipation to experience again the joy of the rest of the song. But each single note is a new creative act, existing only in the present.

The traditional symbolic picture of the *Vishuddhi* (throat) chakra is a lotus flower with sixteen petals. Classically, each petal represents a potential creative ability a human being can develop. Each petal also represents one of the sixteen vowels found in the Sanskrit alphabet. I am again reminded of the power of words over our healing. It is said in the Vedic texts that perfect balance in the *Vishuddhi* chakra opens the person up to the gift of prophecy – the ability to have the words they speak come true.

There are also those who *channel* the words of other spiritual beings. I will talk about this phenomenon in a later chapter, as this doesn't necessarily mean that a channeller has perfect balance in her throat chakra. In some cases the channeller speaks in a foreign or ancient language of which he or she has no previous knowledge – a strange phenomenon now officially termed *xenoglossy.*

The balanced channeller in all these instances will remain aware that their particular gift is that of being able to tune in to these individual wavelengths. The gift does not automatically elevate them into the ranks of the 'highly spiritually evolved'. Most channellers I have had the honor of meeting are happy, grounded and humble people who realize the words they are relaying are not their own. In a similar vein, those in a charismatic church *talking in tongues* ideally realize that they are one part of a congregation as a whole that, after resonating coherently through songs of worship, is acting as a giant collective antenna for another dimension. The experience should perhaps free the church-going channeller to ponder on and wonder about the delights of a shared, interconnected universe, rather than to feel behoven and indebted to a powerful but separate God.

If the heart chakra is to be seen as the gateway to higher consciousness, then the journey through the throat chakra represents our tentative first steps into this bold new frontier. We are now pioneers, permitted to enter into a timeless space of being which somehow hints to us that our creative potential is limitless. For the lucky few, this will happen in their late teens or early twenties, or maybe a few years later when the children have left home. For others, it will follow someone or something opening up their hearts in an act of unconditional love.

For still others, it'll emerge from the most unlikely, even murky, of times – a divorce, an illness or even an apparent disaster – as 'one heck of a silver lining'.

Throat Chakra Exercise

Any exercise using singing or chanting helps the throat chakra achieve balance.

- Breathe in through your nose directing your breath to your navel.
- Allow your belly to rise gently during the in-breath.
- As you breathe out, chant the word **ham** making the word last at least ten seconds. Half the chant can be the **haaa ...** with your mouth open, and half the **mmmm** hummed.
- Try lengthening the chant as your breaths become gently deeper.
- Focus your attention on your voice box, feeling the vibrations spread through your throat and your whole body.

The 6th (Brow) Chakra – Insight, Intuition, and Intellect

If a balanced throat chakra allows us to make our own distinct mark on the fabric of the world, the sixth brow chakra allows us to see it with clarity. For this is where our awareness matures, which is fitting perhaps as the organs it encompasses are our brains and eyes. In our early twenties, we may begin to take stock of our achievements with insights into our journey through the first five chakras. The sixth chakra allows us to make sense of all that has happened to us.

It is now common knowledge that the left and right sides of our brain have broadly different functions. Our left brain is our deductive, analytic side that processes details. The right side processes more abstract concepts, giving us a big picture, an artistic impression into which we can fit these complex pieces. The two are therefore complementary – yang and yin – joined physically by a band of tissue known as the *corpus callosum;* famously more substantial in women.

My medical training was largely aimed at my left brain. I had to learn vast numbers of isolated facts – the names of hundreds of tiny muscles and bewildering chemical equations. All this was of course necessary, but was only possible because, at school, we were disciplined into effective ways to rote-learn. By and large there was no room for debate, no intrinsic meaning to these facts, other than a hope and awareness that they would prove useful in the future. It is because of this training that many people seem in awe of doctors: 'How on earth could you study and learn all that stuff?'

Well, in truth, I found it almost impossible. I was very successful academically when I was allowed to write essays, and employ facts within a framework of my own understanding. I was lucky enough to win a scholarship to medical school with this ability. However, the early 1970s saw the introduction of an exam format that completely stumped me, the multiple choice questionnaire. I started to fail exams, as I struggled to understand the perspective of the examiners. I realized I could only effectively recall facts if I first had a context to place them in. I would look at a collection of possible written answers to a statement and feel completely lost. My heart would sink, and a state of panic would result. I would then procrastinate, waste time and struggle to finish an exam.

Nowadays, we have a broader understanding of the range of processes we use to learn. My struggle would be classed as a type of dyslexia, or learning difficulty, and help would be offered by experienced educational psychologists. However I was left feeling, at the age of twenty, that I had acquired a new state of dumbness. Some years later I began to understand the roots of my 'problem'. I am a person with mixed laterality – for some things such as throwing a ball, writing, inserting acupuncture needles and playing darts, I use my left hand. For others, such as holding a tennis racket, playing a guitar, using a surgical scalpel and playing pool, I use my right hand.

Over the years this has proved to be some advantage, as I have been able to bat for both sides in the battle of the brain hemispheres. I have much sympathy for those whose minds go 'blank' when the word *science* is mentioned.

Over the years, I have learned techniques to help me switch more effectively from the left-brain world of materialistic medicine and science, to the right-brained world of art and feeling. This adaptation has taken many years. As I have already mentioned, and will discuss in more detail in Chapter 4, we have several chances in our lives to fine-tune our chakras.

In my mid-forties, I made a concerted effort to explore my more creative side, writing and performing songs. I made a point of always having a song in progress. I would often awake at 3 am with a tune in my head. I would then rush down to my office and sing the melody line, in *la-la-la* form, into my dictaphone, trying desperately not to wake my family. Often words would come at the same time – much to the amusement of my loyal typist who would have to suffer these bizarre musical interludes between my dictated patient summaries. Occasionally a song would 'burst through' during a consultation, and I would have to frantically scribble out the lyrics in a patient's notes. Luckily this only happened with people I had already got to know well, who understood, and were forgiving of my many idiosyncrasies.

I began to have a deep awareness of how my own education as a child had been incomplete. Such was my focus on 'fact' learning, that my thinking mind had become imbalanced, and overloaded. My mid-forties was also a time I was settling into a routine of gentle meditation, and followed my 'altered state' experience that helped me to decide to change the focus of my medical practice.

There is a fear – I too have experienced this – that venturing into creative and meditative states of being may somehow reduce one's ability to be logical and sensible in a down-to-earth way. Much of this is because in meditation, we have to learn to release our hold on our thoughts and worries. The fear may be that our thoughts will not return.

This of course is not the case. Meditation stills the mind, allowing us to stand outside and select our thoughts. Rather than losing our edge, we become sharper.

Through meditation, our mind becomes open to deciphering original messages from the universal field of consciousness. The melodies and poems that strike such a deep chord within us add a totally original insight to our existence. We do of course use the notes and words we have learned predominantly with our left brain, but these are automatically arranged into a brand new form. Not only are our left and right brain working in harmony, we are at the same time responding to the emotions arising deep within our hearts. Our lower chakras are honored by the infectious rhythm of a song, or the stark, earthly beauty of a piece of poetry.

The Sanskrit name for the brow chakra is *Agya;* translated this means *command* or *knowledge*. It forms the boundary between human and divine consciousness – represented by a lotus flower with two petals. According to tradition, at this level we have almost, but not quite, reached the ultimate state of one-ness with the cosmos. Among the qualities of this chakra are emptiness, truth, consciousness and bliss. The 'third' eye is opening as we appreciate that there is more to the world than that presented to us by our two eyes, and our other senses.

If we turn to the model of the caduceus, we observe a pair of open wings in the area of the 6th chakra. These signify the freedom and expansion that comes with the advent of higher consciousness. Commonly, the wings are thought to represent the two hemispheres of our brain, with the overlapping feathers looking remarkably like the folded, gyrating patterns of tissue that comprise our cerebral hemispheres. They also correspond to the two petals in the Sanskrit *Agya* chakra, openly displaying the rich combination of human and divine consciousness.

So as our 6th chakra opens, we learn to honor our intellect, but to balance it with a sense of wonder and meaning. We also learn to be humble about the knowledge we have gained about our world and ourselves.

Our brain, we are beginning to grasp, is a complex, multitasking, quantum computer, teeming with micro-tubules and perhaps other nano-technology, simultaneously receiving and decoding information from our senses, our body and, of course, the universe as a whole. Balance in the 6th chakra allows us to be deductive, rational and logical – all predominantly left brain attributes – while at the same time we use our right hemisphere to grasp the big picture, feel meaning and purpose, and to think laterally. We can enjoy the daily challenge of completing a cryptic crossword, yet still dance the night away like there was no one looking. We can both analyze and feel, respond intellectually when appropriate, and yet instinctively run for our lives if we are threatened by an act of terrorism.

The formal conditioned Western view of the brain is that it is the creator of consciousness – that somehow consciousness is a by-product of this physical organ. Our consciousness, it is proposed, begins with our birth, and ends with our death. In this book I challenge this theory, (which incidentally remains scientifically unproven), citing modern scientific and traditional wisdom to support an opposing view. Our brain, I suggest, is not the seat of our consciousness; it is merely a vessel through which consciousness is relayed. The Chinese traditionally refer to the brain as 'the hollow organ'.

The Temple of the Soul

The anatomical structure of our brain does give us some insights into just how remarkable an organ it is. A human brain can be divided into three broad parts, each reflecting a different level of conscious evolution:

- The base comprises our reptilian brain, whose function is our physical survival, keeping us on guard for unexpected attack and governing the vital automatic functions of our body, such as breathing and eating. This level of brain activity is as vital to us as the function of our lower chakras.

- The middle level is the limbic (paleomammalian) brain, involved in processing our emotions and the truths that they carry. Parallels can be drawn here with our 4th heart chakra.

- The third level is our cerebral cortex (neomammalian brain) – including our frontal and temporal lobes – and is involved in processing our perceptions and the understanding of our world. It is this 'brainy' part of us that is so highly prized in modern society.

Traditional Eastern philosophies and more modern integral theories, however, regard our intellect as only one element of higher consciousness. They suggest our brains and our body are holographically related, all working as a whole with no hierarchical 'pecking order'.

If we draw a line from the point on our face between our eyes (our third eye) backwards through our skull, we meet a small lake of water (cerebro-spinal fluid or CSF) right in the middle of our brain.

This is our 3rd ventricle, and it sits strategically between these three brain levels, effectively linking up our mind, body and spirit. Floating in this chamber on narrow stalks are the pineal gland, the body's magnetic detector, and the pituitary gland, known as the conductor of the 'endocrine gland' orchestra. The round knob at the top of the staff of Hermes in our model of the caduceus is thought by some to represent our 3rd ventricle.

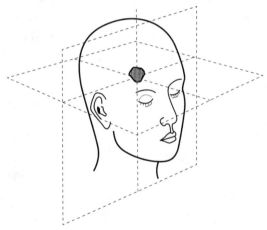

Figure 16. The Third Ventricle: the Temple of the Soul

Our brains are nurtured and nourished by CSF, the most delicate and dilute solution in the body, that flows through a system of lakes (ventricles) and canals to penetrate all areas of our central nervous system from the tip of our spine to the top of our head. The spinal cord, bathed in CSF, corresponds to the staff of Hermes in the caduceus.

I was taught in medical school that the CSF's main function was to buffer and protect the brain, allowing it to float in suspended animation. Just why the third, and two lateral ventricles, existed in this part of the brain remained unexplained. It had not been considered that these lakes could have an important connecting, and conductive role vital to our consciousness.

CSF is a very dilute fluid, with a make-up similar to pure water. Water is now known to be an efficient conductor and amplifier of vibrational energy – whales for example make sounds heard by others, hundreds of miles away in the ocean. The late French medical researcher Dr. Jacques Benveniste has shown that water amplifies the effects of chemical reactions in the body.

Eastern philosophies view the ventricles as transmitting chambers, a place where all the subtle energies from the brain and the cosmos are allowed to mix and mingle, to be amplified and balanced.

I am grateful to Dr Joyce Kovelman, who holds PhDs in both anatomy and psychology, for personally sharing with me her special insights into the role of the third ventricle. In a 2002 article for the journal Spiritual Science that she co-authored with Professor Hoang Van Duc, she fittingly refers to the third ventricle as 'the Temple of the Soul'.

What is Intuition?

One of the common misconceptions about intuition is that somehow it is a state of mind devoid of reason. While it could be argued that intuition is indeed, to quote a dictionary definition, 'knowledge obtained neither by reason nor perception', once an intuitive hunch is well and truly received we need all our experience and rationality to decipher it and to put it to good use. If our brain cells are constantly receiving this infinite supply of information from the cosmos, we need systems in place to prevent our minds from 'boggling'. We still need to be able turn up to work, buy milk and put out the rubbish.

Yet it is when we quieten the day-to-day chatter in our heads that we are most likely to be open to receiving intuitive messages. Edgar Cayce, the famous 20th century American intuitive, would lie down on a couch in a meditative state while receiving information on a subject miles away from his home.

Numerologists focus solely on the numbers derived from a person's name and date of birth, allowing them to tune into information in a pure, uncluttered form. Any other details offered are likely to add confusion, and interfere with the tuning-in process. The experienced numerologist, or intuitive, then uses their logic and common sense to present this to their client in a clear, acceptable form. And because none of us can predict the future accurately – this is because we all have the power and free will to change if we want to – the operator also has to display much wisdom and humility so his reading heals and illuminates, rather than disempowers his client.

This need to remain humble also extends to health practitioners using muscle-testing and pendulum techniques to diagnose illnesses. When performed correctly, these techniques can add valuable insights into someone's healing.

In the ideal situation, the healer and client are joined together as one effective antenna, tuning into the absolute wisdom of the cosmos. But with an imbalanced operator, all sorts of human biases can occur, often due to unresolved imbalances in their own lower chakras. I recently saw a young woman who had a small lump in her breast. Her color therapist had muscle tested her, and informed her that she had 'a serious, invasive cancer' that she could fix with a number of treatments. She told her not to have a mammogram, as this would spread the cancer.

She came to me in a distressed state, and I did feel a tiny lump in one of her breasts. I got her an urgent appointment with a breast physician, who confirmed its benign nature.

Events like this are unfortunately common, and reflect badly on those many natural health practitioners and intuitives who use their skills wisely. My advice is for people to learn to trust their own intuition about their health, and about those from whom they seek help.

Because our health system has been so heavily biased towards a scientifically based, left-brain philosophy, it is understandable that patients are now seeking to achieve balance by consulting caring and intuitive healers. The ideal is for both these complementary models to integrate, just as a healthy brain integrates its left and right sides.

I have tried using muscle-testing and pendulums in my work, but have not found they have helped me. Years of general practice have instilled in me, as they would do in most family doctors, the art of quick, safe assessment. As soon as I greet a patient, my senses are showered with clues, hints and impressions, which contribute towards my diagnosis and treatment.

When I started out in general practice, it was rare for a doctor to see less than forty patients a day. Although this rapid-fire system is hugely flawed, leading to an over prescription of drugs and a co-dependency on doctors, there is no doubt that the sheer bulk of experience instills in the doctor a vast database of knowledge. After twenty years, there is much you can identify instantly.

It is important when muscle-testing someone to realize that you are working in partnership as joint antennas receiving the message from a universal source. I have been unable to convince myself that I am not subconsciously biasing the outcome of muscle testing. I have the same problem with black box machines, as I have learned that the intention of the operator can also show up on the dials.

I do, however, allow myself to test my own intuition, by trying to tune into the needs of a patient before they arrive at my home. I am only able to do this if I have no prior knowledge of their condition, or haven't received a referral note from another health practitioner. Also, I acknowledge within certain intuitive insights I receive during the 'listening phase' of my consultations. Sometimes I will mention these to a patient, but as this could prove distracting and disarming to someone new to intuitive readings, I will often delay telling a patient about this knowledge until a more suitable time when this information can be used wisely.

Much of my work involves helping the person before me to understand her or his own intuitive signals. As they bring these to me in the form of their feelings, their symptoms and their diseases, I act simply as an interpreter of their messages. Their own insights and meanings, if they have difficulty expressing them, are ultimately far more important than any 'brilliant' intuitive hunches that may come my way.

Every symptom and life event we experience has its origins in the vast field of consciousness I have described in this book. The Sanskrit name for this is *Akasha* – literally translated as *space* or *ether*. Traditional texts say that when an individual meditates, his personal consciousness dissolves into the *Akasha*.

A mature and balanced brow chakra allows us to interpret the intuitive messages relayed by our bodies from the *Akashic* field, knowing that it is reflecting a true partnership between body and soul. For some, these explanations come simply as a confirmation of wisdom they are already learning to appreciate. Others may struggle with these concepts.

As we all 'progress through our chakras' we all encounter blocks. Some we overcome, some are left to a later date. Some people have inherited severe emotional and physical problems that make progress difficult, while others are born into angry, abusive environments. For still others, progress can be blocked through addictive substances, be they prescription or non-prescription drugs.

The rising of the *kundilini* progresses like the advancing tide of the sea. Each chakra, it appears, does not have to achieve perfect balance before the next chakra is experienced. However, a problem in a lower chakra – maybe an on-going addiction – creates a block that impacts on the free flow through all subsequent chakras. If we have not had the good fortune to develop creative, loving partnerships with their special spontaneous moments of bliss, it is less likely that we will open up to receiving intuitive messages.

So if as a therapist or a friend you receive an intuitive insight, it is always important to consider if the person is ready to receive the message. The message is only there to guide the person, never to disarm or control. The intent must be to heal. Nothing can be forced, only encouraged.

I am fortunate, as most people come to me ready for a deeper understanding of their health, and we are comfortable to explore important issues with our combined intuition. However, it is possible that their spouse or partner is not yet ready to make this quantum leap, and it is helpful to develop strategies to cope with this. I will describe this dilemma in detail in Chapter 5, as an awareness of ourselves as *human antennas,* although exciting, may well create for us a whole new set of problems with friends, partners and the world around us.

Your Special Intuitive Skills – Honing your Hunches – Brow Chakra Exercise

Intuition is more likely to come when your mind is quietened, free from all the interfering, distracting 'chatter' of everyday life. Any simple meditative or breathing technique will help induce this state. Regular practice will always enhance your intuitive and creative skills.

- Chanting the sound **ohm** while focusing on the area between your eyes further enhances this effect.

   For all of us, our symptoms are a source for our intuitive messages, but your particular brand of intuition is as unique and as special as yourself. There is no one in the world who receives their in(ner)-tuition in exactly the same way as you.

- It may be that it comes as an audible voice in your head. Don't worry; this doesn't mean you have a psychiatric illness (unless the voices are disturbing, or accusatory).
- For others, the words arrive, strangely, in the silence.
- For those of you who are tactile, or tend to get many minor ailments, pay attention to the part of your body that is talking to you. Common tactile messages include: a sensation in your heart, feeling hot, feeling cold, total peace, hairs on end, heart beats quickly or misses a beat, warm fuzzies or just knowing inside.
- If you are someone who thinks in pictures, an intuitive signal may appear 'in your mind's eye' out of the blue, in a flash.
- It may be that you have the ability to see auras.
- Some may see spiritual beings. This doesn't necessarily mean that you are more spiritually advanced; it is not a race after all.
- If you tend to be analytical, and feel you are not 'intuitive', pay particular attention to your dreams. Keep a note pad or dictaphone by your bed, and record the details of your dream as soon as you awake. The insights and meaning may be clear. If they are obscure, you may choose to consult a dream or Jungian counsellor.
- Try writing spontaneously about your feelings; scribble away with gusto. See what comes out. Write poetry or song lyrics. If something emerges that you don't understand, put it aside for a year or two. Its meaning may well emerge.
- Last but not least, learn to accept the wonderful old-fashioned hunch that seems to bypass all your senses, and defies close scrutiny.

The 7th (Crown) Chakra – As One with the Cosmos

You could be forgiven for thinking that achieving balance within chakras one to six is quite enough for any of our lifetimes. The next step which, when fulfilled, sees us merge into a state of blissful unity with the universe may sound rather enticing, but we can be forgiven for being hesitant. It sounds very much like the place in heaven we have been encouraged to apply for once we can fill in an honest CV showing we have behaved ourselves here on earth. Sure we all want to go to heaven, but few of us want to die.

Yet, we are all allowed a slice of heaven. All of us, at some time of our lives, have 'heard the angels sing'. It may have happened on a surfboard or after a hole in one. It is sure to happen when witnessing the birth of your child. It happens every time you cry with joy.

The opening of our 7th chakra allows us to recognize that this pure state of lightness and joy is actually what it is all about. None of these joyful moments relates to time, space, money or desire. All the material things we battle for in our lives pale into insignificance at moments like these.

The crown or *Sahasrara* chakra is situated right at the top of our head. There is, as John Lennon wrote in his great song, *Imagine,* 'above us only sky'. This chakra's lotus flower has a thousand petals – everything unites here. All the colors of the rainbow combine to form a pure white radiance. As the sun rises on our 7th chakra, all ignorance fades.

Many acupuncture meridians merge here – it is the 'Point of a Hundred Meetings' into which I frequently insert a metal antenna in the form of an acupuncture needle (Figure 2). Our 7th chakra opens in all of us to varying extents in our late thirties, as we begin to gain rich insights into exactly who we are. We have to accept that very few humans have ever reached this stage in a totally balanced and sustained way. The ultimate is a stage where desire is replaced by will; where yearning for something we are not and never will be is replaced by a complete sense of comfort for who we are. It is where we are completely at ease with the notion that in our truest form we are perfect and pure – pure beings of consciousness, the living/breathing manifestation of God.

Without the balancing, and often arduous, journey through our chakras, these assumptions could be misinterpreted as mere delusions of grandeur, even dangerous heresies. In fact too rapid a catapulting through the chakras before we are ready – say, as a result of mind-altering drugs – may lead to a disturbing imbalance where we see our individual selves as special and separate from other mere mortals. We will have bypassed our vital heart center, and developed a dualistic – them and us – concept of the world.

So how are we able to touch on the ultimate delights that our 7th chakra offers?

How are we to succeed in being effective *human antennas,* open receivers and transmitters of the blissful timeless network that commands so little air-time on our televisions and radios?

And why on earth should we rely on vague whims, hunches, synchronicities, and telepathic messages when we can now simply dial up anyone on the planet on our phones or computer keyboards?

As I attempt to answer these curly questions, for a few moments anyway, please switch off your TV and mobile phone; and if you must insist on wearing your iPod earpiece, make sure it is playing either Beethoven's Pastoral Symphony or Smokey Robinson's Greatest Hits.

Tuning in to the Ultimate Network (so far)

I was once in a room full of people discussing their near-death experiences (NDEs). My own peak experiences, although wonderful, certainly couldn't compete with their amazing stories in which each of their lives was held in such a precarious balance. I even admit to feeling brief pangs of envy, until I reminded myself that I was really fortunate to have avoided such brushes with death. Hopefully, I then thought, I don't need a NDE to help others – listening in and 'getting the general gist' is maybe enough. All those who I have met that have had NDEs are likewise happy to avoid a repeat run of the circumstances that so threatened their lives. They are however, as a direct result of their NDEs, able to derive deep insights on the human condition; many extract the essence of their experience, and transplant it into their everyday lives. Life becomes more immediate.

While out for a walk, they are first to notice the early signs of spring, the buds forming on a tree, the first bluebell to flower. The colors of nature are, well, more colorful, and the scents more vibrant and evocative. Their body-less experiences have served as instant reminders to them that there is more to their existence than their physical bodies.

Yet, somewhat paradoxically, they embrace their bodies, and all facets of the natural world, as true living miracles. The entire process of life is seen as a highly efficient and inspired network within which we as humans play a hugely privileged role. We are, it appears, the only species of animal that lives with an awareness of our own impending, and inevitable death. And we hold the dubious privilege of having evolved to the point of our development where we have the power to obliterate our own planet. The future of our world is now in our hands – an awesome position of responsibility that each of us struggles to come to terms with as our 7th chakra opens.

Our 7th chakra also helps us understand that in every moment of our adult lives, we have complete free will; at every living moment we have at our disposal an unlimited number of choices, as portrayed by the thousand petals on our lotus flower.

Alongside this, we are also part of an invisible network of being, bound seamlessly by compassion and love, which sets each scene in our lives. This is the *sacred (Akashic) field,* within which our world unfolds. Our lives become guided by events that sit outside our conditioned framework of time and space.

As we develop an awareness of the *synchronicities* in our lives, it dawns on us that our intuition is merely a reflection of a sacred universal field that is manifested in us. Balance in the 7th chakra allows us to have the best of both worlds. On one hand we regard ourselves as part of one massive universal organism, receiving guiding messages from events unfolding around us, while on the other hand we are able to make proactive decisions at just the right time. We may not be able to control the iron's temperature, but we have learned to bide our time patiently, and then 'to strike while the iron is hot'.

One further vital ingredient is needed, however, to make this brew truly potent. We must infuse our actions with the purest of *intent*.

Synchronicity and Serendipity

I am constantly amazed by the synchronous events that occur in my practice. If I am faced with a particular dilemma about how best to advise someone on his or her health, then undoubtedly someone else arrives the next day with a ready-made solution. It may be that I am struggling to suggest a way a distressed mother can deal with her wayward, drug-dependent son, or the name of a good cranio-sacral therapist in a particular suburb of Auckland.

On one occasion, two women with the same rare medical condition booked in to see me on consecutive days. I had not encountered this disease outside a textbook in 25 years of practice. Moreover, each patient had been told that they were the only person in New Zealand with this condition. And so, with their permission, I introduced them to each other, resulting in a healing relationship that has lasted to this day. A synchronous experience such as this provides a memorable and solid foundation on which a structure of change can be built.

Being open to spontaneous synchronous events is not a substitute for effort and persistence. Such events often occur to give us encouragement when the going becomes tough. *Serendipity* is the word used to illustrate an event that happens 'by accident' but turns out to bring unexpected good fortune. One famous example found in the history books of modern medicine is Sir Alexander Fleming's serendipitous discovery of penicillin.

Just as we all have had the misfortune to find, behind a pile of books, a half-finished mug of coffee harboring two weeks growth of foul smelling slimy mould, Fleming turned such a grim experience into something that has saved thousands of lives. He had the presence of mind to notice that the mould growing on a Petri dish, forgotten for days on a shelf of his laboratory, was destroying the bacteria growing there.

Serendipity first appeared in the English language after the eighteenth century letter-writer and author Horace Walpole's short story, *The Three Princes of Serendip*. This mythic fable was set in Persia, although its origins were thought to be Indian. It is a complex tale of three princes, from a Far East island of Serendip, that set out on a journey to prove themselves capable of becoming rulers. They succeeded, not as a result of painstaking planning, but through a combination of astuteness and an innate ability to 'ride their luck'.

A modern author, John Barth, reset the story of Sinbad in a mythical island of Serendip, in *The Last Voyage of Somebody the Sailor*. I quote:

"You don't reach Serendip by plotting a course for it. You have to set out in good faith for elsewhere and lose your bearings serendipitously."

So much of healing depends on the ability to change to meet the circumstances that confront us. It calls for us to be utterly adaptable – proactive one minute yet surrendering to 'what is' the next.

When we are sick and low in energy, we can least afford to be led laboriously up the wrong garden path. Synchronous experiences are a godsend for the sick, as they occur as a trusted guide to preserving precious reserves of energy. They bypass that draining phenomenon we call worry, and demand only the briefest of responses – a simple 'aha' is all that's needed.

Often, blessings come to us in disguise. An illness such as cancer or multiple sclerosis may reveal to us just who and what is important in our lives. It certainly isn't what we have planned, but every week I hear people who have experienced these conditions tell me that 'they wouldn't have changed a thing'.

So the subtle partnership of synchronicity and serendipity amounts to rather more than just a terrifying tongue-twister (which of course it is). An awareness of the importance of this awesome winning combination is the secret key to unlocking a life full of treasures.

Getting Connected

Those doctors who, like myself, practise complementary medicine, tend to see many patients for whom a standard, orthodox Western medical approach has failed to make a significant difference.

People with connective tissue disorders fall into this unfortunate category. Conditions such as rheumatoid arthritis, lupus and multiple sclerosis not only produce wide-ranging and confusing symptoms, but also the course of the illness is bewilderingly haphazard. Added to these illnesses are many other rarer conditions, and unclassified illnesses that each defy an accurate diagnosis.

Earlier, I discussed how our connective tissue is not simply our internal structural scaffolding, but that it also has the property of connecting us electrically with the outside world. It is this network that the acupuncturist taps into when inserting a needle into a point on a meridian. This connective tissue network – our cytoskeleton – extends into every cell in every corner of our body, carrying with it, messages about our outside world. I suggested that when our electrical system is balanced, healing from another dimension is facilitated. In short it is our connective tissue that allows us – and all other animals and plants – to be effective antennas.

Our immune system also connects us to our world – in general people with connective tissue disorders have immune systems that, rather than solely defend them against invaders, have turned on their own bodies.

Formal medical treatments are focused on quietening down this overactive process using suppressant medications such as steroids, or even stronger drugs. These drugs need to be used cautiously because of long-term side effects, but do help make sufferers' lives worth living. Naturally most people want more than this, and are keen to involve themselves in their healing.

Support groups for sufferers of multiple sclerosis, as for those with cancer, have been shown not only to provide emotional and practical support, but also to lead to less frequent relapses in their conditions. This is one example of how effective networking with the outside world helps create healing and balance inside the human body. It appears, therefore, that one way of making a difference for people with connective tissue disorders is by helping them to become connected to the world in a meaningful way.

In simple terms, this often means becoming who they are, rather than the person people expect them to be.

Mary and Bill's Story

At 57 Mary was the envy of all her friends. Her husband Bill, six years older than her, had been a highly successful businessman with a chain of bookshops. In his early sixties, he sold out, leaving them with the time and money to enjoy their retirement while they were both fit. Mary had helped manage their largest store, and was loved and respected by her staff and many loyal customers. When they sold, she felt it was best to leave although the new owners offered her a smaller store to manage. Her two daughters had left home several years before, but were living overseas. One was married in London with a young child, and the other was living alone in Sydney where she had a successful marketing job. Tragically, her youngest child, their only son, had drowned in a boating accident when he was only five.

Mary enjoyed her golf and bridge, and settled into a comfortable life of leisure when Bill retired. However after three months, she noticed she couldn't swing the golf club with the same freedom, feeling stiff and sore in her shoulders. Over the next few days, the pain became deeper and more widespread – her arms and even her hips were sore. She booked to see her doctor who arranged some blood tests. She was now worried, as it was like nothing she had ever had before – she feared the worst. Could she have bone cancer, or a serious form of arthritis?

In fact, the tests showed her to have PMR (Polymyalgia Rheumatica), a connective tissue disease that presents as widespread inflammation of muscles. He told her that the only treatment was to be on steroid medication, but there was a risk that her bones would become brittle with osteoporosis with prolonged use. Mary did feel much better once she started the medi-cation, but began to gain weight – another side effect of steroid use. After two months, she was keen to reduce the dose, but every time she tried, her symptoms came back with a vengeance. Her doctor referred her to me, as Mary was keen to see if acupuncture could help her overcome this hurdle.

So Mary arrived at my home, and we started to talk about how this illness was impacting on her life. And how ironic it was that she should be so afflicted with PMR at a time in her life which, to the outsider at least, seemed so perfect. Then I asked her whether her life of leisure since her retirement was really as ideal as it seemed.

She replied that in the weeks before the onset of her illness she had a growing feeling of dissatisfaction. On one level it was fun playing golf and bridge, socializing with other women, but on a more profound level she felt she was no longer contributing to the world. In fact, she harboured a sense of deep emptiness – a void that wasn't being filled. We then talked about the loss of her son 23 years before, and it was clear that there was much grief still left inside her. Her years of working and coping had meant that much of her grief had not been openly expressed.

I arranged for her to see a grief counsellor attached to the local hospice. I then performed some simple acupuncture, using only the 7th chakra, 'Point of a Hundred Meetings'. We talked more of how meaning and purpose had left Mary's life; how she had become more of a spectator than a participant. She returned the following week having met with the grief counsellor. She had cried for much of the week, and now realized how much grief she had kept inside over the years. She also recognized how much grief Bill also had been holding, and with some gentle encouragement he too received counseling. We continued with Mary's acupuncture treatment, gradually reducing the steroids over the following weeks. This time the pains didn't return. Mary was impressed and grateful for the valuable help offered by the hospice counsellor; so much so that she decided she would become a volunteer for the hospice, providing practical assistance for the families of those dying.

Her life gained meaning once more, and to this day she remains pain free without the need for medication.

Mary surrendered to the fact that she needed to begin to resolve her grief, and recognized that her body's symptoms were leading her to this point. She submitted herself to the caring help offered by others. But she was also committed to playing an active part in her healing process. Synchronicity and serendipity too played their part.

Mary was guided to a hospice where she received the care she needed. The comfort she gained from this led her to fulfill her own need to play a significant and satisfying healing role in the community. Her husband Bill also devoted time every week to the hospice, becoming an active member of the fundraising committee. So there were numerous valuable spin-offs from Mary's healing course.

Mary's story tells us much about the value of balance in the 7th chakra. It is in this center that we learn to appreciate the fine line between submitting to what is, and acting with our infinite and free will. Too much of the former means we become a victim to life, blaming fate or even God's will, for all our misfortunes. On the other hand, if we exert too much free will, wanting to control every event around us, we exhibit all the dubious qualities of a 'control freak'.

The 7th chakra helps us recognize that we are all connected, and that healing flows freely and gracefully to others when we are motivated with the right intent.

Grace and Intent

Gaining access to this interconnected world poses a dilemma for modern human beings. How is it that we find it so difficult to live in a state of one-ness in a world that indigenous cultures have taken for granted for millennia? What is it we have to do to sample the carefree delights of this heaven on earth? We quite rightly strive to achieve our full potential by setting ourselves testing goals. We are encouraged to reach for the stars, yet this is a realm that seems to exist just beyond our grasp. The harder we try, the more elusive it becomes.

The illustration of the Superior Condition, on page 35 (Figure 1) gives us a clue on how to open this door. We are all accustomed to doors into hotels and supermarkets that open automatically as we approach them. An infrared sensor detects our presence as we move towards them. However the door that allows access to this realm requires a special maneuver; the sensors only seem to work if we take a backward step. Then, rather than having to stride forth through the open door to sample the delights held beyond, we find that they automatically come to surround us. The picture shows the therapist achieving a Superior Condition by separating himself from his subject. Although he has not physically moved away, he is no longer touching him, or exerting a hypnotic spell. Clearly, his intent is to detach himself from the outcome. He has released his control, and surrendered to a process he may be humble enough to admit is beyond his understanding.

A balanced 7th chakra allows us to be comfortable with what we don't know. We have learned to value our intellect, but are in no way put off by how little we really know. Our ego doesn't get in the way. No longer do we have to prove our worth to anyone. Soon after starting to practise acupuncture, I became aware of how interfering my ego could be on the outcome of a treatment. If somebody told me they had been given acupuncture before by another therapist with dramatic relief, I was very keen to at least match or even better this result. Unfortunately, without exception, this I failed to do. I had to learn to curb my strong competitive nature – what worked effectively for me on the golf course, was a hindrance in my quest to heal.

I still struggle with these desires; if a doctor who is rather skeptical refers a patient to me because he has run out of other ideas, I find myself hoping that this will be the case that makes him see the light. But these feelings, it seems, can subtly influence the outcome by clouding my intent. Healing firstly requires a pure intent, shared equally between healer and healee. This heart chakra attribute fittingly lies at the heart of healing. This is why so many attempts to measure the effects of healing practices and such related phenomena as telepathy and psychic awareness, are so far off the mark.

Once one introduces strict, man-made controls, or financial incentives, we upset the delicate balance achieved by pure intent. These are the conditions that live within the lower chakra world of 'we win/you lose' that are altogether out of place at these levels of consciousness. I will examine this issue later when I discuss the difference between healthy and unhealthy skepticism.

It is by applying the right intent, that we are allowed graceful access to dimensions beyond our current knowledge. For some, this is an indescribably blissful place where angels sing or deceased loved ones live on, whereas for others it is simply a place of comfort and peace. A balanced 7th chakra allows us to become aware that miracles are taking place in our midst all the time.

Mary and Bill's story may not make headlines in the national newspapers. If you look around, you will discover many stories just as touching.

As an exercise, try making a point of noting how many such acts of grace and kindness come into your awareness over a week. This is a great way of becoming aware just how extraordinary we all are, or at least can become.

Tuning In and Tuning Out

Earlier in this section, I described two tall buildings. One of these was the Sky Tower, rising high above the city of Auckland. From a platform near the top, one can see for miles around. Reaching way above is a radio-transmitting spire, while way below, the sturdy base houses a bustling casino.

Reaching the dizzy heights of our own crown chakra gives us a true perspective on our lives. We are now aware that our physical presence here is only one version of reality. We have learned to recognize synchronicities that remind us that time and space are, as Einstein said, 'modes by which we think, not conditions in which we live'.

As a mature *human antenna,* you realize you have always been in intimate radio contact with the whole universe, but have been unable to appreciate it; the reception has been rather blurred.

Now it's as if a veil has been lifted from your eyes. You appreciate at last that all living things share this gift of instant communication, but that only humans are fortunate enough to be able to talk about it.

Your self-esteem is now strong enough to allow you not to judge those who scoff at your ideas, preferring instead to use your awareness to help and heal. You know that it is the power of intent that allows you to transmit a message; small messages with just the right intent can reach anywhere in the universe, no matter what the level of background 'buffering' interference.

When you step into the real world, which of course you never actually left, you now do so with an understanding that you can step outside whenever you want to. You no longer feel trapped, controlled or addicted. You can switch in and out of *antenna* mode at will. And when one of your friends asks you that curly question: 'And why on earth should we rely on vague whims, hunches, synchronicities, and telepathic messages when we can now simply dial up anyone on the planet on our mobile phones or computer keyboards?' your reply is simple. 'I am, my friend, only interested in the truth.'

You have learned to trust that, as a *human antenna,* you have your own, in-built spam filter. Half-truths and scams just don't get through.

In *antenna* mode, you only receive the whole truth, and nothing but the truth. And, of course, the *human antenna* doesn't need replacing every six months.

The Kaimanawa Wall – Stepping into the Unknown

The Kaimanawa Wall in the central North Island is a place shrouded in mystery and intrigue. To some it is a sacred ancient site of healing, dating back many thousands of years. To others it is simply a collection of stones, a natural artifact exposed by erosion but carrying little meaning or historical significance. In March 2004, New Zealand hosted an international Medical Acupuncture conference in Taupo, just north of the famous lake that lies at the heart of the North Island (Figure 17). My friend Dr. Gary Cook, one of New Zealand's foremost authorities on our country's sacred sites, had talked to me several times of this place. I was therefore keen to visit it, and allow our overseas guests to experience a special part of New Zealand that the guidebooks may not mention.

Figure 17. Lake Taupo, New Zealand
Compare this figure with Figure 16, page 143.

Accompanying us was an experienced local guide and Wall enthusiast, Vernon Smith, and my friend and mentor Dr Steven Aung from Edmonton, Canada. Also with us was an elder of the local Maori tribe or 'iwi'. A group of about fifteen set out in a convoy of cars and minivans from our hotel on a cool misty morning, with just a hint of rain in the air. On the way, our guide explained one theory that this wall was part of a larger pyramidal structure that had decayed over many centuries, becoming overgrown by the forest. An ancient tribe, so the story went, used to gather here for worship and healing. We had asked the Maori elder's permission in advance to explore the site, and requested that he perform a blessing on behalf of his 'iwi'.

As we neared the Kaimanawa forest, he explained how we must treat the forest and site with the greatest respect. Both Vernon and Steven nodded in agreement. As well as being a Western physician, Steven is a qi gong master, and a committed follower of Buddhism. Along with all those of his faith, he shares the same deep respect for the forest held by the Maori and all indigenous people around the world. I felt truly privileged to be in the presence of three such wise and modest shamans.

Our convoy came to a halt in a clearing in the forest, and we gathered together in the light rain. Our guides advised us on the rules of protocol we were to follow. We were to act as honored guests of the forest, treating it with the respect we give to a dearest friend who has invited us for a meal at her home. Firstly we were to listen for the call of the forest birds, and recognize this as a welcoming greeting. Secondly, under no circumstances must we urinate in the forest. This was unfortunate as most of us, including myself, had had a couple of cups of coffee at breakfast. To our relief, we were allowed to answer our own particular calls of nature at the edge of the grassy clearing, but only after we had asked permission of the surrounding bush. Within the context of the trip, I have to say, none of this seemed too bizarre. We then slowly proceeded up the road towards the wall.

I was surprised that our guides stopped after less than 100 meters, and pointed to a mossy bank on the right side of the road. There, inlaid into the bank, were the upright stone plaques of the Kaimanawa Wall. All of us had driven right past it ten minutes before and had completely missed it. After the blessing, some of us hovered tentatively around the wall, while others respectfully touched the stones. Soon we headed up the steep bank, keen to explore the site in full. Steven would go from tree to tree gathering 'information' by placing his forehead gently on the bark. In true shamanic tradition he was being guided towards somewhere important.

Eventually, after a climb of about fifty meters, we reached the top of a small rise. Upon it stood a magnificent tree and again Steven went through the ritual of placing his forehead, his third eye, on the trunk. 'This is the one' he exclaimed. He then described how the structure hidden beneath our feet had been shaped like an ancient Mayan pyramid. The trees that had grown over it through the centuries had done so in a particular pattern. Right at the top was the most significant tree of all. To use acupuncture terminology, this tree was growing over the site's 'Point of a Hundred Meetings', having the same 'antenna' effect as a needle placed in someone's head.

I remembered visiting Stonehenge several years before. One explanation in the guidebook was that the stone structures were sitting on electromagnetic ley lines, acting as conducting channels in precisely the same manner as acupuncture needles on points on the body's meridians. After climbing down the bank, we returned to our cars, and travelled back to the conference center. It seemed for each of us the experience had been profound, but in ways we were struggling to explain.

I was aware that more conference delegates were keen to visit the wall that afternoon, and I volunteered to take another small group there, this time without our guides. So we set off in one minivan early in the afternoon, as the weather began to deteriorate. While driving, I tried to explain the differing theories on the origins of the Wall. Although I was keen not to prejudice their up-coming experience, I did try to describe the morning's findings, albeit in a rather matter-of-fact way.

I sensed that this group was rather more skeptical than those who had visited in the morning; none were regular meditators or had participated in anything quite like this before. One young man, a partner of a doctor attending the conference, was a structural engineer by profession. Firmly and politely he offered me his opinion. 'It seems most likely, Robin, that there is a logical explanation for this wall. From what you have told me, I suspect that it is a naturally formed artifact.'

After arriving, I found myself taking on the role of protective host and guide. In retrospect, my attempts to explain the sacred rituals that we needed to observe were rather half-hearted. I was more concerned that everyone was safe, and was going to have a good time. I even forgot to listen to the birds. In the morning session I had been the keen and carefree student, gently guided and tutored by wise sages. I had been happy to simply drift along with nature. By the afternoon though, I had reverted back to my organizing and rescuing mode, which carried with it the burden of responsibility. Everyone in the party was to be satisfied.

After a few minutes at the wall, I led them up the bank towards the tree that had so intrigued us all that morning. I had a firm idea of exactly where it was as I had made a point of committing the surrounds photographically in my mind just a few hours before. But on this occasion, the more I looked the less I found. There was no sign of the tree I so wanted them to see and touch. Nothing appeared like it had that morning.

It was now raining heavily, and despite the protective canopy of the forest we were all getting cold and wet. I became disorientated. Although we were less than 100 meters from the road, I had no idea which way to turn. People were beginning to scatter, and I feared we would lose somebody.

Admitting that I too was lost, I handed over responsibility to the young, and rather skeptical, structural engineer. He immediately took charge of the situation, and looking around quickly found the path that lead us all safely to the road.

As I drove back, all my passengers told me how they had enjoyed the experience, despite the difficulties we had encountered. They remained open-minded but generally unconvinced that the Kaimanawa Wall was part of an ancient and sacred site of healing.

We arrived back at the conference center in good spirits, although rather wet and bedraggled. I was greeted by Steven, who seemed to have already guessed that not all had gone completely to plan. 'I really wondered if you would be able to find it this time,' he said. He had a knowing look on his face. I proceeded to tell him of the afternoon events. A good friend, who was listening in, seemed highly amused by my story. He was sure, he said chuckling away to himself, that I must have had 'a secret pee' in the bush. I blushed guiltily.

Steven reassured me that there was rather more to it than this. 'This is very interesting,' he said calmly. 'I think the tree will only appear when you are truly ready to see it.'

I have thought about this day at the Kaimanawa Wall frequently since. Did I miss the tree the second time because I was disoriented and inept? Quite possibly; or could it really be that, as modern physics would suggest, our world around us collapses down from a field of infinite possibilities into our familiar, tangible form only when we observe it? That we are co-partners in the creation of our world. Somehow we only see what our level of consciousness permits us to see.

On the first occasion I was in a receptive, open and relaxed mode, emotionally and physiologically balanced. By the afternoon, I was in my worried, logical, 'left brain' mode.

I really don't know.

I do know though, that this is a classic 7th chakra test, helping me to become comfortable in my not knowing. And I do know for me, the Kaimanawa Wall, on that day, in its own unique way, cast its special spell. And its magic and mystery lingers on.

7th Chakra Exercise

- Try to spend a short time outside every day, focusing on how every element of the world is working in harmony.
- Stay in the present, aware of how everything just 'is'.
- Become aware of the abundance that surrounds you.
- If you are in a natural environment, listen out for the birds.
- Watch the bees and insects.
- If you are in a city, watch people of all races interact peacefully.
- Release the need to understand or know.

4: The Human Antenna Through the Years - The Maturing Soul

Applying strict time-lines to the growth of the human soul can present problems.

Our lives seldom progress in an ordered linear manner. We are more likely to follow the cycles of nature, which is part of the philosophy at the heart of Eastern and indigenous cultural beliefs. We only have to observe the advent of a new season to understand this model. As winter turns to spring, generally the weather becomes warmer. However, each new day is not necessarily warmer than the last.

The chakra model is a useful guide map on which we can plot the progress of our human soul. We can appreciate that each level builds onto, and encompasses, the last as life events guide us towards achieving a point of balance.

So far I have tried to explain the holographic nature of our universe, and how the conscious evolution of our own society is reflected within each of us; and of course vice versa. But it is also important to develop practical models we can all call on and use in the context of our busy lives. One such model I have already integrated into the last section aligns the growth of our chakras with our ages from zero to thirty.

In my work, as each new patient recounts their life story in their own way, I find myself probing them for evidence of significant events at certain times of their childhood. For example, could their irritable bowel have its roots in an unhappy event at the age of eight or nine, when overpowered by an insensitive adult or bully? Similarly, could an imbalance in the thyroid gland in the throat chakra represent a time in their late teens that prevented their true voice being heard, and stopped them pursuing their vocational goals?

In this section, I extend this model to cover our soul's journey, from cradle to grave. Perhaps more accurately, from conception to the time our matured soul is released. You will now have realized that you have been an antenna for another dimension from the moment your father's sperm beat fifty million others to your mother's egg, or even earlier than this, as each individual sperm has a spiral shaped powerhouse called a mitochondrion.

And soon after this, when – nestled securely in your mother's womb – your first cell, a fertilized egg, divides with 'radio-controlled' spindles pulling your nucleus into two, and then into four, and so on, until you are fully grown. Then throughout your life, when many trillions of non-local interactions between your DNA and microtubules help lay down the matrix, the living 4-D map, within which your body is continuously being formed. So each of us has in fact been a fully integrated *human antenna* all along; only now have we reached a stage we can become fully *aware* in our lifetime of exactly what this means.

As we mature, we begin to learn just how and when to use the gifts that this model bestows on us – how to act with good intent, just when and how to pray and how to recognize and value our intuition. But it also bestows on us responsibilities that extend beyond helping and healing our fellow man. We carry a conscious awareness that is unique on our planet – we have become guardians of the earth and all its inhabitants.

And when, ultimately, our time on earth has run its course, each human soul is released back into the timeless state in which it feels most comfortable. Someone told me recently that 'we are the light, not the light bulb'. But it seems the bodies that house our souls are very special and economical light bulbs – when they eventually blow, the light lives on forever.

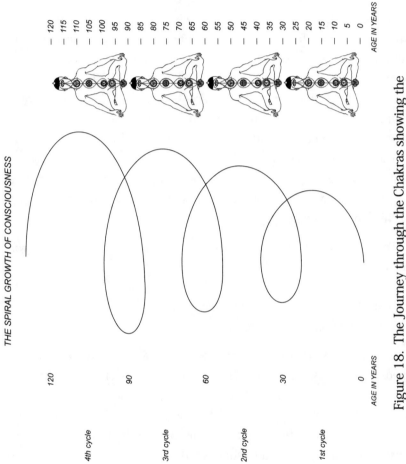

Figure 18. The Journey through the Chakras showing the journey of the individual and 3–4 cycles of generations

The Generation Game

Let's now consider what happens to us during our stay here on earth. One simple model that 'works for me' sees the chakra cycle repeat itself as we experience each new generation.

Say we progress on our journey through the chakras, eventually gaining some insights on who we are 'soul-wise' by the time we are thirty. We then decide to have a family. As we raise our children we gain new insights about our own early years. In many ways we relive those years again, with our children teaching us much about ourselves. We may begin to understand the difficulties our own parents faced, and learn to dissolve any grudges we may continue to bear against them. Our children therefore become partners in our forgiveness of others.

They also teach us how to play, and to how to re-discover the world of fantasy. This process continues as our children become teenagers and young adults. They never hesitate in the slightest way to tell us when we are acting hypocritically.

Teenager: 'Grandma said *you* used to stay out till midnight when *you* were eighteen.'
or

Dad: '*I* would *never* have said that to *my* father!'
Teenager: 'Yeah, right Dad . . .'

And of course there is always the classic raising of the eyes to the heavens whenever we utter some highly predictable words of advice.

Somehow, although I would never let them know at the time, rather than being soul-destroying for the hapless parent, all these excruciating tactics are more likely to be nudging our souls in the right direction. So whenever one of my daughters suggests that I ' . . .get a life, Dad', I stop to consider that maybe, you just never know, she is helping me do pre-cisely that.

When the time eventually comes for our children to leave home, we are presented with yet another opportunity to grow creatively. For women, the menopause is a time characterized not only by distressing symptoms such as hot flushes, but frequently by a surge in creativity. For many this is a time where they re-evaluate their lives, and begin to find their true voice. Some may return to their academic studies, this time doing exactly what they choose. Others may unearth hidden artistic or musical talents.

Many honor their inherent understanding of holistic principles by committing themselves to the practice of yoga, Pilates or meditation, or by training in one of the many healing arts.

All of these changes are soul-enhancing, allowing intuition to flourish. They are all activities that help ease open the door to higher levels of conscious awareness. It is important for me to stress here that those who do not have children, either through choice or infertility, are in no way disadvantaged. It is even possible that they have more time to develop their creative skills, and reach their full potential in their jobs. All of us absorb and reflect the energy of the generation that succeeds us.

Gay couples, by sharing happiness and love with their partners, achieve a healthy balance in their heart chakras, thereby opening the door to higher levels of consciousness. Many gay women and men are already innately gifted creatively and intuitively; probably a reflection of their finely balanced male and female energies. So their souls are ideally placed to flourish, especially with the active support of a more open-minded society. Laws permitting gay marriage and the adoption of children by gay couples are a reflection of modern society's own heart chakra – or green 'meme' – opening.

Barriers are broken down, as discrimination is replaced by integration. We then have the ultimate win/win situation, as highly creative souls are free to prosper, adding color and joy to the lives of all.

The Later Years – Living with Dying

Married or single, straight or gay, we are all, thankfully, likely to become wiser with age. Over the years we have learned to ride the bad times, and to appreciate the good times, while accepting that both have helped us become better-rounded, well-balanced human beings. Our hard edges become softened, our egos less precious. We are older souls. It is likely too that we have had close encounters with death. We may have witnessed at first hand the death of a parent, or a friend – profound events that have left a lasting impression on how we perceive life.

It is sometimes only by becoming totally lost in the darkness of our grief that we can begin to find some clarity on aspects of love and life that have always confused us. Nowadays, a funeral is often an open expression of love; glowing tributes flow graciously and eloquently from loved ones' lips, and broad warm smiles shine through tears of sadness and joy. As I absorbed the beauty and honesty of such a ceremony recently, I was reminded of our true, often untapped potential to create heaven here on earth.

As we age, we also begin to come to terms with the nature and inevitability of our own death. Unfortunately, our continued witnessing of thousands of violent deaths on our television and movie screens may have conditioned us into fearing that our own deaths will be unduly traumatic or painful. We may then view death as an unnatural, rather than a natural process. It is only by experiencing the peace and dignity of someone close to us 'dying a good death' that we can begin to become immune from this modern, fear-based epidemic.

With age, we form our own opinions on whether death indeed constitutes the final moment of our being, or whether it signifies a transition to another dimension. Until recently, this dilemma was totally a matter of faith; even a rationalist who insisted that we just disappear had nothing tangible to base this idea upon. I was discussing this recently with a well-travelled older man who had a terminal illness. He told me that several years ago he had asked a wise Taoist monk in China whether humans reincarnated. 'I am sorry I can't tell you as presently I am not dead' was his simple reply.

Science, only now, is beginning to address the question: 'What happens to us when we die?'

The physics of the past 100 years has allowed us to consider that energy and matter are interchangeable; that our physical world is only one version of reality. Using this paradigm, at every living moment, we are continuously incarnating, or collapsing down, into our physical form from a universal field of timeless consciousness. One consistent model, recognized by past life therapists and channellers of esoteric wisdom, regards our physical existence here on earth as vital for the overall growth of our individual eternal soul. As our soul exists outside time and space, it cannot be separated from the consciousness of the universe; so as the vibration of each individual soul rises, so does that of the universal soul. The consistency of reported findings in near-death experiences is one line of evidence that supports the theory that consciousness exists beyond the body, and survives death. Another piece in the jigsaw has been put in place by the life's work of Dr Ian Stevenson, a Canadian born psychiatrist from the University of Virginia. He studied over 2,500 cases of children who had remembered previous lives. Amongst his findings were many children who had birthmarks at the sites on their bodies corresponding to lethal penetration injuries of those who had recently died. These birthmarks, like a child's memory of past lives, tended to fade as the child reached 6- or 7-years old. Most of the children were from Eastern countries whose citizens retained a strong belief in reincarnation. We now have scientific models that begin to explain such bizarre findings.

Firstly, we have seen how each cell, through its DNA and microtubular structures, can act as an *antenna* for the universal or Akashic field. Dr Rupert Sheldrake's hypothesis of *morphic resonance* sees similar individuals 'sharing' and 'transmitting' information within this field. As such information exists as the fundamental matrix on which our physical body forms, it is possible that a holographic imprint from someone dying, is transmitted onto the matrix of a tiny embryo at, or soon after, the time of conception.

Could it also be that the conscious acceptance of reincarnation in the community creates a background resonance that facilitates this process?

Most of the other examples of telepathic communication mentioned in this book, whether with the living or the dead, have been enhanced by feelings of love. Even those who doubt that consciousness survives physical death would find difficulty convincing even the most hard-hearted that love completely fades away with death. It seems unlikely to me that they could attend a modern funeral, Maori tangi or any other cultures' observance of the passing of a loved one, and remain unconvinced that unconditional love is the link between those who live and those who have died.

Does Our Light Really Go Out?

One day I turned on our trusted family TV set – the one in which we kept the Wombles – to be greeted by a tiny white dot in the middle of the screen. I pressed the on-off switch twice. Even then, five years before owning our first home computer, I was well versed in the art of re-booting. There was now absolutely no response – nothing, not a dickey bird.

This was eight years after the initial Wombles incident, and though my growing daughters were no longer worried that the jolly, furry creatures may have been trapped in the darkness within, they instructed me, nonetheless, that I simply *had* to buy another television straight away, this time with a big screen, as that night there was to be showing this new cartoon series that all of their friends were crazy about. In it, I was informed, there was this 'way cool' ten-year old boy with spiky blond hair, whose Dad was really stupid, and liked beer and the old 70s music I liked, and who kept saying 'Doh!'.

So, seeking another opinion on the state of our old family friend, I phoned the TV repairman, who on hearing the story and the age of the set, informed me in a kind and gentle way that it really was a 'goner'.

With a heavy heart I headed out to the garbage dump with its remains in the trunk of my car, reminiscing about the life of something that had been 'one of the family' for so many years. Thinking back to the antenna incident, I realized that the set was teaching me yet one final valuable lesson – this time about the nature of life and death. For although the TV's body had grown old and died, the places and characters, including the Wombles, that it had brought into our lives, lived on. It had really only been a relay station for our favorite channels.

When our own bodies fail and die, I thought, it doesn't necessarily mean our favorite networks die with them. Our bodies have only been the means by which we have got our messages across to others; our messages are really who we are.

Like the Taoist monk, I honestly don't know what happens when we die. However, I suspect we return fully to the reality of a timeless state, completely away from the pressures and pain of this life. As the most consistent, timeless and placeless thing I have experienced here on earth is *love,* it seems likely to me that this is what envelops us when we die.

Those who have had profound near-death experiences seem to report that they begin to drift into an overwhelmingly gorgeous state of heavenly bliss, before their rude awakening back here on the physical earth plane.

I have read many reports of those under hypnosis giving detailed reports of past lives, and of 'times' between lives. They report wonderful mountains, birds and happiness all around. Life previews are conducted in magnificent lecture theaters; and everyone around acts in a non-judgmental and supportive way. However, I wonder how much of this is really a projection by people who, understandably, are using their earthly experiences as their sole frames of reference. Could it be that if these events occurred, they would have happened in a totally different dimension? The interpretation we give them under hypnosis is merely in a language and form we can understand with our earthly experience. Like a dream, it is the message, and the metaphor that counts.

If we do indeed, on dying, return in an enriched form to an eternal state of 'nowness', at one with God and the universe, isn't it incorrect to refer to this as the *afterlife?* In eternity there is no before or after, only now. And it is only when we enter the 'now' here on earth, that we catch a glimpse of heaven. If our measurements of time and space are simply fabricated artifacts of our worldly existence, how correct is it for us to refer to *past lives?* If, while under hypnosis, someone recollects a past life, is it possible they are really time traveling, connecting and resonating instantly with someone similar who in earthly terms did live and die many years before?

Similarly, when we contact, with the help of a medium, a loved one who has died, are we naïve to imagine that the spirit world in which they now live is somehow a beautified version of our own world? Is this not simply another projection based on our experiences, locked here within the confines of time and space? It is perhaps more helpful to consider that only a part – the physical body – of our loved one has died. Their soul, being eternal, lives on.

In fact it could be said that, after its earthly experience, it has never been in better shape. And anyway, does it really matter? Experienced hypnotherapists who guide us through 'past lives,' and mediums who help us contact those who have died, do so because this can lead to peace and healing in our lives here on earth. They help us live our lives in full brightness, and not under a cloud of worry about our own death.

I suspect that it is really only this end result that matters, and this is the reason why I lend encouragement to patients who are keen to journey down these roads. My only advice is that they trust their intuition about the therapist, and avoid those who appear to over-power them.

The Eternal Flame

One elderly man recently explained to me how his Christian faith had been renewed by his near-death experience (NDE). Since his experience though, he had developed a whole new perspective on the story he still regarded as 'the greatest ever told'. Prior to this it had been Jesus' suffering on the cross, the crucifixion itself, which carried the greatest significance.

Now, he told me, these harrowing images no longer dominated his faith. The part of the story that now carried the greatest meaning for him was the *resurrection,* the return to a pure and blissful state of consciousness. His understanding now was that this story was not just about one man in the Middle East who had achieved Christ consciousness, but about the potential for all human beings to be 'as one with God'. He told me, with a twinkle in his eye, that he now considered himself a 'died-again Christian'.

Like many others who have had NDEs, he had a renewed awareness of his need in this life to create an environment of peace and balance. The words *'on earth as it is in heaven'* now assumed a different emphasis. Rather than this being a phrase that separated heaven from earth, he now understood that the two were not mutually exclusive. He now could identify the presence of heaven here on earth – as *earth* was indeed, *'in heaven'*.

This was not to suggest that he viewed the world solely through rose-tinted glasses. He only had to open a newspaper, or turn on his television, to realize there was a 'hell on earth' too.

Richard and Jackie's Story

This year I met Richard, a remarkable man in his early thirties with an advanced stage of bone cancer. By the time he saw me, the cancer had already spread via his bloodstream to his lungs. The tumour had started in the bones near his right wrist and surgeons had amputated his arm near the shoulder in an attempt to restrict its spread.

Richard had also undergone a course of chemotherapy and radiotherapy, but this had failed to stop the cancer spreading. He was still hopeful of being healed.

He had attended a world-class meditation retreat in Australia, meditated with his partner Jackie every day, and was keeping strictly to a vegetarian diet. But despite this, he was beginning to accept that his time here on earth was limited. So the three of us talked frankly about his situation. I remember how peaceful and calm he was, and how very relaxed I felt in his presence.

Jackie, who had accompanied Richard on his visit to me, sat serenely and supportively beside him. Asking what it was he wanted from me, he replied: 'Precisely this. Your support and possibly a confirmation that I am not missing out on anything. And maybe some gentle acu-puncture, as I have always found this helpful in keeping balanced and relaxed.'

Over the years, I have seen many people who have had limbs amputated. Some have developed phantom limb pain, where pain is felt in the area of the lost limb even though it no longer exists in physical form. Even in the absence of pain, the amputee can frequently still feel the presence of his limb positioned in a specific way. I asked Richard about this. He told me that although he had no sensation of pain, he could always feel the presence of his arm. It could assume a variety of positions, and even at times seemed to move about. On this occasion Richard could 'feel' his right arm tucked close to his chest with his elbow pointing outwards, and his wrist cocked inwards.

Several years ago, I was asked to see a young lady with a severe pain and blood vessel disease who had had her right leg amputated because her foot was rapidly turning gangrenous. Unfortunately, the same situation was now occurring in her left leg, which was causing her severe and unremitting pain. I couldn't perform acupuncture on this area as it was infected, and far too sensitive, so I chose to use a point on her left ear. This gave her immediate, but not total relief.

She told me she could feel the 'ghost' of her amputated right leg. More remarkably, when I put my hand on the place she felt her ankle lay, she responded by telling me she could feel my touch. I found this difficult to believe, as the conventional wisdom was, and still is, that a limb exists in phantom form after amputation because the areas in the brain involved in processing the function of the arm remain. The memory of the limb is therefore held within the brain's matrix. This could not explain though, how she could actually feel me touch the 'ghost' of her right leg.

Still rather skeptical, I asked if she would mind wearing a blindfold so I could repeat the test. She kindly agreed and she was still able to tell me exactly where and when I was touching her phantom leg. She could even guide me to touch the individual toes of her amputated right foot.

Of course, this finding suggested something really bizarre; that a non-physical presence of her leg – a field or matrix of information – actually continued to exist precisely where she felt it to be. Unfortunately, her disease rapidly advanced, and surgeons amputated her left leg soon afterwards. As she was so sick, I felt uncomfortable about pursuing her for a more formal set of experiments. However ever since that time, I had been on the lookout for patients who had suffered amputations, and who could feel others 'touch' their phantom limbs. Most of those who came my way over the next couple of years could tell me the position of their lost limb, but none could feel my touch in the way this young lady had described.

I had begun to wonder if this experience had been an artifact, a one-off finding possibly exaggerated by this poor lady's extreme sensitivity and delicate state of ill health. I explained this story to Richard and Jackie who were similarly intrigued. I went through the procedure I had used before, this time being guided by Richard, with his eyes closed, to a place I was 'touching' his phantom right wrist – the site where his tumour had originally grown on his physical arm. He told me he could feel a faint presence, and I asked Jackie if she wished to touch the same area.

Jackie's touch proved to be more potent than mine. Not only could Richard feel her touch more definitely, Jackie herself was aware of a tingling sensation in her own fingers when 'contact' was made. I suggested this was something they could gently explore together at home, and possibly gather some meaning that could aid Richard's healing. I was happy to leave this in their capable hands, literally, and dedicated the rest of the consultation to giving Richard his acupuncture treatment.

As they left, I lent them a copy of Rupert Sheldrake's book Seven Experiments that Could Change the World in which there is a chapter specifically dedicated to the phantom limb phenomenon. Within it, Rupert raises the possibility that a morphic field of information could actually remain after the amputation of a limb.

I saw Richard and Jackie only twice more, but kept in regular phone contact. About three months later I received an e-mail from Jackie with the sad news that Richard had died. Soon after this she visited my home, returning the book. We reminisced fondly about Richard, especially how dignified he had been throughout his difficult illness.

I asked whether anything had come of our 'experiment'. Jackie replied that, over the following weeks, there was no doubt that Richard could feel her touch on his phantom arm. I then asked if this had carried with it any special meaning for them. 'When he could feel me touching his phantom hand, and I could feel him, we were both reassured that something, somehow, carried on existing, even when all physical evidence of this part of him had gone. When Richard lost his arm, we were able to share the grief together. Then we gained great comfort in discovering, together, that something very special remained in its place.'

She went on: 'Richard's body may no longer be with me, but I feel Richard's presence all the time.'

5: The Female and Male Antenna

There is a popular book by psychologist John Gray that suggests men and women are so unalike, they might as well come from different planets. The book, and its many sequels, has continued to top best seller lists around the world. There is even a musical stage show based on the book that played in Las Vegas.

The message, of course, is a positive one – we should honor and respect our own and our opposite gender's unique talents, traits and foibles, ultimately achieving loving and harmonious relationships.

But when we turn our attention to the tricky topic of intuition, there are many who proclaim that men and women do not even share the same solar system – we inhabit, they say,totally different worlds – light years apart.

Recently I was discussing this with a Maori student at Massey University here in Auckland. Not only was he studying four separate degree papers, he was also a writer, an independent film producer, and a composer of music. And the proud father of an eighteen-month-old boy. His problem was that he was literally becoming dizzy with the amount of information he was having to cram into his brain. There were even times he was passing out, collapsing suddenly to the floor. To make matters worse, his creativity was not flowing as richly as usual.

On asking him whether this pattern had happened before, he replied that it had been a recurring problem. Over the years he had seen many doctors, and had undergone a myriad of sophisticated tests and scans, without any definitive diagnosis ever being reached.

He then said that he wasn't surprised that the doctors had drawn a blank, as his condition was, at its roots, spiritual in nature. I shared with him that I was writing this book about how we all were relay stations for consciousness and creativity, and how best we could create the ideal conditions in our lives and our world for this to happen. He told me that he already understood this, as this was precisely the holistic world view held deep within Maori culture.

He had come to see me because he had seen my photo on the wall in the student health center waiting room, and felt that I would understand. I thanked him for the trust he showed in me. Over the next few minutes we shared our ideas and experiences, discussing in particular the prevailing view – misguided to both our minds – that men were somehow less intuitive than women.

The solution to his problem, we decided, was to request from the university that he focus on only two academic papers for the rest of the year. The academic program had placed undue load on his deductive left brain, and as a result his central nervous system – and whole being – had become imbalanced. Reducing his commitments would restore harmony and balance to his mind and body.

The meeting ended in an exchanging of e-mails, and with the traditional Maori *hongi,* where our two noses and brow chakras touched gently once, and then once again.

The following day, a sixteen-year-old secondary school student returned to see me for her fourth acupuncture treatment. She had been suffering from an extreme fatigue state for several weeks, and while I was treating her I had become aware of her exceptionally bright and enquiring mind. Encouraged by my meeting at the university the day before, I again described my interest in consciousness, sacred geometry and telepathy.

"Those are all the things I ask my teachers about, but no one seems to know what on earth I am on about!" she said despairingly.

She went on to share with me her theories of time reversal and teleportation together with her understanding of crop circles, the Golden

Ratio and much more besides. Her mother, who was with her in the room, looked on with a broad smile that expressed both pride and amazement.

I then explained how, in my experience, many young people who suffered from extreme fatigue states had an abundance of the special qualities of sensitivity, wisdom and intelligence. For these, and there are growing numbers, *education* should be as the word translates from its Latin origins, a 'leading out' of wisdom not simply a cramming in of facts. According to traditional Chinese medicine, over-thinking and worry depletes the spleen energy causing fatigue and immune problems.

Our intuition is a state of knowing – a reflection and passing-on of universal wisdom. When we tap into our intuition, we therefore avoid the need to weigh up the pros and cons of argument, and to expend energy worrying. Unfortunately, the more intelligent a child appears to be, the more information she is fed. She ends up with more facts at her disposal, more choices, and of course more worries. It is all the more important then for gifted children to honor their intuition, with programs of relaxation or simple meditation. They should also be helped to recognize the early signs of burn out.

In this chapter, I will discuss how the consciousness of men and women can evolve side by side, with each 'side' helping the other. Over the past few centuries in the West, both men and women have had to suffer many indignities as hierarchical societies and dictatorships have tended to suppress their individual expression of creativity and intuition. Men have been required to follow orders, becoming blind to their intuition, while women have had their intuition patronized as being something devoid of reason, definitely inferior to logical thought.

It is not an exaggeration to say that the suppression of intuition has contributed to a huge loss of human life. Millions of men (and women) have fallen in battle. Women have been hunted down, demonized and burned at the stake as witches.

The Sacred Feminine

The space shared by a mother and her child is sacred. From the very moment of conception, an intimate bond is formed that lasts forever. For nine months, two individual bodies and souls reside together in harmony, each leaving an indelible imprint on the other that survives their physical separation at the time of birth.

The bond of love that holds a mother to her child is non-local, unconditional on matters of time and space. All of us, men and women alike, are welcomed into the physical world enveloped warmly and securely within this cradle of love; our mother's love, before and after we leave the womb, serves as our initiation into a world that is interconnected in ways beyond the physical. Milk from a mother's breast is not only nutritionally ideal for her baby; it is a gift of love from deep within her heart chakra.

Even though our conscious rational mind may not remember them, experiences shared with our mothers within this gentle and peaceful environment will have a profound influence on how we open ourselves up to loving partnerships throughout our lives. It also nurtures deep within us a sense of trust and of belonging to a wider community. We can grow to become effective participants in the world, thereby achieving our greatest potential. A mother's love sets us safely on a course that runs less risk of being hijacked by our own ego.

Of course women who become mothers experience this bond from both perspectives. In many ways, they become doubly wise. Mothers and their daughters are particularly powerful intuitive combinations – this is brought home to me regularly in my practice. The incidence of *telephone telepathy* between mothers and daughters who consult me is huge! This is the commonly expressed experience of having someone phone the moment we turn our thoughts toward them.

In 2003, Rupert Sheldrake conducted a series of experiments to test the validity of telephone telepathy. The results of 800 such trials suggest that it is a significant phenomenon, more so between people who have strong social and emotional bonds. I am sure that the prevalence of texting telepathy will be just as significant once mothers become as adept as their teenage daughters at this bewildering art.

This form of non-local connection is much more likely to exist when the two parties are compliant – in other words when their heart chakras are open and communicate in unison. In my experience, mothers have less obvious telepathic experiences with their teenage sons, but this may be that, for teenage sons, admitting such things is definitely 'uncool'. Also, I have had less opportunity to discuss this with teenage boys. Most hate going to the doctor with their mothers anyway, and when they do, tend to shrink down in their chair, look vacantly out of the window, and disagree (monosyllabically) with everything their mothers say.

I suspect that sons have the potential of being just as receptive as their sisters to telepathic communication with their mothers, once they have learned to let down the protective guard of their ego.

Several years ago, I awoke one morning having just dreamed of my mother. But it was unlike any dream I had experienced before: in the briefest of moments, her smiling face had flashed before me – like a photographic slide on a screen. And, rather strangely, it was the youthful face of my mother in her late thirties. An hour after I got up, my father phoned from a hospital in England, saying my mother had been admitted with a suspected mild heart attack.

He went on: "Everything is going to be OK, but we were both very worried when she was in the ambulance an hour or so ago. She kept saying she so wished you were here."

Women in Search of Their God

Perhaps the greatest privilege afforded me as a doctor is the opportunity to hear and appreciate a wide range of spiritual beliefs Women unfortunately develop more than their fair share of chronic illness, and inevitably at their time of greatest need they question long held issues of faith. If their illness is life threatening, and they reflect on their own mortality, these issues become all the more urgent.

Women in these situations have been my most valuable teachers; the insights that women have brought to the spiritual dimensions of all our lives in recent years have lead to a rapid maturing of all religious practice around the world.

My own approach is to avoid projecting my own understanding of spiritual matters during a consultation. None of us ultimately knows all the answers. Although those who hold strictly fundamentalist beliefs, be they Christian or otherwise, are less likely to seek me out, when they do

I try my best to honor their beliefs. One of the landmark studies on the healing effects of prayer on heart patients in San Francisco involved 'born again' Christians praying at a distance for patients they knew only from photographs. Most churches, whether fundamentally or liberally based, provide supportive counseling and a willing network of concerned friends. There are now many studies that show that regular church-goers tend to heal more quickly, and live longer than non-attenders.

However, I see a growing number of women who feel alienated from institutionalized religion – some even harbour traumatic memories of mistreatment and abuse by officials of the church during their childhood. Frequently these injustices leave deep emotional scars. These experiences may condition them into reacting to future illnesses with overwhelming feelings of guilt and shame.

A question they frequently ask themselves, and sometimes me, is "What have I done to deserve all this?"

As a child, I attended what is best described as a 'middle-Anglican' church. The classification in use then divided churches into 'low' or 'high' – the former being more informal and liberal, and the latter more imposing and ritualized. Our church definitely belonged to the former. The God they seemed to talk about was a kindly but rather strict old man, who I pictured as a slim version of Santa Claus. He was rather pale and grey without Santa's rosy cheeks. Like Santa, though, he had this amazing ability to gauge, and respond to, the needs of all people on the earth. Santa proved this by responding, with amazing accuracy, once a year to my scrappily written request for Christmas presents, whereas God was there 24/7 answering my prayers. This made my God extremely intelligent, incredibly busy, and very tired. I remember wondering whether God and Santa were related.

Over the years my understanding of God has evolved. Rather than continuing to take on the identity of an elderly wise man, I now regard God more as a pure manifestation of love. An invisible thread that connects us all – more an entity than an identity. A God that is present when we invite a stranger into our home, when we help the victims of a tsunami or hurricane, and when we forgive. It is there when a mother feeds her child.

There are still times however, when I find this updated version of God too difficult to visualize. When I feel fragile and the need to pray, I find myself returning to the comfort of the more tangible God of my youth. If I were to rationalize this, I would say I was retaining this image as a Jungian archetype, a figure that epitomizes those values I hold most dear. However, I have found too much thinking gets in the way of prayer; the only real reason I return to my old grey gentleman God is that, at times, it is easier.

However for many women the God of their youth did not appear so benign. He was portrayed as a figure to be feared – a judging, patriarchal Lord so very removed from their own being. He seemed to represent a male dominated hierarchical world-view, a black and white world of good and evil, of power and revenge. For many women brought up in the Catholic faith, the church's honoring of Mary, the mother of Christ, has not been enough to redress the balance.

A mother often puts her own healing in second place behind that of her child. It is only when her child reaches an age of independence that she may give herself the space to heal. There are some instances, for example when her child lives a life addicted to drugs, when this state of delay lasts a lifetime. When confronted by a life-threatening illness such as breast cancer, a woman frequently questions her role her on earth.

"Am I here to suffer for others?"

"Do I really have to put myself and my needs in second place all the time?"

"What changes do I have to make to give me the best chance of survival?"

But happily it is not only serious ill health that acts as a catalyst for women re-owning their spirituality. Equal opportunities in education and the work force have empowered women to study, research and openly express their deeper needs. Not satisfied with a hierarchical interpretation of the scriptures, many women have embarked on their own journey of spiritual discovery finding comfort and meaning in other world religions, either singly or in combination.

Along the way, many have discovered their own practical healing gifts. Many find Eastern models of healing that link spiritual, emotional and physical aspects of health honor an inner purity; a vision of God held within each sentient being. They may discover, or perhaps more accurately rediscover, a God of healing and balance, an expression of pure unconditional love that doesn't need to own a face. A God – or Goddess – they can again recognize within their own being. A God of all things.

In some cases, this leads them back to their Christian faith – but this time returning to the Bible to read not only the words but also what lies between them. Christianity, Judaism, Buddhism, Hinduism and Islam are no longer seen in isolation, as competitive and conflicting forces. Rather, a common ground of compassion is sought within these teachings. So the feminine values of nurturing, forgiveness and healing are now beginning to change the face of religion, helping to break down the imposing walls that have stood for centuries as a testament to human, sadly often male, ego.

The story of Christ is also evolving. It is not only Dan Brown's popular *The Da Vinci Code* that has made many re-evaluate Mary Magdalene's role as a significant spiritual figure. The 20th century discovery and translation of the Gnostic gospels – which include the Gospel of Mary Magdalene – all elevate Mary's role in the New Testament.

Whether or not Mary was married to Jesus, and indeed gave birth to his child, is now a matter of much debate. Personally, I regard the historical details as less important than the beneficial effects an open discussion of this sensitive issue may have on healing. To me, a natural – more feminine – balance is now being brought back to Christianity that better serves both women and men in their hour of greatest need.

However, there are many times I am reminded of just how painful and difficult it still is for some to heal.

Cherie's Story

Recently, Cherie, a distressed woman in her late 40s came to see me. She was suffering from insomnia, depression and palpitations. I asked her about any events in her life that could have caused this.

She started to cry, telling me her eighteen-year-old son Gary had committed suicide the previous year. Her own marriage had ended some years before, and she was now living on her own.

She reached into her handbag, and showed me a photo of a fit teenage boy clutching a surfboard. As a father of teenage children, I could barely imagine what she was going through.

I asked her whether she was receiving any grief counseling, and she replied that she was.

"They are helping me come to terms with the fact he is now in hell," she explained, now deeply distressed.

"Who is it that says he has gone to hell?" I asked.

She told me that she was seeing a counsellor from her church, and this was their, and her belief. She named the church, which I knew to preach a fundamentalist version of Christianity.

After a period of silence, I asked her what she would like me to do.

"Just make me feel better, please," was her simple request.

I suggested that I should first perform a thorough physical examination, and then we could have a talk. I could see that this was not quite what she expected.

"Can't you just fix me with some acupuncture? My friend says it makes her feel wonderful."

I responded that in my experience, acupuncture worked better if it was part of an open healing relationship. I explained that it would be ideal for us, together, to try and understand what her body was trying to communicate.

"Maybe we could talk about the grief you feel for Gary, while I help you relax with some gentle acupuncture."

Rather reluctantly she agreed.

After the check-up, I used a couple of acupuncture points to help her relax. I was still feeling rather uncomfortable, as despite my concern for Cherie's distress, we had not achieved an ideal state of harmony together. Part of this was a resistance within me, as I felt I was being asked to 'fix' something in a way that wasn't appropriate.

I decided to discuss with her, in as gentle a way as possible, her own understanding about God – and of heaven and hell – as it was clear that she was wrestling with the idea that her son was continuing to suffer incredible torment. It would be nice, I thought, to establish some common ground.

She responded only with more tears; so after another brief period of silence I said, very tentatively:

"There are some who feel that God exists within us all; it is a God of love, and peace, and comfort."

Cherie glared at me.

"You are you not one of those New Age doctors are you?"

Trying not to react defensively, I explained that I had my own beliefs and understandings, but that it was also important for me not to impose these on others. I briefly recounted my own journey in the hope that Cherie would find some point of empathy.

Unfortunately no such point was reached.

The best I could do was to avoid harbouring any feeling of personal frustration, and to wish her well.

We made no further appointments, but I encouraged her to feel free to keep in touch. To date, somewhat predictably, this hasn't happened.

As she left my home, I remember reflecting on how so many people must be suffering their own private version of hell – right here on earth.

Female Intuition

"Is it your hormones, or is it me?"

In retrospect this was a brave (or foolish) question to ask of Trish in the early days of our relationship. Like most men, I was confused how a certain, in my view perennially witty, comment made by me one week could elicit such a different response the next. At the beginning of the month I would be rewarded with a gentle chuckle and peck on the cheek. Later that month, the same ounce of charm would go down like the proverbial lead balloon. My only feedback would be an icy glare.

And this was precisely the response I received to my naïve, and somewhat dangerous question.

Over the years, I have learned that Trish is a most tolerant, evenly balanced woman. It is the varied perception of the world that all women experience at different times of the month, that allows them to cope with change, in my view, far better than men. We tend to be more dogmatic, and dare I say, at times rather pig-headed.

One interesting study in 1989 shows that women hear more negative words such as 'rage,' 'anger' and 'sadness' in the time before their periods. Research has shown that it is the right hemisphere of our brain that is primed to hear these negative words, whilst the left side hears positive words such as 'joy' and 'love.' Dr Christiane Northrup is a gynaecologist and author who has long promoted the important role intuition plays in the health of all women. She proposes that the hormonal changes (low levels of LH and FSH) in the menstrual cycle before ovulation lead to a predominantly left brained 'happy' mood. After ovulation, and before the period, the levels rise and the right brain kicks in.

Dr Northrup proposes that this right brain 'perspective' is more a true reflection of the world around the woman. Whereas in the early part of the cycle negative 'realities' are blocked out, later on her intuition is on red alert. Where she was satisfied with her lot early in the month, she now sees the need for change – that she deserves generally a better deal in life. It could be said that she is no longer in a 'fool's paradise'.

Many women tell me that that their intuition and creativity are at their most acute in the time before their periods. It appears this is when they are indeed more efficient receiving, and transmitting, *human antennas*.

Dr Northrup describes this monthly ebb and flow, or waxing and waning of intuition as being replaced at the time of the menopause by a more constant flow. In hormonal terms, both LH and FSH now remain persistently raised providing, she proposes, a steady nurturing environment for creativity. It is certainly my experience that the menopause frequently heralds the full flourish of a woman's creative potential. There is now a heady mix of wisdom, intuition and assertiveness that acts as an essential balance in a predominantly left-brained Western world. No wonder women prefer to call their hot flushes 'power surges'.

It has taken me many years to attempt an answer to that smug question I asked of Trish long ago. I would have to conclude that, in retrospect, it was also a rather silly question. It is now clear that it (I forget what exactly *it* was) was due to *both* Trish's hormones *and* me.

Although I would pick my time to let her know.

The Connected Man

Men are shrouded in mystery. Despite being one myself, the best I can usually do when faced with a middle-aged man's health problem is to join him in the void.

There are exceptions of course; he may have come along clutching his hand encased in a bloodied oil-soaked rag from his shed after an unfortunate encounter with the wrong end of his chainsaw.

"I did it cutting up the firewood, Doc," he might say.

He may have completely severed three essential tendons, rendering him unable to drive or use a computer for three months, but he can take solace, and some sense of pride, in that this was an injury incurred battling extreme forces of nature, while fulfilling his solemn duty to his wife and family.

His wife, who would have had to leave the cooking to her non-communicating teenage son and daughter to drive him to the clinic, would likely interpret things rather differently.

"Stupid idiot," she might say rolling her eyes. "Third time this has happened in five years. Too mean to buy us one of those gas fires with fake logs. Just as good – in fact better – and they come with a remote. Tell him Doc, he won't listen to me."

Usually, however, the solutions to a man's problems are less obvious. Together with Australia, New Zealand shares the highest incidence of male suicide in the developed world. Why is it that here in a land of exquisite beauty, first class education and endless job opportunities, a significant number of men are opting to end their lives prematurely?

None of us yet has the answers to this. But I have certainly become aware of the sense of isolation, and meaninglessness, within the lives of many men who have consulted me over the years. Frequently relationships lie at the heart of their problems. Relationships with their wife, partner and perhaps most important of all, with the world.

Research clearly shows that men live longer and happier lives when married, or in a long term relationship. Women however thrive when they have a network of women friends. When their spouse dies, statistically a man's health takes a dive, and his life expectancy shrinks. Whereas a woman, figures show, can take on a new lease of life.

It seems that we, as men, have a lot to answer for. As I became interested in deeper aspects of healing, I realized how important it was for me to form an honest partnership with each patient. Each has proved to be unique, and some of course more satisfactory than others. I am only of any use in my role if such a partnership is formed, as all healing is self healing, and at my most effective I am a co-channeller of a balancing universal field. To achieve this, we need to share a space, and together hold a joint intent for healing.

Women, I have to say, tend to be a lot smarter at this than men. I have mentioned some of the reasons for this already. These are attributes of a healthy heart chakra – a woman is more inclined to open her heart to another, and share her emotions. She can often do this more successfully with her friends than with her husband or partner. He may have extreme difficulty expressing his own needs. The door to his heart is closed, or at the best hanging ajar.

The opening of our heart chakra heralds in a totally new perspective on life. No longer do we need to be locked in battle in competition with others, and prisoners to our own egos. Instead we are involved in true partnerships, connected to others and the natural world.

We learn to savour the present, less consumed by worries and fears. We become more alert to possibilities, less like victims, more contented and more giving.

So why is this step up so threatening for us as males? The answer probably lies in our conditioning. After all, for centuries men have been trained to dissociate from their emotions in battle; empathy for an opponent in one-to-one armed combat leads to hesitation and, more than likely, our death. We have been trained to follow orders, to honor and obey. Our wives were in turn expected to honor and obey us – and of course to love us.

I am fortunate to be a member of the first generation that has not had to go to war. So for most baby boomers (and those of generation X and Y), we are in the process of exploring new horizons. Those who venture into the territory of the heart from the conditioned familiarity of the black and white, win/lose world of our warrior ancestors, are setting foot in a world of the unknown. Women know that this is a world of love. We, as men, are often not so sure.

A man may fear losing his power and status. He may fear losing his competitive edge if he were to become somehow softer and more well-rounded. But despite this apprehension, deep down, somewhere in the dark recesses of his soul, he remains discontent with his lot in life. Climbing another rung on the career ladder, surpassing his projected sales figures, and landing that big contract no longer give him the buzz he experienced years ago.

What has happened to the spontaneity, the joy, the meaning in his life?

I have seen many men pass through their own *'Dark Night of the Soul'*. Some would say that the plight of the sixteenth century Spanish saint, John of the Cross, has little in common with that of a modern executive trying to reach a meaningful balance in his life. St John was interrogated, tortured and imprisoned at the age of thirty-five for challenging the ritual and dogma of the Catholic Church. While incarcerated in a tiny closet that had previously been a bathroom, he began to write poetry. Miraculously he escaped through a tiny window in his cell, and found refuge in a nearby convent. Now in an understandable state of bliss, at one with his God, he wrote more poetry and prose describing his ordeal – since translated as *The Dark Night of the Soul.*

St John's story is one of triumph of soul over ego; it is as relevant today as it was over four hundred years ago. For example, the elation felt by many who have reported NDEs (near death experiences) is reminiscent of John's own blissful experiences.

Over the years I have lent the translation to several men, and women, who were at a crossroads in their lives and for them it has served as a powerful, and reassuring metaphor for their own journey. For men, in particular, who struggle with their own deeply perplexing issues, it provides a welcoming glimmer of light and hope at the end of a very dark tunnel.

Living the Single Life

Before I discuss how our spiritual growth can flourish within a close relationship, it is prudent to mention that there may be times in our lives when, by choice or otherwise, we are very much on our own.

It may be that these times, despite often being hard and lonely, provide the space we need for our conscious awareness to grow without the complications that a relationship may bring.

If we learn to appreciate and savour these still points in our lives, a balanced mix of male and female energy is likely to come our way nurturing us, even healing past traumas.

It Takes Two

Thankfully, most of us do not have to endure the extreme discomfort of St John's dark night before our lives become lighter, and more meaningful. Time, the ultimate healer – within this dimension at least – is on our side. Life events, smooth and rocky relationships, and the school of hard knocks all guide our growth. If we learn to live life in the present, much of this process takes care of itself.

Even within a meaningful long-term relationship, our spiritual growth is unlikely to be in total synchrony with our partner. Commonly, women who gain fresh insights into their own spirituality from their illnesses fear 'outgrowing' their partners. In my experience, this is a realistic worry. If it is the relationship that lies solely or partly at the root of a woman's illness, it is highly likely that it will not survive unless her partner addresses his own issues. Both parties have to make changes if deep healing is to occur.

However, in the ideal situation, there will indeed be healing in both partners. A woman with breast cancer, for example, will gain the freedom to express and fulfill her needs, while her partner learns to value each day, being more spontaneous and 'in the moment'. Both hearts thus heal in their own way, and a new-found freedom flourishes within the relationship. And yes, they live happily ever after.

Max and Kim's Story

Kim, an elegantly dressed women in her late forties, came to see me with headaches, insomnia and dizzy spells. All the tests had proved normal, and she told me she needed 'balancing'.

The major stresses in her life revolved around her husband Max. They had been married for over twenty years, and she still loved him "to bits".

"But I'm not sure I like him very much now!" she despaired. "He works late every night, comes home, has his dinner and goes to sleep. He doesn't work weekends, but he needs the whole of Saturday to recover

from the week. He walks around the house like a zombie – I am unable to hold a conversation with him till midday Sunday. Then on Monday, it all starts again."

"Last Saturday, I just erupted and said all sorts of things about him I now regret. He just stormed off up the road saying he can't change. He's back now, but I can't go on like this."

I agreed, saying that it would be ideal if I had a chat with Max. I had met him before, and he struck me as an intelligent, thoughtful and kindly man.

"I don't know if he'll come. I'll do my best to get him here. What time do you work till?"

To my surprise, Max agreed and our first consultation was both frank and fulfilling. He realized his marriage was under strain, but it was his business that was to blame.

"I have gathered together a staff of twenty over the years. Quite frankly, there are two people not pulling their weight. They have been there from the start, and I have noticed they have lost all passion for the job. I know their families, and although I know I have to, I just can't give them the sack. So instead, I am finding myself doing much of their work, and I know I'm in a serious state of burn out."

I agreed that this was indeed a difficult situation. I felt that I had not the expertise to advise him on these business matters, but recommended a business consultant I knew well. In fact, Max reminded me a lot of him.

I heard nothing for six weeks, when Kim phoned to tell me she was sleeping well, and her headaches had all but disappeared. She thanked me profusely for linking Max up with my friend. They had "hit it off like a house on fire," and had restructured the business completely. What was more, the troublesome two employees had decided to leave of their own accord.

"Oh yes, and we are taking tango lessons every Friday."

Togetherness Exercise

Demonstrating our love for another comes through a willingness to make our partner's life better. This often involves stepping into the unknown, recognizing and changing a pattern of behaviour that has become deeply conditioned in us. Max demonstrated this by turning up at my rooms with his intent focused on making such a change. The rest fell neatly into place.

When we initially fall in love, all this is second nature. We are in the embrace of change and wonder; our conditioned isolated selfishness fades into the background. With time – and luck – this phase of romantic love eventually matures, leading to a partnership that is practical, sustainable and less possessive.

However, it may also become safe, predictable and less fun.

This exercise needs to be practised at regular intervals. It applies to different and same sex couples equally.

Make a booking for two at your favorite restaurant. Request a small corner table, with a single fresh rose in a small vase, and a solitary candle.

After arriving at the restaurant, order two glasses of your favorite drink. Once your glasses are filled, look your partner directly in the eye – the way you did during the first few weeks of your romance.

Move your left hand towards your partner's, touching it over the middle of the table.

While maintaining your gaze, lean gently forward, carefully avoiding tipping over the vase and singeing your hair, beard or eyebrows on the candle.

With your right hand, pick up your glass, synchronously, with your partner, moving it gently towards his or hers, stopping skillfully with less than a centimeter to spare.

Focus inwardly on your heart, and the heart of your partner. Visualize that the two are beating as one.

You now become aware that your two glasses are traveling the remaining few millimeters, as if by remote control, on their own.

All you need do is hold onto your glass.

You will now observe a magical sound – best described as a 'clink'.

If you listen very carefully, you will also hear something else.

Together, and in perfect harmony, these following two simple words will escape effortlessly and spontaneously, from your, and your partner's, lips.

"To us."

Now, mindful still of the candle flickering precariously beneath your chin, move in even closer for this, the grand finale:

Plant the briefest, and most delicate, of kisses on his/her lips. (With repeated practice, this maneuver is guaranteed to become more accurate and coordinated.)

While still maintaining eye contact, lean back gently, returning to your original upright seated position.

It is now, and only now, that you can ask the waiter for the menu.

6: Skeptics, Psychics and Savants

"We don't see things as they are, we see things as we are."
–Anaïs Nin

"I'd love my husband to come, but I'm afraid he's very skeptical about acupuncture. He can't understand how sticking needles in my feet and ears can help my headaches."

It has been important for me to try to understand skepticism. I have learned that it comes in many forms; ranging from a healthy curiosity that balances a thirst for knowledge with the humble awareness that there is so much in our universe that will remain unknown, to a cynical dogmatism that overrides and belittles the beliefs and wisdom of others. The word *skeptic* is derived via Latin from a Greek term meaning 'one who inquires or examines'. At one end of the spectrum, the inquiry is seeded in the realms of wonder – to quote J. B. S. Haldane: 'There are more things in heaven and earth than are dreamed of'. At the other, there is a strict fundamental adherence to what has been discovered through rational thought, and recorded by rigorous scientific method.

To the most extreme in this category, the real world only exists within the confines of their own senses; consciousness, if it exists at all, arises from somewhere deep within the fertile pastures of their highly developed brains. The more rational, and brainier, a human becomes, the more likely is he to know the answers. Those who have not reached this advanced stage of highly ordered intelligence need to be protected from the hoards of charlatans, cranks or frankly stupid New Age extremists who are out to undermine human progress with bizarre, ill-conceived theories. Worse still, they will say, are all those crackpot psychics and clairvoyants who are in business solely to swindle naïve, frail little old ladies out of their hard-earned life savings by preying mercilessly on their fears, making them believe there is an afterlife where they can find their dearly departed loved ones. Many modern day skeptics I have talked to regard themselves as guardians of the truth, protectors of the vulnerable and infirm.

So who was the original skeptic?

It is generally agreed that the first school of skepticism in the West was founded by the Greek philosopher Pyrrho (c.360–c.270 BCE). Pyrrho travelled with Alexander the Great to India, where, so the story goes, he met with 'naked wise men' known as *gumnosophistai*. What exactly happened in this encounter has not been recorded, but it seems to have had a deep effect on Pyrrho. He returned to Greece a changed man. No longer was he interested in lengthy intellectual debates with other philosophers on the meaning of life that would last long into the night. This he now regarded as a tiresome waste of time. Instead, he had become comfortable in not knowing; he no longer grasped at every opportunity to develop a rational argument to prove a point. He adopted the deeply relaxed state of *ataraxia,* or apathy. Happiness and wisdom were his ultimate goals; he renounced all desires and beliefs, freeing himself from the cloud of unhappiness that inevitably accompanied them.

It appears Pyrrho had left Greece for India an uptight activist, to return a laid-back mystic.

You will now recognize in the new Pyrrho many attributes of a balanced seventh chakra. His had been a journey to higher levels of consciousness, leaving behind his own internal world of conflict dictated to by his ego. Furthermore, like Fibonacci centuries later, he introduced a powerful Oriental ingredient to the Occidental palate – a touch of Eastern yin to the Western yang.

Of course his opponents in ancient Greece, the Dogmatists, thought he had taken leave of his senses – which in a way, I suppose he had. In fact, there are reports that Pyrrho wandered around in a dream-like daze, needing to be accompanied at all times for fear of his being hit by a carriage, or falling down a cliff. But despite this, Pyrrho was apparently hugely popular especially with artists and poets, with a monument being built in his honor after his death.

Organized Skeptics' Groups

Pyrrho's brand of skepticism seems at odds with the philosophies of modern day skeptics' groups. Over the years, I have placed myself somewhat in the firing line of such groups, as many are highly critical of doctors who lend credence to what they regard as 'alternative medicine'. The wording of their official documents has often been very strong. For example, The US Council for Health Fraud, in its statement on acupuncture, claims that its *'theory and practice is based on primitive and fanciful concepts of disease that bear no relationship to present scientific knowledge.'* It then claims that *'research over the past 20 years has not shown that acupuncture is effective against any disease'*.

The current New Zealand skeptics' website, is highly critical of the 14% of doctors practising acupuncture in this country. We do so, apparently, solely on the basis that *'3,500 years of clinical observations by the Chinese are reliable evidence of its efficacy'*.

And their stated views on ear acupuncture? *'The concept of the auricular homunculus (the inverted baby pattern) is a scientific absurdity.'*

It is rather sobering to discover that a proportion of the thinking population regards one as a deluded, simple-minded fraud. There have certainly been times in the past I have felt annoyed, and threatened by the statements of such groups. But I now resist entering into battle with the holders of such a mindset, even though their claims can be easily countered with modern scientific fact.

However, I believe it is possible to view the opinions and actions of organized skeptics' associations in a positive light. I continue to visit websites such as quackwatch.com so I am alerted to all the counter arguments to holistic theories. Skeptical criticism has undoubtedly contributed to the improved design of scientific trials in psychic research.

Researchers such as Martin Rossman have found that parapsychology now uses 'double blind' protocols more consistently than all other branches of science – including medical science.

So it is important to keep the dialog open, even with the most closed-minded of skeptics; this allows the truth to eventually emerge through a mist of dogma and self-interest. During his last visit to New Zealand in 2002, I attended a public meeting with His Holiness the Dalai Lama. After his address on the nature of happiness, he invited questions from the large audience. One person asked:

"Many of us in New Zealand are very concerned about the plight of your country, Tibet, in the face of the Chinese occupation. What is it that we can do to help you and your country?"

The Dalai Lama thought for a moment. His reply carried a simple message.

"We should", he said, "convey our personal under-standing of the situation when talking to visitors from mainland China." He suggested we employ no coercion, simply the setting out of a reasoned argument from a concerned bystander. He implied that with education and awareness, the truth will become apparent – without the need for conflict or undue argument.

I have found that those who carry within them a degree of understandable and healthy skepticism respond generously to my gentle and honest – if sometimes garbled – attempts to explain the basis of my work. But ultimately, knowing comes from experience; action speaks louder than words. I have seen many a professed skeptic arrive at my rooms grimacing and bent double in pain, to leave several minutes later smiling and straight.

Open-minded skeptics are inclined to trust their experiences, and to adapt accordingly. It is certainly not my role to change or convert anyone; in fact I tend to subscribe to the theory that no one can effectively 'change' anyone else. This has to come from somewhere inside themselves.

Louis Armstrong, perhaps the most influential figure in popular music in the 20th century, said it best:

"There are some people that if they don't know, you can't tell 'em."

Open and Closed Minds
in the Consultation Room

The paradigm I am presenting in this book poses real problems for a follower of a scientific model that represents us all as solely material, physical beings completely separate from each other. There are many who claim despairingly that all this talk of instant interaction at a distance turns much of science on its head.

I am not a pure, experimental scientist with a reputation to protect. For such a person, esoteric concepts such as love, intent and prayer are best kept outside the laboratory door. Indeed, the validity of their life's work may well have depended on their being detached from such influences; they may have been rewarded for compartmentalizing their lives.

But for a doctor or health care professional, life is never quite so ordered. Every few minutes, we encounter a chaotic mix of science, fear, worry, pain and, of course, love. Separating out each ingredient within a consultation does not do justice to the final dish. The physical, the emotional, the spiritual and the scientific are all indelibly blended together.

What is more, the *human antenna* model doesn't separate the doctor or healer from the patient. They are both in the bubble together – along with the surroundings, the receptionist, and even the goldfish (in its bowl) in the waiting room. In the interconnected, participatory world there is no real distinction between the observer, and the observed.

But for healing to occur, something else has to be there in the mix; a catalyst that defies measurement. A heart-felt state of being that harmonizes but never controls. An *intent* that carries with it goodwill and kindness.

It needn't be elicited overtly though a prayer, or even through words. It does however need to be shared; someone who comes along solely to please someone else, comes along with a blocked intent. A diehard skeptic who scoffs at the notion of forming a healing partnership, preferring instead a quick fix, creates a barrier to his own healing. By handing over total responsibility to another, he remains disengaged from the process. It could be said that his controlling head is disconnected from his sharing heart.

An animal, a trusting dog for instance, has no such mindset. There is no background interference from an overactive mind, no bravado or ego. No preconceived notions to block the faith in one's own ability to heal. Rupert Sheldrake's research on the telepathic nature of animals, and the growing use of homeopathy and acupuncture in veterinary clinics, all suggest that it is our overly rational human minds that unnecessarily complicate the natural process of healing.

However, for those humans who are open to such matters, the healing process begins as soon as they make the appointment. This is when the intent becomes fixed. It may then be forgotten consciously, lying dormant inside, only to be re-awakened in the car in their trip to the therapist's rooms. Once a patient's intent is set, the therapist's work becomes much easier. If we imagine the healing process as a slice of chocolate cake, the consultation is simply the tasty icing on top.

But what is the effect of a negative third party?

For healing to be effective, it is a shared activity. It is a true partnership with its source within the heart chakras of the participants. If an angry or controlling third person is around, particularly if they are in the consulting room, the purity of this partnership can be muddied.

There can be disruption on several levels. Two of these are easily explained.

Firstly, both therapist and patient may feel distracted, so the focus is somehow diverted away towards a third party. The distracting person may or may not be trying to actively disrupt proceedings.

Secondly, either the therapist or the patient may feel tense, unable to enter into the relaxed state ideal for healing.

However, is there a third, rather less obvious, subliminal force at play? Could the intruder impose his negative intent directly on the unsuspecting subject, casting a jinx or curse on proceedings?

If this indeed happens, the implications extend far beyond the confines of the therapist's room.

The Experimenter Effect

To attempt an answer to this question on the power of positive and negative intent, we need to move from the consulting room to the research laboratory.

For instance, does the intent of someone conducting a scientific experiment have an effect on its outcome?

Does a scientist who is open to such concepts as extrasensory perception and telepathy achieve a different result, in an identical experiment measuring such effects, to one who is very skeptical?

In 1997, parapsychology researcher Dr Marilyn Schlitz investigated these very questions in an experiment with a skeptical researcher, Richard Wiseman. Marilyn Schlitz first became interested in psychical research as a student in 1977, and impressed with Russell Targ's remote viewing research, began running experiments of her own, together with other psychologists at Wayne State University. Her first study involved a self-confessed psychic as a subject but did not produce positive results. It was only when they substituted themselves as remote viewers that they obtained significantly positive results. One explanation for this was that the ego of the psychic blocked the remote viewing effect.

Over the years, Marilyn has conducted many remote-viewing experiments; one involving an agent in Italy and a subject in Michigan demonstrated the strongest effect known at the time in the published literature. Another experiment tested whether mice sleeping in one room could be aroused by the intent of a human 'sender' in another room. The mice lay on photocells that recorded any movement. A variety of people from healing professions, including doctors and nurses, attempted to wake the mice but failed to produce consistent results. It was only the researchers themselves that could do this.

The study that led to the collaboration with Wiseman was performed in California with Dr Ed May. The researchers recorded the physiological changes in human 'receivers' in one room, at the precise moments they were being stared at on close circuit television by 'viewers' in another room. Under randomized and controlled conditions they got statistically significant positive results. Richard Wiseman was naturally skeptical of the findings, and proceeded to conduct his own experiments under identical conditions in his own laboratory. His results were overwhelmingly negative. When Schiltz visited his laboratory and repeated the experiments herself, she replicated the same positive results she had produced in her own laboratory.

This line of research is still in its infancy, but if the Experimenter Effect becomes accepted as a bona fide scientific phenomenon, the ramifications are far reaching. If it becomes apparent that the expectations, beliefs and intent of the experimenters can have an effect on the outcome of a study, the way we conduct all research, including trials on pharmaceuticals, will come under renewed scrutiny. Moreover, it will lay down a dramatic challenge to the prevailing and dominant version of the scientific model that separates subject from object, and us, as observers, from the world around us.

Natasha's Story

Natasha Demkina is the seventeen-year-old schoolgirl from the Russian city of Saransk who was the subject of the 2004 Discovery Channel TV documentary 'The Girl with the X-ray Eyes'.

Natasha has gained a reputation in her neighborhood for diagnosing medical conditions intuitively. To use her own words, she is able to "look deep inside people's bodies, watch their organs at work and spot when things go wrong."

She first became aware of her gift when she was 10. While at home with her mother, she suddenly had a vision. She saw inside her mother's body, and started to tell her exactly what it was she could see. Her gift has evolved and she explains it like this:

"Now, I have to switch from my regular vision to what I call medical vision. For a fraction of a second, I see a colorful picture inside the person, and start to analyze it."

Keen to gain more credibility, Natasha agreed to submit herself, and her 'gift', to the scrutiny of Western scientists. The television documentary focused on the series of experiments set up in New York by the Committee for the Scientific Investigation of the Paranormal. The principal investigators were psychology professors Richard Wiseman and Ray Hyman.

The main experiment involved Natasha facing 7 subjects, in the presence of the investigators. The subjects were not allowed to speak, and wore blindfolds. Natasha was given 7 cards, each with a specific medical condition written on it. She was asked to match the cards with the people in front of her.

Natasha and her agent were first asked to agree to the experimental protocol that stated:

"If Natasha correctly matches fewer than 5 target medical conditions, then the Test Proctor will declare that results are more consistent with chance guessing and does not support any belief in her claimed abilities."

Natasha in fact managed to identify 4 out of the 7. The investigators pronounced Natasha's effort a failure. When questioned by journalists about why she at least guessed four correctly, Professor Wiseman replied:

"At best, she's done this a lot and she has real expertise to look at people and make reasonably accurate diagnoses. But at worst, there is something else going on."

He was suspicious, but had no proof, that Natasha had been cheating, receiving helpful text messages from her companions during the test – something that the experimenters had expressly forbidden.

At the end of the program, Professor Hyman summed up:

" . . . my hope for Natasha is that she will grow up . . . and give up this aspect of her life . . . I don't think it is good in the long run for any of us to be living an illusion."

As I watched the program on television, I became increasingly disturbed. Firstly, I could see no scientific rationale behind the decision to claim 5 out 7 correct answers were needed for Natasha to be successful. In fact, using the standard statistical method of appraising scientific experiments taught at secondary school, the likelihood of achieving 4 hits out of 7 by sheer chance turns out to be *one in fifty*. In other words, statistically, this is a very significant result. Other research scientists, including Nobel prize-winning physicist Professor Brian Josephson, have since voiced their concerns about the investigators' poor experiment design, and subsequent conclusions.

My concerns, though, spread beyond the purely academic. The experiment seemed to be conducted within an overpowering atmosphere of experimenter control. I identified that, had this been occurring in my own consulting room, I would have been unable to do my job unless the controllers left the room.

The subjects themselves had been blindfolded in an attempt to limit sensory clues. However, this would also have limited the formation of a true healing partnership that would act as a catalyst for intuition. Physical presence, and the use of our senses, allows us to bond harmoniously with others. Blindfolding the subjects, although understandable from a standard scientific perspective, interferes with the formation of this resonance.

We had also had no information about the intent of the other subjects. Again, unless all were in total harmony, there would be 'lines' of interference throughout the room. Given this, plus the conspicuous presence of the film crew and their equipment, it becomes more and more remarkable that Natasha achieved what she did.

And if, as Marilyn Schlitz's research suggests, there is such a phenomenon as an Experimenter Effect, then this also was likely to be at play, independently of all these other forces. The overriding intent of the experimenters was made crystal clear in their closing remarks.

So at best, this experiment fails to prove, or disprove, anything. If Natasha's gift is to be studied seriously, experiments need to be designed with full knowledge of all these issues. At the very least a supportive, harmonious environment needs to be created for a study such as this.

But this program affected me in a still more profound and emotional way. Natasha was about to embark on her own career in medicine – she is now a student at Semashko's Moscow Medical University. Every year, young medical students, both male and female, visit my rooms, keen to nurture their own healing skills. They are eager to use their innate gifts alongside the new technology of modern medicine. They instill in me great hope for the future, and give me the confidence to continue on my own journey.

My hope for Natasha is that she places the rather patronizing judgments of two middle-aged male investigators, whose reputations have been forged on debunking human psychic ability, firmly in context. May they only strengthen her resolve to use whatever gifts she retains wisely.

To quote Natasha:

"The dream is, if I preserve my gift, to use it but on the basis of proper medical knowledge."

If this comes to pass, medical science will surely be the winner.

Autistic Savants

One rare group of humans who are challenging our preconceived notions of consciousness, and how we use our brains, are the so-called autistic *savants*. Also known somewhat unfairly as idiot-savants, these individuals can perform extraordinarily complex feats of mind power in a flash. Perhaps the most famous is Kim Peek, who inspired Dustin Hoffman's character in the movie *Rain Man,* who could count thousands of matchsticks at a single glance. Then there is the prodigiously talented artist, Stephen Wiltshire. On one occasion, after flying over central London in a helicopter, he returned to his studio and recreated the exact scene on canvas. It was perfect to the most minute detail, including every window in every high rise block.

Equally impressive is the case of the young Englishman Daniel Tammet, a mathematical genius who demonstrated to an audience that he could recall pi to 22,514 decimal points – without a single error. Unlike many autistic savants, he has a rare insight into his condition, and is able to describe the process he experiences when performing his feats of mind power. As a child, his brother asked him to multiply 82 by 82 by 82 in his head. After 5 to 10 seconds the answer flowed out of his mouth.

He describes how numbers appear to him as shapes, colors and textures.

"When I multiply numbers together, I see two shapes. The image starts to change and evolve, and a third shape evolves. It's mental imagery. It's like maths without having to think."

About 1% of those with autism have these dramatic savant abilities – it is considerably rarer in the population at large. So what is it about the condition of autism that creates an environment for such acts of genius?

Autism is a condition first recognized as recently as 1943. Its incidence in America has risen tenfold in the past twenty years, and this is not simply due to better awareness or reporting. People with autism have extreme difficulties in aspects of life many of us take for granted, although the severity of their symptoms varies considerably. They tend to have a block to forming relationships, and interacting with others. They tend to be rigid, mechanical and emotionally distant.

Their brains often seem totally obsessed with detail; Daniel Tammet describes how he can only rarely go to the beach, as each time he has an overwhelming compulsion to calculate the total number of pebbles within sight.

Medical science has been unable to pinpoint a structural abnormality in the brain specific to autism, despite the use of sophisticated modern MRI scans. At the forefront of research into autistic savants are psychologists Allan Snyder and D. John Mitchell from the Center for the Mind at The Australian National University in Canberra. They are studying the effects of a Transcranial Magnetic Stimulator, a machine that can turn on and off different parts of the brain.

By inhibiting the parts of the brain involved with coordinating functions – the capacity to think conceptually and contextually – they are discovering that they are unlocking savant-like skills in a wide range of people.

There is much debate about the nature of savant ability. It is generally recognized, though, that most savants have a degree of brain damage, suggesting that each of us has the latent potential, in theory, to perform our version of these extraordinary feats. It appears that neurological damage – in Daniel Tammet's case he suffered a major epileptic fit at the age of 3 – somehow blocks the normal pathways in the brain that tend, in most of us, to override these single-minded acts of genius.

So what do these remarkable autistic savants add to our understanding of the *human antenna?*

Their gifts are certainly not due to high IQs or expensive education. This is not a learned behaviour in the traditional sense – a savant such as Daniel will produce an answer to a complex arithmetic problem considerably faster than the cleverest professor of mathematics. Another savant is able to play all the songs heard on a radio note perfect on a piano, despite never having had lessons.

This instant receiving of undiluted information is more consistent with our non-local model of consciousness. It seems that autistic savants have a special ability to tap into a quantum field of universal wisdom. For most of us, this would be blocked from our consciousness by the background interference from all the other information reaching us via our senses. For the sufferers of autism, these pathways so vital for our connection to the physical world seem to be malfunctioning, resulting in the extreme difficulties they encounter in day-to-day life.

It could be said that they are indeed remarkable *human antennas* – but few of us would envy their plight. Their perfect reception of specific 'wavebands' comes at a considerable price. The ideal pattern of growth for the *human antenna,* as presented in this book, relies on our first being suitably 'earthed' – as represented by our journey through the first three chakras. It is through this process that we find how to relate to each other, and the world around us. When this has achieved some balance, we progress through the heart chakra to the realms of higher consciousness. On the surface, the results achieved through this climb through the chakras may not appear so dramatic as those produced by gifted savants. But infused as they are with compassion and the intent to heal, they carry with them a profound message of hope for our future.

Gifted savants such as Daniel Tammet provide us with a tantalizing taste of the true limitless nature of human consciousness. His is also a story of hope for those who have autism, and suffer from disabilities that the general public struggles to understand.

Daniel has succeeded in articulating the highs and lows encountered in the life of an autistic savant. He has succeeded, too, in forming a loving relationship with his partner.

And his remarkable public display of brilliance in spending five hours faultlessly reciting the infinitesimal pi to over 22 thousand points was no ego trip. It carried with it the very humblest and noblest intent.

"I memorized pi to 22,514 decimal places, and I am technically disabled. I just wanted to show people that disability needn't get in the way."

Mediums and Magicians

To the ardent skeptic, a medium performing on stage or on television is either a confidence trickster, or someone completely deluded. In the case of the former, the performer is aware how to manipulate his or her subject with a series of leading questions, carefully observing the answers given together with clues from the subject's body language. In the latter, the poor deluded medium does all this unknowingly.

A skilled magician, the skeptic will claim, uses this technique of 'cold reading' consistently without claiming special powers. Interestingly the most vocal and committed skeptics, such as Robert Wiseman and James Randi, are also professionally trained magicians. It upsets them that by inferring that the world of 'illusion' has some reality, celebrity mediums create wealth and fortune for themselves at the expense of the aggrieved and gullible.

In other words, the unscrupulous medium or psychic is on one gigantic ego trip, whereas the scrupulous medium is literally and simply 'away with the fairies'.

I feel it is important to introduce some balance to this line of thinking. Carefully examined, this extremely skeptical viewpoint appears to be more of a judgment on the frailties of the human condition than a serious examination of the art of mediumship. The world the skeptics are describing is the win/lose world of material gain and loss. The world of personality and self-esteem as represented by the first three chakras. The model I have presented in this book sees access to higher levels of consciousness best achieved by progressing through the heart chakra to chakras five and beyond. This is a path beyond ego.

Our ego, and an unhealthy over-reliance on our expertise and reputation, serves as a block to accessing higher realms of consciousness. The reception is at best very murky. For this reason, I prefer to work alongside psychic practitioners whose practices grow via 'word of mouth'. I am also cautious of anyone who promotes himself in the media as a 'psychic to the stars', or uses any phrase that claims how 'successful' he is at his art.

Similarly, I see considerable risk in a psychic or clairvoyant adopting the role of 'fortune teller'. Every moment of our lives presents us with countless choices. We have at our disposal an infinite number of ways of expressing our free will. Those who try to plot our course for us rob us of this special human right to choose. Human consciousness only continues to grow and expand because we embrace change and take risks.

Frequently I hear the question:

"Why was it that Princess Diana, who frequently consulted with the best psychics money could buy, had no prior warning of her fatal car crash?"

Hopefully, the insights I have just presented serve as a healthy contribution to this debate.

But let's now return to our 'celebrity' medium, trusting her to be both honest and intelligent. That even though her marketing may be somewhat garish – television and popular newspapers are, after all, mainly personality driven – she carries within her a deeply held intent to heal and to serve.

What possible valid explanation is there for what we are observing in a public 'medium' show?

Firstly, we must consider the audience. Most will attend with their own deeply held intent to contact a close loved one who has died. It is also likely that they intend to feel better or in some way heal, from this encounter. Like my own patients coming to see me, their own healing process starts as they make the booking.

Then, we need to consider the group effect. Imagine we are now in the audience. As we mix and mingle with others with similar intent, our receptivity is further enhanced; many hearts locked together in a sharing partnership. Any personal feelings of self-importance and isolation are duly released. (We all experience this as we become part of an audience, listening in silence and spontaneously laughing and clapping together. In doing so, we become part of a larger collective *human antenna*.)

If, sitting beside us, is a close family member also keen to contact the same loved one, our reception becomes even more potent and clear.

So, the scene is set. The medium now appears on the stage. She quickly begins to establish rapport with her audience. This helps reduce her own nervous tension, while opening up her own heart chakra. A sharing, resonant harmony is now established within the theater, further clearing any blocks within the medium herself. She is very much like the conductor of a symphony orchestra; a guiding, coordinating figure in control, but allowing her performers considerable artistic freedom. She immerses herself in a supportive environment of trust; her intuition is allowed to flourish.

The special gift of the medium now becomes evident. She allows herself to tune into a particular individual or couple, somewhere within the sea of faces in the audience. This she *allows* to happen *intuitively*, rather than her *choosing* her subject *rationally*.

Once the subjects are duly identified, the medium engages in the familiar pattern of greeting and the exchanging of ideas and pleasantries, thus allowing for yet further resonance. I would suggest that, in the ideal situation, this interchange is more accurately a 'warm' rather than a 'cold' reading of her subject.

This process in turn allows a shared field of intuition to blossom between the medium and subject(s). Together they are tapping into a timeless non-local dimension beyond the time and space of their earth-bound existence.

This is the quantum *Akashic* field – I have used several terms describing this realm – from which our physical reality 'collapses' down. This is an eternal field of consciousness existing beyond our body and brains, and out of reach from our five senses. It is an eternal consciousness that survives death, because our lives are only temporary.

We are all linked within this consciousness by something that we learn to recognize here on earth, but that continues to defy our methods of measurement. That something is, of course, love itself.

It is this, the true essence of a departed loved one, that I propose the medium is helping her subject identify. This essence never dies, living on in all those who were touched some way while he or she was physically alive. Rather than regarding this person as being transported into another world or *'afterlife'*, I prefer the notion that their soul continues to be ever present – eternally resonating within a loved one.

The only valid reason for someone consulting a medium or psychic is to make that person's life more fulfilled. It is most simply a healing interaction, often helping to disperse harmful feelings of guilt or fear.

And finally, one further question begs an answer: Just what, and where, is the *spirit world?*

There are some physicists who suggest that a medium is somehow accessing other *parallel universes,* each consisting of multi-dimensional layers of existence beyond our wildest imagination. Our deceased loved one, they suggest, has only departed from our familiar four-dimensional world.

In the future, some of these new cutting-edge theories may well prove to be correct. However, for the present I prefer to regard the *spirit world* as a world intimately connected to, and inseparable from, our own. It is where we already are, no more or less of an illusion than the computer, desk and window I see before me now. Our physical world is a miraculous manifestation of an all prevailing whole – seen uniquely through our eyes.

Just as the revolutionary French novelist Anaïs Nin was to remark, "We see things as we are".

Some Remarkable Human Antennas

"Firstly I feel so small as if I am surrounded by another being, enclosed, warm and completely protected as if I am a child in the womb. I am also conscious of his words.

The emotion of love is all around and through me."

These are the words of Thomas Ashman describing his experiences in the 1970s as a medium for St Stephen, known as the first Christian martyr. According to the New Testament book of Acts, authored by Luke, Stephen preached in the name of Jesus after the crucifixion, and was tried by Jesus' enemies for blasphemy. He was duly dragged out of the court and stoned to death by a mob.

Thomas was not an overtly religious man, born to a Catholic mother and Jewish father in London. He left school at the age of sixteen, having learned no other languages, joining the RAF at seventeen in 1943. On discharge in 1948, he married a Polish refugee in England, earning a living in business and hotel management. He married again in 1974 – this time to Olive, a New Zealander.

It was Olive who first heard Thomas talk Latin while he was asleep, recording his words on tape. The spiritual being subsequently revealed himself as St Stephen, and Thomas's mediumship continued for seven years. Stephen usually talked through Thomas in a rather strange brand of English, but occasionally added in words from a specific ancient Greek dialect peculiar to his time and region. This too was taped, and after several years independent scholars have confirmed that these indeed were words from an ancient language long since extinct.

A retired Anglican minister, Reverend Michael Cocks from Christchurch, New Zealand also witnessed many of the sessions, and chronicled the whole experience in a book, *The Stephen Experience*. Here, Stephen's teachings are documented in full, and are mostly of a deeply spiritual and metaphysical nature. Reverend Cocks is at pains to describe the experience as something rather more than simply one discarnate soul being channelled by an individual. He has a long and scholarly interest in psychical research, and he sees his own involvement, and that of several other intimate parties, as important catalysts for the process. He describes several synchronous events experienced by the group of investigators after the channelling sessions stopped; something they regarded as a confirmation that his was truly a shared experience.

I was privileged to be a small part of this experience, as Michael facilitated a workshop devoted to the Stephen Experience in May 2004 in Auckland. I was one of several doctors, scientists, psychologists and teachers who were able to question Michael about these events, and, as the others, was impressed by his clear intention to treat the whole exercise with dignity and reverence. I personally found Stephen's teachings profound, and very much in line with the new thinking linking quantum physics with consciousness and spirituality.

It also introduced me to the intriguing concept of *xenoglossy*, whereby a channel, or medium speaks in a language he has never learned – or even heard – before. It is a recognized phenomenon with a few other convincing cases recorded in the 20th century.

In 1931, a young girl from Blackpool, England, started to speak an ancient Egyptian dialect, channelling an entity known as Telika-Ventiu who had lived in approximately 1400 BCE. Witnessed by the Egyptologist Howard Hume, she wrote 66 accurate phrases in the form of ancient hieroglyphics, and spoke in a tongue that had been extinct for thousands of years.

In another case, a blond, blue-eyed eleven-year-old boy talked to a doctor under hypnosis in an ancient Chinese dialect. This was recorded on tape, and identified by a professor of oriental studies at the University of California as a recitation from a forbidden religion from Ancient China.

So these rare cases of *xenoglossy*, together with the remarkable, proven feats of the savants, provide us with further evidence that human consciousness can transcend the recognized confines of time and space. It is also evident to me that these are events that require investigation in an atmosphere of utmost respect, reverence and diligence. The stories often carry with them profound messages for mankind and the future of our earth, and so we would be wise not to sensationalize the findings, nor exploit the bearers of these tales.

Certainly, these were the views of another remarkable 20th century channel of esoteric wisdom, Alice Bailey (1880-1949). I discovered Alice Bailey's teachings by accident one day in an Auckland bookshop sometime in the early 90s. I was amazed to see a whole row of books, volume after volume, all in blue, and all by the same author. There were intriguing titles such as *A Treatise on Cosmic Fire*, and *Esoteric Healing*. As I flicked through the pages, I wondered how on earth any one individual, in one lifetime, could acquire such wisdom. Noticing that the prose was presented in a rather strange jargon, and determined to understand more, I bought one volume – her unfinished autobiography.

In it she describes how the teachings are, in fact, those of The Tibetan, a channelled spiritual master also known as Djwhal Khul, or simply DK. In 1919, after sending her children off to school, Mrs Bailey (as she like to be called) sought a few moments of peace on a hill near her home. It was here that she first heard a 'voice' imploring her to write several books. She initially rejected the experience, describing herself as skeptical of psychical matters. However the voice had promised to return in three weeks, and it was only then when this indeed happened, that she began to become "curious".

Over the following weeks she began to write the first chapters of her first volume:

"I simply listen and take down the words that I hear and register the thoughts which are dropped into my brain."

With experience and time, this process changed from being one of *clairaudience,* to one close to pure telepathy, where a voice was no longer actively heard. She would occasionally change DK's phrasing to make the teachings more palatable for the modern Westerner, but was careful, by and large, not to tamper with the material coming through her.

She was also careful to say that her process was in no way related to automatic writing, warning of the dangers that may ensue if the aspirant lets "any part of his equipment out of his control. When he does, he enters into a state of dangerous negativity".

Alice Bailey warns that the material received when one surrenders one's own consciousness entirely to the channelling process tends to be inferior, leading to the dangers of obsession. She seems to be describing the need for the channeller to be involved at the highest conscious level, with the purest of intent.

Of all Alice Bailey's teachings, it is her *A Treatise on White Magic* that resonates the most strongly with me. A white magician is one that translates the energies and aspirations of higher consciousness to other beings here on earth, through passionate acts of love, creativity and healing. Using our *human antenna* model, this divine information is received 'vertically' through our crown chakra into the vortex that accompanies a balanced mind and body.

It is then projected 'horizontally' through our heart chakra, in the form and expression of positive emotions that are shared by all, and serve to unite humanity. Poets, artists, writers, actors, musicians, and inspired world leaders, are all white magicians. So too are all parents, grandparents and teachers who expose our children to this magic.

The potential is within us all – every single one of us can learn to be a co-creator of white magic. The balanced *human antenna* not only reaches for the stars; he/she captures them safely for others, keeping them secure for generations to come.

7: Living as Human Antennas

*"The intuitive mind is a sacred gift and the
rational mind is a faithful servant.
We have created a society that honors the
servant, and has forgotten the gift."*
−Albert Einstein

We live in constant and instant connection with nature.This is our natural and normal state of being. Nothing I describe in this book is *super*natural or *para*normal. It is perfectly natural to reach out to a child in distress, and clothe him in love. It is then perfectly natural for that child to grow up securely in the inevitability that giving and receiving love is perfectly normal. It is perfectly natural for us to love and respect the natural world by seeking it out in its purest form, allowing it to balance and heal us at the time of our greatest need. As we are within nature, and nature is within us, it is only natural, and smart, for us to return this sacred favour by ensuring that our world and environment is balanced and healed.

The story of the *human antenna* is a perennial and abiding love story. Our non-local connections are fostered by love, and the reasons for this are as practical as they are divine. Understanding the role of love in someone's life is the essence of my daily work. It is love that is at play when a mother brings her sick child to the doctor, and when a daughter sits alongside her elderly mother with arthritis, explaining to me how she really has a lot more pain than she is admitting.

I remember one time at the end of a busy day I was listening to a person's story for the first time. She had for years been suffering from the most distressing migraine headaches, forcing her to spend much of her life in a darkened room in severe pain. Nothing she had tried, and no doctor or health professional she had consulted, had been able to bring her any relief. For me it had been one of those days – nobody I had seen was getting better. I was tired and hungry. So, for all these reasons and perhaps others more hidden, as this poor lady was recounting her sorry tale I started to cry. Then she cried. For a time, we cried together.

To this day, it remains the most potent and effective therapeutic intervention I have ever (inadvertently) instigated. Aided by the most gentle and delicate acupuncture – she had a morbid fear of needles – her migraines rapidly improved to the stage she could return to work, suffering for only a couple days a month. At the time, I had no idea that such an unplanned and spontaneous shedding of emotion could be anything more than rather embarrassing and unprofessional. It was only a few years later, when she returned for further treatment, that she told me that this had been the turning point for her.

So for me the understanding that spontaneity, letting go and 'not knowing' may play an important part in my work has been greatly comforting. Understanding that it is compassion itself that lies at the heart of healing, releases us from the pressure of demanding so much of ourselves. Often we are meeting and communicating for reasons beyond our immediate comprehension. Sometimes, all we have to *be* is to *be ourselves*.

Our very presence may be enough to elicit deep healing. To one patient, without my knowing it at the time, I may represent the son who died at birth; to another, the father she never had. Honoring these special roles may be all that is truly required of me.

It may seem from our newspapers and televisions that ours is a world dominated by suffering, pain, greed and aggression. But there is also a world, just as real, where people connect with each other through small, but significant, acts of kindness. It is when we connect, harmonize and resonate together with noble intent that we make the most difference.

We have seen how forming trusting bonds with others, and with the world around us, leads us on the journey to higher consciousness, aligning our soul to our personality. This precious balance allows events to fall into place, as we follow the signs provided for us by a universe in synchrony. By developing trust in our intuition, we free ourselves of excessive worry and fear. For my own part, this has helped me cope better with the many complexities that confront a doctor in the 21st century – understanding the vast number of treatment options now available, deciphering research material and becoming IT literate, to name but a few.

I am convinced that trusting one's intuition helps clear the way for a better retention of this knowledge, much as a walk in the fresh air every day clears a muddled mind. It also makes for a life that constantly delights and surprises. Everything, just everything, in our lives becomes interesting and meaningful.

The holographic model I have presented in this book suggests that this state of interconnectivity is an abiding law of the universe, reflected uniquely within each and every one of us. As it epitomizes all that that is good and loving, it can truly be regarded as divine and sacred. This is where our unique consciousness, our soul, resides; the quality, special to us, that doesn't diminish with time and distance; the part that projects from us instantly with every single act of kindness we perform.

It is also the part of us that doesn't die. It is free from the pain, the worries and the fear we all encounter, and try to overcome, during our stay here on earth. When we begin to consider the possibility that our consciousness survives our death, we fear dying less, and enjoy happier and more peaceful lives. As this realization becomes fulfilled during this century, it will have a major impact on how we practise medicine.

We are as one with all others, whatever their race or religion. So too are we one with our earth. Our physical bodies carry the same sacred proportions as all of nature – from the tiniest single-celled organism to the largest galaxy. We all manifest from the same source. If we look above while the sun shines through the rain, we see all the colors of our chakras displayed within a bow of radiant light.

Our earth, and its surrounding biosphere, carries these very same patterns. Way beneath our feet lies the red core of our earth that unselfishly provides us with the minerals and oil that sustain our physical being. Above this is the yellow clay – that magical medium in which, many millions of years ago, the chemistry of life was born. It is within the green space above this – our planet's very own heart chakra – that we have been permitted to perform our own special magic. It is here on the surface of the earth, that we have evolved physically, emotionally and spiritually to a point that we are beginning to open our hearts to embrace our greater role.

And above our green and pleasant landscape is a canopy of blue and indigo, and at night a blackness, stretching out forever into the infinite realm of the unknown. As far as our extended minds allow us to travel. A realm beyond time and space, from which we are all continuously manifesting.

So we stand, like a giant tree, tall and magnificent with our roots firmly in the earth. But ours is an earth that is now under real threat. We must bear some responsibility for this; in order to support our burgeoning population we have stripped the earth of many of its gifts that sustain natural life.

By destroying the equatorial rainforests, and by our fervent burning of fossil fuels, we have caused an imbalance in our ecosystem that is contributing to the climate changes we are all experiencing. It appears our polar ice caps are melting and the water temperature of our seas is rapidly changing. The warm waters to the east of the United States and Mexico are setting the scene for destructive and frequent hurricanes. The cooling of the seas in Northern Europe threaten to divert the warming gulf-stream away, leading to the possibility of a new ice age in that part of the world.

There is, however, evidence that global warming is not all the fault of human negligence; a series of photographs taken over the past six years as part of the Mars Global Surveyor mission, suggests that the ice on Mars's south pole is also melting. We are in the midst, it appears, of a cyclical period of rapid climate change affecting our whole solar system. Added to this we have an impoverished Third World suffering deeply from the devastating effects of famine, disease and natural disasters; and the ever-present threats of terrorism borne out of funda-mentalist idealism.

From my perspective, if we are to adapt adequately to these enormous challenges, it will require an unselfish degree of cooperation between all people of all nations, the likes of which we have never experienced in our history. This is no time for humans to harbor personal guilt, or deep resentment for the past actions of others. It is a time for forgiveness, and an escape from the destructive actions brought about by human ego.

The *human antenna* model causes me to have real hope that we can, indeed, rise above these significant, at times overwhelming, threats to our future. It is a model evolving within our consciousness that recognises a universal truth: each of us exists, at our most profound level, in an interconnected state with each other, and with all of nature. It is only through acts of compassion that we are learning to gain true access into this realm of reality. Then, and only then, does it reveal itself to us – perfectly, with great clarity, and in an instant.

We have, I believe, only touched on the vast potential held by the collective human mind. Our bodies contain trillions of tiny antennas, communicating in perfect harmony with themselves and with our universe. On a larger scale, our living earth provides shelter for more complex, fully integrated antennas – all the plants, trees, and animals are linked together in a worldwide web to which we are only beginning to regain access.

And in the midst of our natural world stands the *human antenna* – a vortex of universal wisdom encased within a perfectly designed body. Every single experience we encounter here is leading us to become co-creators of our planet's destiny. Only now are we developing an awareness of just how immense an honor this is; an honor that has been bestowed on each and every one of us.

And one, I believe, that we are highly likely to live up to.

Journey's End

As I gaze out of the carriage window, I realize our journey is coming to an end. The train is slowing, and it appears we are approaching a station. It all looks strangely familiar – I do believe it is the very station from which we departed some time ago. It seems our journey into the unknown has brought us right back to where we started.

Yes, it definitely is the same station. I remember seeing that man with the blue peaked cap sweeping the platform; only now I notice how broad his smile is – how contented he looks.

Now we have come to a gentle stop, and I see that the platform is full. Outside our carriage there are now more people keen to travel into the unknown. It would perhaps spoil it for them if we were to let on that this was a circle line. Better maybe that they discover this for themselves.

I see an elderly man with rosy cheeks wearing overalls. He has white paint in his hair and on his hands. He is heading for our carriage.

And over there is a family – a fair-haired father is talking earnestly on his mobile phone (I can just catch a glimpse of the ear-piece of a stethoscope poking out of his jacket pocket). Beside him is a woman with golden brown curly hair; she is glowing and radiant. Just behind her, I see a blond teenage girl proudly clutching the brand new Harry Potter book, while her young brother has his head down low over his prized Game Boy, his small thumbs quivering furiously on either side of the tiny LCD screen.

And just beyond them is a young woman in her twenties, with a shaved head, wearing the purple and yellow robes of a Buddhist monk. Next to her is a nun, who has eyes of aquamarine. I wonder what they are laughing about.

And in the corner, two young men with dark hair and straggly beards are talking to each other intently. One is wearing a small black cotton skullcap and a Star of David pendant; the other is clutching an old book, its tattered cover bearing a title in faded Arabic writing – I recognize it as a copy of the Koran.

It appears they all want to board our carriage. But I see there are only a few seats left, and it would be a shame if someone had to stand. So it is perhaps best that I take my leave of you.

But before I go, I would like to thank you all for listening to me with such patience and good humour. Now it is the turn of one of you to recount your own special story. You may want to mention to the new travellers some of what I have recounted – or maybe not. It is entirely up to you.

As for me, it is time I made my way home.

For home, I am led to believe, is where the heart is.

Appendix 1: Shedding New Light

"Be as a clear glass through which God can shine."
–Meister Eckhart

The Human Antenna is in a constant state of receiving and transmitting messages. Some of these messages, such as light, sound and heat are readily identified by our human senses. Others are more hidden from us and only identified by very sensitive individuals, or by sophisticated electronic detecting machines.

As soon as I started to perform acupuncture on patients in the early eighties, I became aware of the Chinese concept of qi, the subtle energy of life. I was amazed only two weeks after starting to practise my newfound healing art, to hear people tell me they could 'feel something moving' inside their bodies during a treatment session. I was even more amazed to discover that the lines these movements followed coincided, as often as not, with the body's meridian lines mapped out on the vast paper charts that covered my consulting room wall. As the years went by, I learned to practise the art of qi gong (translated as 'working with the qi') aimed at balancing and preserving this energy. In China I even witnessed how physicians could be so in control of this mysterious energy that they could heal others without even touching them.

Over the past thirty years, scientists from the East and West have searched for this hidden life force – a quest that is forging a valuable link between ancient Eastern wisdom and cutting-edge Western science. One of the world's leaders in this pioneering work is German biophysicist Fritz-Albert Popp, who has detected a special 'light' emitted and transmitted by all living beings. He names this subtle energy – biophotonic energy – and the particles that are involved – biophotons. [1]

Through sensitive electronic devices he has succeeded in measuring this energy as it is emitted from both plant and animal tissue. Other researchers have studied its wave-like properties in an attempt to understand just where this energy fits within the whole spectrum of electromagnetic energy. Interestingly, the consensus is that it most closely resembles the widely spaced waves of sound, rather than the narrower waves of light. Some have speculated that this allows the 'beams' of biophotons to travel through the body more effectively with less resistance.

Popp's experiments have revealed fascinating insights into the nature of this subtle, yet vital energy. He, and other physicists, discovered that cancer cells emit more biophotonic energy than healthy tissue, suggesting that this is truly a sustainable and renewable resource in healthy tissue. Healthy cells are less inclined to lose energy – actively recycling it. It appears that the rampant, uncontrolled multiplication of cancer cells outpaces the body's ability to reabsorb this energy, leaving the sufferer of cancer drained and weak.[26]

Another study revealed that someone in a balanced, calm, meditative state emits even less of this energy. In other words, in this state we are more likely to conserve our vital energy with resulting health benefits.

There is also speculation that biophotonic energy is processed by the DNA[7] within the nucleus of each cell, and then fired out of the cell in a coherent laser beam with 'the trajectory of a bullet'. Others have speculated that the body's connective tissue – in particular the helical shaped microtubules, flagellae and collagen molecules, are all involved in propagating these beams of biophotons within the body.

I vividly remember the first time I witnessed a laser light show at a rock concert in the eighties. To the amazement and delight of the crowd, beams of green light were projected onto a screen of artificially produced clouds of smoke above our heads, forming vast three-dimensional images that pulsated wildly and synchronously with the music. I recall thinking this was one psychedelic trip that could be enjoyed by all present, and not exclusively by those who had chosen to supplement their experience by indulging in a variety of mind-altering substances.

Just as in a laser light show, our own internal beams of biophotons beams interact and interfere with each other forming a truly holographic field or matrix. Only in our body this show is complex beyond our wildest imaginings, with many trillion sources all firing at once. It is even envisaged that our growth and regeneration all unfolds within this hidden matrix, which, when we are in perfect health, is in perfect harmony with our natural environment.

Figure 19. Spiral Vortexes of the Quantum Foam

Detailed theoretical models of this process have been proposed over the past twenty years by pioneering, broad-minded scientists. Physicist Bevan Reid describes a step-by-step process whereby the 'virtual' energy of pure space literally converts initially into these beams of biophotons, which in turn form the foundation matrix for living matter.[8]

But before we describe this fascinating and complex act of conversion occurring at every given moment within all of us, maybe we should examine the special, sharing relationship we all have with the space between us. Scientists are now beginning to understand just how and why our physical body of cells, our hardware, is in constant communication with this mysterious, ubiquitous, 'virtual' energy of space.

But surely space, we have been led to believe, consists of simply nothing – zilch – the empty area into which everything else fits? Not so, according to quantum physicist, and one-time colleague of Albert Einstein, John Wheeler. All space, including the proportionally vast areas within our atoms where no particles exist, comprises an infinite number of tiny spiral vortices, or wormholes, collectively known as the 'quantum foam.'[9] Each one, according to this theory, acts as a portal to the entire library of universal information; each one a mini star-gate to other dimensions (Figure 19).

Reid proposes that this space energy 'stored' within the vacuum of a symmetrical spiral makes contact with our dense living tissue, and then converts into the coherent laser-like beams I have already described. These beams of biophotons then contain both the infinite store of information from space, and also further information acquired from this collision with the physical hardware of our bodies.

Our physical bodies are wonderfully efficient memory storage devices; complex computers containing the history of everything we have experienced. So it is proposed that space energy, on making contact with our bodies – our uniquely personal database of experiences – instantly downloads this vital information storing it away in its own vast files for posterity.

There is, therefore, a constant and harmonious exchange of information between each of us, and indeed all sentient beings, and the invisible field of universal consciousness. This process is known as resonance.[10] So space energy is being continuously updated and upgraded by contact with our bodies – meticulously recording within its vaults all our earthly

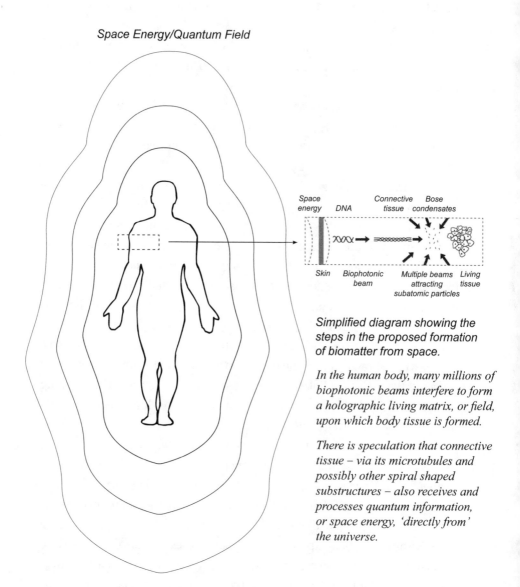

Figure 20. Bosons Interacting with Microtubules and Cells

experiences. This record is enriched beyond measure by that special gift so valued by all human beings – the free will with which we are all so generously entrusted.

So every deliberate act, every thought even, in every one of our unique lives contributes in a significant way to this universal, timeless field of consciousness.

As each of us evolves spiritually, so in turn does the field. If we fully embrace this model, we human beings inherit an awesome level of responsibility. We are clearly, it would appear, co-creators of our own, our planet's, and our universe's destiny.

But wait, as every good television infomercial breathlessly informs us, there is more!

It is our own bodies that also stand to benefit immeasurably in this co-operative venture. To explain this, let's now revisit the intricate process whereby interfering beams of biophotonic energy (another name for biophotons is bosons) – derived from space energy, and processed through our DNA and microtubules – form a field or matrix within which our physical tissue manifests (Figure 20).

Scientists have recently discovered that electrons and other subatomic particles are attracted to this field, condensing onto and within its matrix, in precisely the way a cold glass attracts water onto its surface. The resulting mixture of particles is known as a Bose condensate.[11] It is speculated that this process then progresses into the formation of the very living tissue – our structural proteins – that we can see and feel with our senses.

Many of these far-reaching concepts are based on complicated mathematics. However, in a bold set of experiments between 2001 and 2005, Russian scientist Peter Gariaev and his team at the Quantum Genetics Institute in Moscow have already demonstrated many of these effects in the laboratory. In one experiment, the pancreases of poisoned rats were completely remodelled into healthy tissue using a laser beam from a 'quantum biocomputer'. This machine had previously scanned the pancreas of a healthy rat of the same species, recording quantum information emitted by this healthy tissue's DNA. The information in the form of a laser beam was then directed back into the poisoned pancreases of the diseased rats. ninety percent of these fully recovered – with completely healed pancreases – compared to a control group in which all died. [12]

If these early experiments can be validated by further studies, the scientific and medical implications are truly startling. Simply stated – our life force and the physical reality of our bodies have their origins within the invisible world of space.

In other words, the space that surrounds, bathes, perfuses, and engulfs the Human Antenna not only provides the medium through which vital messages can be received and transmitted. It also holds within its mysterious realms the very essence of our being.

As a child I remember asking my Sunday school teacher what, on earth, was "this thing called the Holy Ghost." I could understand, or so I thought, the first two parts of the Holy Trinity – the Father and Son – but the third one had me completely flummoxed.

What was more, its very name scared me – or 'spooked me out' as my children would now say. Needless to say, I never really received an answer I could understand – even though I would pose the same curly question many times to many people over the ensuing years.

Maybe now, nearly half a century later, a meaning – aided by modern science – is beginning to dawn on me. And it appears the soft light of this dawn is shining down from somewhere I would have least expected.

Appendix 2: Tapping Into the Now

"In art, the hand can never execute anything
higher than the heart can imagine."
–Ralph Waldo Emerson

Over the years, I have explored ways of making acupuncture gentle and unthreatening, so that even the most sensitive people can tolerate, even enjoy the experience. Fortunately the more sensitive a person is, the more likely she or he is to respond to the most delicate of procedures.

In general, children are both less complicated and more sensitive than adults. They are also less likely to have been conditioned into thinking what is, or isn't, possible in health, and in life in general. So when I choose to join them on the floor of my waiting room, armed with my portable infrared laser and a pen, and ask them whether I can draw funny pictures on them, they are usually neither surprised nor openly skeptical. If I can then enter into their special world of play – access to this place is definitely by invitation only – so much the better. A good trick, I have found, is to pick up a plastic building brick and place it precariously on my head. This seems to grab the child's attention, and engender some degree of confidence in me. (From experience though, this act is unlikely to have the same effect on adults.)

By engaging in play this way, we achieve a lovely state of resonance with each other that continues into the next stage of the 'treat'ment.

If a little girl has, for instance, a tendency to suffer frequent colds and ear infections, I begin by drawing a picture over each of the relevant acupuncture points on her arms and legs. I ask her to tell me exactly what to draw – teddy bears, pussycats and sausages are very popular. (Boys tend to choose alligators and tanks in addition to sausages.) I explain that this is all about getting her better, something she is likely to accept without any undue comment.

I then place the tip of the infrared laser over teddy's, or pussy's, nose and ask her to press down the switch on the laser's plastic handle, explaining that together we are making teddy, or whoever, better. This ritual is then repeated on the other drawings – even the sausage receives therapy.

Of course, if repeated visits are necessary, my drawing skills tend to be tested to the limit, as more and more complex animals and shapes are requested.

I have always been pleasantly surprised just how successful this playful and fun approach has proved to be over the years. It seems that by entering into a child's special and mysterious world of play, and by involving her in the healing process, genuine therapeutic rewards are reaped.

This degree of personal involvement is essential for the deep healing process at all ages. Adults who follow their intuition and instruct me exactly where I should insert my acupuncture needles, seem to do exceptionally well, even though these points may vary from what I consider the ideal Chinese prescription. A loved one gently touching the points as illustrated in Figure 13, tends to produce a more profound healing effect than myself.

Throughout this book, I have outlined exercises to enhance your healing, encouraging you to be creative as possible once their essence has been learned. In recent years, therapies involving tapping or touching acupuncture points have become extremely popular. Evidence is mounting from clinical trials, that these techniques are both effective, and safe, for an increasing number of conditions, especially phobic and anxiety states. So far, only one study withstands the strictest scientific scrutiny. This shows Emotional Freedom Techniques (EFT) to be significantly successful in treating people with phobias of insects and small animals.[13] Other promising studies are presently awaiting publication in respected peer-reviewed scientific journals.

EFT is perhaps the most well known of all the Energy Psychology practices. There are now many books and websites helping people learn these self-healing exercises, and I have listed those I recommend in the Resource section at the end of this book.

I offer here a brief outline of the process I use, together with my understanding of the possible mechanisms at play in this new, exciting healing art.

All practitioners agree on the need for a scoring system for the condition, giving us instant feedback on just how effective we are being. In the case of a spider phobia, this must be the feeling (out of a score of 1 to 10) immediately experienced, there and then, as soon as the word 'spider' is brought to mind. Cravings and addictions are similarly scored. If using the technique for currently experienced pain, then this too is scored out of ten.

Before starting, I recommend a gentle abdominal breathing exercise, with a meditative focus on the breath. This promotes an atmosphere of inner peace, and physiological balance, ensuring the body is at its most receptive to the messages we are about to convey.

The Tapping Session

1: The Heart-Opening

This is perhaps the most vital step in the whole process. Allowing our selves to be open to healing, to truly deserve it, is essential to its success. So this involves tapping with three fingers seven times over a point on our chest, our heart chakra, saying out loud:

"Even though I have this problem (say an excessive fear of spiders) I really love and respect myself."

An alternative tapping site is the heart protector acupuncture point two inches above the crease on the inside of the wrist. This can be done effectively under a newspaper on a train or bus, without attracting un-due attention.

As conditioned perfectionists, we tend to judge ourselves harshly. This simple exercise seals within our body a state of self-forgiveness, completely free of judgment. We are thus embued with a true intent to be healed, in resonance with our own higher selves.

Note how the problem is first stated in its truest form, immediately followed by the most positive affirmation of all – the declaration of love for one's self. Thereby a perfect balance is achieved between the opposing forces of negative and positive, vulnerability and control, opening our heart chakra to the non-local, zero point dimensions described in this book. (See Fig 21.)

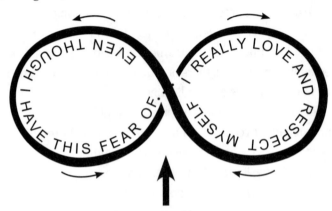

Heart Balance

Figure 21, The Self-acceptance Statement Connects Us
with Infinity

2: The Left-Right Balance

With our hearts now suitably open and engaged, we can turn our attention into becoming even more effective Human Antennas.

This second part of the protocol involves tapping a point on the back of our hand, between the bones that lead to our ring and little fingers. This is on the Chinese Triple Energizer meridian, which as the name implies, acts as a bridge connecting our three major Chinese energy zones – the upper, middle, and lower body. In Vedic terms, the Triple Energizer opens the connections between all our seven chakras. Balancing this meridian also stabilizes any tendency for our body to overreact to threats to its safety, ensuring that we are cool, calm, and collected.

While we are harmonizing our mind and body in this way, the protocol suggests we also engage in simple tricks aimed at balancing the left and right sides of our brain, and body. These comprise various rotating eye movements, and the humming of a well-known tune, such as 'Happy Birthday'. This understandably is the part that most find rather bizarre. In fact, laughing at this point helps rather than hinders, as it further lightens the heart, and is a great 'brain gym' exercise on its own. If in public, it is perfectly all right to roll the eyes behind closed lids, and to just imagine a tune.

I personally find the 'Pink Panther' theme tune the most effective, as it always makes me laugh.

3: The Meridian Balance

This part involves tapping seven or so times over a point on each of the meridians, while mentioning, without judgment, the problem to be helped. (See Fig 22.) Again a lighthearted approach is needed, without heavy analysis. So if we have an unhealthy fear of spiders, we just say the word 'spiders' while tapping.

This final procedure is precisely the same as the time in my own consultations that I address the dis-ease of the person with an acupuncture

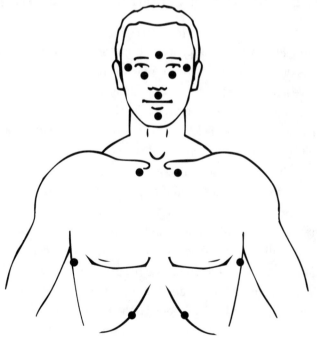

Figure 22, Common Tapping Points

treatment. If using needles, I would naturally select fewer points than this, to minimize any undue distress. As the tapping method is so quick, easy to learn, and of course completely painless, this concern is not an issue.

However, many people ask me for simple effective shortcuts – something they can use under the boardroom table. In response, I tend to select one or two acupuncture points I consider to be the most potent for the condition we are addressing. As the resolution of so many of our health issues involves self-forgiveness and opening ourselves up to healing, the heart protector point on the inner wrist often proves to be the single-most important of all.

If we are doing this for the first time for a particular ailment, it is advisable we repeat the whole procedure (steps 1–3) one or two times. We can then score our progress in precisely the way I described at the outset. It is important to end the session with an affirmation of thanks, or a blessing, for our newfound health benefits. This also helps ground us, as we integrate back into the world.

Adapting and Understanding the Tapping Points

Adapting EFT to more complex emotional and physical conditions may require considerable guidance from a health professional. As all chronic diseases have a mixture of physical, emotional, and spiritual causes, skill is needed in overseeing someone as layer after layer of conditioned thoughts, fears, and worries are peeled back. The whole process of deep healing commonly leaves the healee feeling, at times, vulnerable and emotionally exposed. So although these exercises are easy to learn, support from someone experienced is best sought for more complex and longstanding conditions.

With these precautions in mind though, EFT and other Energy Psychology techniques are largely both safe and effective. But do we truly understand exactly how and why these bizarre tapping exercises work?

In short, the most honest answer is 'not really'. However, as these exercises are performed on recognized points of energy exchange on Chinese meridians, it seems reasonable to start looking for clues within the ancient texts of Chinese medicine.

So far, EFT and other Energy Psychology practices have been mainly used to help clear the body of anxieties and phobias. The organ system in Chinese medicine that relates to fear and sensitivity is the kidney. Unlike our largely physical focus in Western medicine, the Chinese kidney is an energetic system incorporating, body, mind, and spiritual dimensions. The Chinese kidney system is also not simply confined anatomically to the paired physical organs of the kidney we know in Western conventional medicine. It also includes the adrenal (or suprarenal) glands involved in producing adrenaline and steroids, both necessary, in balance, for our appropriate fight-or-flight reactions. So already, associating the kidney with the emotion of fear seems less bizarre, even for those of us heavily conditioned by the scientific method.

Closely aligned to the emotion of fear is our innate sensitivity to the world around us. Those of us who are very sensitive tend to have 'thin skins' and, at times, this can lead to a condition known in the West as a nervous disposition. There is, however, positive news for those of us who are sensitive; when in balance, we are exquisitely tuned into our environment, leading us to an enhanced state of spontaneity and creativity. Many creative people, including artists and actors, have sensitive Chinese kidney systems; and in Eastern terms sensitivity, when in balance, is regarded as a definite strength.

The color associated with the Chinese kidney, is black – the very color we all closely associate with the emotion of fear. The associated sense organ is the ear – with soothing words and music regarded of great value as healing aids for imbalances of the Chinese kidney energy. And the element most linked to the Chinese kidney is, naturally, enough water. Both Chinese and Western medicine agree that it is our kidneys that largely govern the balance of water in our bodies.

So what does modern science now have to say about water?

Strangely enough for a liquid that is so vital to life, we are only beginning to discover the unique properties owned by water. If, as recently as five years ago, one was to suggest to a group of scientists or doctors that that molecules of water retained memories – the very theoretical basis of homeopathy – the reaction would not likely to have been pleasant. I speak from bitter experience in this matter.

But somewhat appropriately, the tide now appears to be turning.

Biophysicist Monika Fuxreiter of the Hungarian Academy of Science in Budapest has demonstrated that water molecules play a vital part in the manufacture of our body's building blocks, our proteins, by our DNA. In fact, water molecules, while attached to DNA, relay information to proteins and amino acids at a distance, informing them of the precise sites on the DNA molecule they are to bind. It follows that this information must first be stored as 'memory' within the molecules of water for this guiding process to occur.[14]

The pioneering work of Japanese scientist Dr. Masaru Emoto has now reached a wide audience largely through his books and the movie "What the Bleep do we know?" Millions of people around the world have marveled at his photographs of water crystals, whose structure is dramatically affected by music, words, and most importantly, the intent behind the words. Although others are yet to replicate his work, we are discovering that water is indeed a quantum elixir. For over sixty years, scientists have attempted to modify our weather patterns by dispersing crystals of silver iodide into the atmosphere, attracting to their surface water molecules, in crystalline form, in a process known as 'cloud seeding.' The shape of these water crystals has been shown to exactly match the crystals of silver iodide, even though no chemical transfer is known to take place.[15]

It is also now known that the atoms within water molecules remain entangled even after they have been physically separated. It is speculated that this is one of the properties at play in homeopathy. A homeopathic remedy becomes more potent with each successive dilution – something that has been dismissed by mainstream scientists for decades. In classical homeopathy, the therapist vigorously shakes each dilution in an action known as 'succussion'. It is speculated that this shaking ensures a breaking of the bonds between molecules, allowing messages to be passed onto, and then amplified by, the newly added molecules of water.

However, as demonstrated in Emoto's work, there is perhaps another vital factor at play in the whole process of preparing a homeopathic remedy – the compassionate intent of both the therapist, and the person seeking healing. Is this the element that has been ignored for so long by mainstream scientists, working within a paradigm that separates the healer from the 'healee'?

People of all cultures and religions have for centuries used 'holy' water in their blessing rituals. As a baby, water blessed by a minister was poured onto my forehead – over my third eye – as I was baptized into the Christian faith. The minister then painted a sign of the cross over this very point.

In another well-known Christian ritual, as a sign of profound respect and commitment to their faith, it is traditional for followers to demonstrate the 'sign of the cross' over their upper bodies – touching points on their forehead, abdomen or chest, and each shoulder. Different denominations teach different techniques – in some orthodox churches crossing the heart in the wrong direction risks evoking the devil.

The healing techniques used in Energy Psychology are open to all people of all religions, and, if performed out of order, bear no such negative connotations. They simply carry with them the intent of compassion, and love, to one's own self. The acupuncture points on which we tap with our fingertips are known vortices of subtle energy, each with their own central core opening to infinite realms. (See Fig 23.)

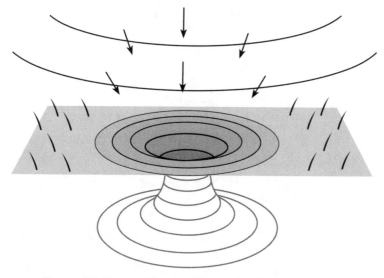

Figure 23, Energy Flowing Through a Skin Acupoint

The meridians that lead to the heart chakra start and end in our fingers. A circuit is therefore made connecting these points with our own heart – now laid open by our intent to self-heal. We are in precisely the same state of connection with the field as illustrated in Figure 13 – only this time we are going solo! See Fig 24.

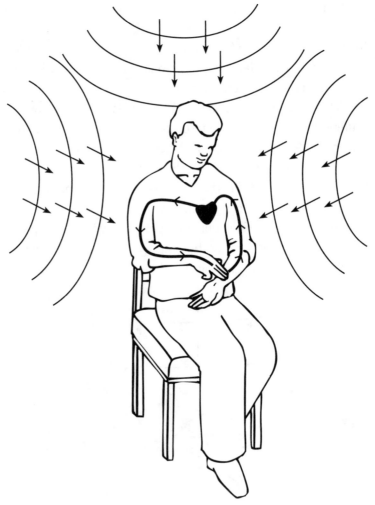

Figure 24, Universal Energy Flowing Through the Heart Meridian

We now know that our bodies can also be regarded as complex and sophisticated quantum computers. By recalling fears or memories, without judgment, while tapping over the body's keyboard – its acupuncture meridian system – it is as if we are simply highlighting useless files, then pressing the delete buttons! They disappear in a flash because, despite having caused havoc in our lives for years, they take up remarkably little memory space. They may well have dragged us down for years, but in fact they weigh absolutely nothing!

The software that stores these memories, I would speculate, is our body's water. A special and dynamic software package that we are continually updating with every sip we take, and every word we hear. It holds our true essence and unique story, yet is always simply 'passing through'. In its remarkable journey through each of us, it is perpetually receiving and passing on information, until it returns, older and wiser, to the waterways of the earth and the sky.

But perhaps the most profound clue in solving the mystery of exactly how, and why, 'tapping' is such a potent therapy, lies within the name itself. An elusive something that just can't be found in longer, more sophisticated, words, such as 'psychology' or 'psychiatry.'

The clue reveals itself in all its glory when we recall, from our high school English lessons, that the word 'tap' is an onomatopoeia – a word that, when spoken, sounds like the very sound or action it is describing. A tiny, monosyllabic word that describes an act that is over as soon as it begins.

Each tap introduces a guiding, compassionate presence into our bodies – severing ties with the past that no longer serve us. We are thus engaging in the act of breaking unhealthy timelines, resetting our lives into a healthy present, ensuring for ourselves a healthy future.

So when we 'tap' our body with an open heart and a pure intent, we are really instilling into ourselves a noble truth.

A truth to be found only in the here and now.

References

1. Professor Popp is a member of The International Institute of Biophysics, in Neuss Germany. Comprehensive details on his, and other biophysicists', research on: www.lifescientists.de/index. htm.

2. Ruth, B. und Popp, F. A., Z. Naturforsch. 31c(1976), 741.

3. Popp, F. A., Ruth, B., Bahr, W., Böhm, J., Grass, P., Grolig, G., Rattemeyer, M., Schmidt, H. G., and Wulle, P., Coll. Phenomena 3 (1981), 187.

4. Schamhart, D. H. J. and van Wijk, R., *Photon Emission from Biological Systems*, eds. B. Jezowska-Trzebiatowska et. al. Singapore: World Scientific, 1987, pp.137–152.

5. Grasso, F., Grillo, C., Musumeci, F., Triglia, A., Rodolico, G., Cammisuli, F., Rinzivillo, C., Fragati, G., Santuccio, A., and Rodolico, M., Experientia 48 (1992), 10.

6. Kim, J., Choi, C., Lim, J., et al. "Measurements of Spontaneous Ultraweak Photon Emission and Delayed Luminescence from Human Cancer Tissues," *Journal of Alt. and Comp. Med.* Oct 2005, Vol. 11, No. 5: 879–88.

7. F. A. Popp, Q. Gu and K. H. Li Mod. Phys. Lett B8 1269 (1994).

8. Reid, B. L., On the nature of growth and new growth based on experiments designed to reveal a structure and function in laboratory space. Parts 1 and 2. *Med Hypoth* 29, 105–144 (1989).

9. Wheeler, J., Ford, K., Geons, *Black Holes and Quantum Foam: A Life in Physics*. W. W. Norton, New York 1998.

10. Reid, B. L., "Attempts to identify a control system for chemical reactions residing in virtual energy flows through the biosystem." *Med Hypoth* 52, 307–313 (1999).

11. There is debate whether this fragile state can arise at "warm" temperatures above absolute zero. However, there is support for the theory that living systems create the dynamic environment for this – and superconductive states – at body temperature. www.quantumconsciousness.org.

12. Crisis in Life Sciences. The Wave Genetics Response. P.P. Gariaev, M.J. Friedman, and E.A. Leonova-Gariaeva http://www.emergentmind.org/gariaev06.htm.

13. Wells, S., Polglase, K., Andrews, H. B., Carrington, P. & Baker, A. H. "Evaluation of a meridian-based intervention, emotional freedom techniques (EFT), for reducing specific phobias of small animals." *Journal of Clinical Psychology*, 59, 943–966 (2003).

14. Fuxreiter, M., Mezei, M., Simon, I., and Osman, R., Interfacial Water as a "Hydration Fingerprint" in the Noncognate Complex of BamHI. *Biophysical Journal*, 89:903–911 (2005).

15. Matthews, R., Water – The Quantum Elixir. *New Scientist*, 8 April 2006. Magazine issue.

Bibliography

And (Robin's) Recommended Reading

Attenborough, David. *The Private Life of Plants: A Natural History of Plant Behaviour.* London UK: BBC, 1994.

Bailey, Alice A. *Unfinished Autobiography.* New York, USA: Lucis Publishing Company, 1973.

————. *Esoteric Healing.* New York, USA: Lucis Publishing Company, 1971.

————. *Treatise on White Magic.* New York, USA: Lucis Publishing Company, 1970.

Barth, John. *The Last Voyage of Somebody the Sailor.* Doubleday Publishing, 1992.

Blake, William. *Songs of Innocence.* New York, USA: Dover Publications, 1971.

Capra, Fritjof. *Tao of Physics.* London, UK: Flamingo. 3rd Edition, 1992.

————. *Web of Life: A New Understanding of Living Systems.* New York, USA: Anchor Books, 1996.

Chopra, Deepak. *Quantum Healing: Exploring the Frontiers of Mind-Body Medicine.* New York, USA: Bantam Books, 1989.

Coelho, Paulo. *The Alchemist: A Fable about Following Your Dream.*

USA: HarperSanFrancisco, 10th Edition, 1995

Cook, Gary. *The Secret Land 2, Journeys into the Mystery.* Christchurch, New Zealand: StonePrint Press, 2002.

Emoto, Masaru. *The Hidden Messages in Water.* Oregon, USA: Beyond Words, 2004.

Davies, Brenda. *The Rainbow Journey.* London, UK: Hodder and Stoughton, 1998.

Dossey, Larry. *Reinventing Medicine: Beyond Mind-Body to a New Era of Healing.*

San Francisco, CA, USA: HarperSanFrancisco/HarperCollins, 1999.

Gardner, Laurence. *Lost Secrets of the Sacred Ark: Amazing Revelations of the Incredible Power of Gold.* London, UK: HarperCollins, 2003.

Gribbin, John. *Companion to the Cosmos.* Boston, USA: Little, Brown and

Company, 1996.

Jahn, Robert G. and Brenda J. Dunne. *Margins of Reality: The Role of Consciousness in the Physical World.* San Diego, USA: Harcourt Brace, 1987.

Kelly, Robin. *Healing Ways: A Doctor's Guide to Healing.* Auckland, NZ: Penguin Books, 2000.

Laszlo, Ervin. *Science and the Akashic Field: An Integral Theory of Everything.* Rochester, USA: Inner Traditions International Limited, 2004.

Lawlor, Robert. *Sacred Geometry: Philosophy and Practice.* London, UK: Thames & Hudson, 1982.

Maciocia, Giovanni. *The Practice of Chinese Medicine.* London, UK: Churchill Livingstone, 1994.

Myss, Caroline. *Anatomy of the Spirit: The Seven Stages of Power and Healing.* USA: Random House Value Publishing, 1997.

Nogier, Paul. *Handbook to Auriculotherapy.* Maisonneuve. France, 1981.

O'Donohue, John. *Anam Cara: A Book of Celtic Wisdom.* London, UK: Bantam, 1998.

———. *Divine Beauty: The Invisible Embrace.* London, UK: Bantam, 2003.

Oschman, James L. *Energy Medicine: The Scientific Basis.* UK: Churchill Livingstone, 2000.

Paramhans Swami Maheshwarananda. *Yoga in Daily Life. The System.* Vienna, Austria: Ibera, 2000.

Pert, Candace B. *Molecules of Emotion: The Science Behind Mind-Body Medicine.* New York, USA: Simon & Schuster, 1997.

Purce, Jill. *The Mystic Spiral: Journey of the Soul.* London, UK: Thames and Hudson, 1974.

Radin, Dean. *The Conscious Universe: The Scientific Truth of Psychic Phenomena.* New York, USA: HarperCollins, 1997.

Schlitz Marilyn, Tina Amorok, Marc Micozzi, (Ed.) *Consciousness and Healing: Integral Approaches to MindBody Medicine.* Philadelphia, PA, USA: Elsevier/ Churchill Livingstone, 2005.

Schulz, Mona Lisa. *Awakening Intuition: Using Your Mind-Body Network for Insight and Healing.* New York, USA: Harmony Books, 1998.

Sheldrake, Rupert. *A New Science of Life.* London, UK: Blond and Briggs, 1981.

———. *Seven Experiments that Could Change the World: A Do-It-Yourself Guide to Revolutionary Science.* New York, USA: Riverhead Books, 1996.

Shepherd, Charles. *Living With M.E. – Chronic Post-Viral Fatigue Syndrome.* London, UK: Vermillion, 1999.

Starr Miribar. *St John of the Cross: The Dark Night of the Soul – New Translation.* London, UK: Rider Books, 2002.

Stearn, Jess. *Edgar Cayce: Sleeping Prophet.*New York, USA: Bantam Books, 1989.

Swanson, Claude. *The Synchronised Universe: New Science of the Paranormal.* Tucson, USA: Poseidia Press, 2003.

Talbot, Michael. *The Holographic Universe.* London, UK: HarperCollins, 1996.

Tolle, Eckhart. *The Power of Now: A Guide to Spiritual Enlightenment.* Vancouver, Canada: Namaste Publishing; New World Library, 1998.

Wilber, Ken. *A Theory of Everything.*Dublin, Ireland: Gateway, 2001.

Recommended Listening

Cohen, Leonard. *Dear Heather.* Columbia Records, 2004.

Recommended and Related Websites

Dr. Steven Aung
Physician, Qi Gong Master
www.aung.com

Dr. Stuart Hameroff
Anaesthetist. Consciousness researcher
www.quantumconsciousness.org

Professor Brian Josephson
Nobel prize-winning physicist
http://www.tcm.phy.cam.ac.uk/~bdj10/

Dr. Joyce Kovelman
Psychologist and anatomist
http://www.essentialsforasoul.com/

Dr. Rupert Shedrake
Biochemist and cell biologist
www.sheldrake.org

Journals and Research

British Medical Journal Online
http://bmj.bmjjournals.com/

Research on Savants and Psychic Healers
www.guardian.co.uk

The Lancet
http://www.thelancet.com/

The New Scientist
www.newscientist.com

The Journal of Reproductive Medicine
www.reproductivemedicine.com

The History of Amphetamine Abuse
www.amphetamines.com

Research on Ancient Skepticism
The Metaphysics Research Lab, Stanford University
http://plato.stanford.edu/

Research on Plant Growth
Stanford Report – Stanford University News Service
http://news-service.stanford.edu/

Organizations of Skeptics

New Zealand Skeptics
http://www.skeptics.org.nz

Quackwatch
Quackwatch, Inc., which was a member of Consumer Federation of
America from 1973 through 2003, is a nonprofit corporation whose
purpose is to combat health-related frauds, myths, fads, and fallacies.
http://www.quackwatch.org/

Progressive Organizations

Australasian Integrative Medicine Association (AIMA).
Promoting the integration of holistic and complementary medicine with current
mainstream medical practice, in pursuit of a complete whole person care.
http://www.aima.net.au/

Science Medical Network.
The Network is a transdisciplinary forum for the exploration and
investigation of the interface between science, medicine, and spirituality.
www.scimednet.org

The Emergent Mind.
An open venture between scientists, scholars, meditators, and all those
who believe that we are approaching a conceptual threshold in our
understanding of how physics, physiology, and consciousness interact.
http://www.emergentmind.org/

Foresight Nanotech Institute.
Foresight Nanotech Institute's mission is to ensure the beneficial
implementation of nanotechnology.
http://www.foresight.org/

The Gawler Foundation.
The Gawler Foundation is committed to an integrated approach
to health, healing, and well-being that includes the body,
emotions, mind and spirit.
http://www.gawler.org/

Good Company Pacific.
Promoting the emergence of a compassionate and creative
culture that nurtures the well-being of all peoples and evokes our
highest potential. http://www.goodcompanypacific.com/

The Ground of Faith.
Exploring science, mysticism and experience together.
http://homepages.ihug.co.nz/~thegroundoffaith/

The Institute of HeartMath.
The institute's primary mission is to facilitate people in finding
the balance between mind and heart in life's decisions.
http://www.heartmath.org/

The Institute of Noetic Sciences.
Exploring the frontiers of consciousness to advance individual,
social, and global transformation.
http://www.noetic.org/

New Zealand MindBody Network.
Promoting a greater understanding of MindBody healing in
Aotearoa/New Zealand.
http://www.mindbody.org.nz/

Society for Scientific Exploration.
Providing a professional forum for presentations, criticism, and
debate concerning topics which are for various reasons ignored
or studied inadequately within mainstream science.
http://www.scientificexploration.org/

Index